D0816148

PACE YOURSELF

Ric Engram

THOMAS NELSON PUBLISHERS
Nashville
❖ *A Janet Thoma Book* ❖

Names of the people mentioned within and details of their lives have been changed and altered to protect the identities of actual people.

Published in Nashville, Tennessee, by Thomas Nelson, Inc., and distributed in Canada by Lawson Falle, Ltd., Cambridge, Ontario.

Printed in the United States of America.

Scripture quotations are from THE NEW KING JAMES VERSION of the Bible. Copyright © 1979, 1980, 1982, Thomas Nelson, Inc., Publishers.

Library of Congress Cataloging-in-Publication Data

Engram, Ric.
    Pace yourself / Ric Engram.
        p.   cm. — (Serenity meditation series)
    ISBN 0-8407-3323-2 (pbk.)
    1. Compulsive behavior—Religious aspects—
Christianity—Meditations.   2. Twelve-step programs—
Religious aspects—Christianity—Meditations.
3. Devotional calendars.   I. Title.   II. Series.
BL624.5.E54   1991
242'.66—dc20   91–28456
                                                    CIP

Contents

Introduction

It seems that in our society today, drivenness has become an accepted way of life. The pressure to achieve, to succeed, to obtain, and to improve has pushed millions of people onto the treadmill of compulsive behaviors. Every day they face the prospect of trying to be and do more, only to once again feel shortchanged in their quest for personal fulfillment. *We Are Driven* (Nashville: Thomas Nelson, 1991) was written by Drs. Robert Hemfelt, Paul Meier, and Frank Minirth to help people see that recovery from these addictive behaviors is really possible. And *Pace Yourself* is meant to be a daily supplement to that recovery, following the same outline and emphasizing the same techniques as *We Are Driven*.

In one sense, this has not been an easy assignment, because I struggle with issues of compulsiveness in my own life. Yet in another sense it has been a refreshing journey for me to rediscover how practical and relevant God's Word remains in addressing the difficult issues of life. My hope and prayer for you as you meditate on His promises is twofold; that you may come to recognize through the personal stories that you are not alone in your struggles, and realize that you *can* have victory, for "with God all things are possible" (Matt. 19:26).

God bless you,

Ric Engram

Part 1

UNMASKING
COMPULSIONS

I thought about my ways,
And turned my feet to Your testimonies.
—PS. 119:59

As each of you begins the difficult task of recovering from your compulsions it is important that you have a direction. To simply state "This is my problem, and now I know that I am going to get better" is not really beginning the healing process. In order not to stand still, you always must be moving forward.

As this verse from Psalms states, the considerations of your ways should lead you toward God even though your behaviors have been leading you away from God for many years. The wonderful promise of God's Word is that as you consider your ways in the light of what God has said, you realize that you cannot do anything without His power. Indeed, to consider your ways without that light is to slip further into attempting to better yourself through your compulsive behaviors.

While it is not intended to be a substitute for your own meditation on God's Word, this book will be a source of encouragement and challenge along the way. May it be a help to you as you move toward completeness and wellness found through Him.

Lord, as I go through the difficult task of considering my thoughts and ways, may they always lead, however small the steps may be, in the direction of Your love and wholeness for my life.

The wisdom of the prudent is to understand his way,
But the folly of fools is deceit. —PROV. 14:8

Several weeks ago, my young daughter came into the room and requested we play a game of hide-and-seek. I agreed and we decided that she would be the one to hide. So I closed my eyes and counted to ten. When I opened my eyes she was standing in front of me with her hands over her eyes. I playfully pulled her to me and asked her why she had not gone and hidden somewhere. She took her hands away from her eyes and looked at me astonished. "How could you see me when I had my eyes closed?" she asked. "Just because you can't see yourself doesn't mean that no one else can see you," I responded.

That was the way Karen had been dealing with her painful past. She tried to believe that if she just closed her emotional eyes and pretended that her pain did not exist, it magically would go away. Yet in recovery, she realized that rather than pretending, the only true way to help those issues disappear was to face them directly and begin confronting them.

Father, help me remove the hands of deceit from my emotional eyes.

Beware lest anyone cheat you through philosophy and empty deceit, according to the tradition of men, according to the basic principles of the world, and not according to Christ.
—COL. 2:8

Have you ever been cheated before? Perhaps you were cheated when you were younger, playing some childhood game, or even as an adult by some door-to-door salesman with false promises and empty claims about his product. How does it make you feel when you find out that you have been cheated? Perhaps you feel angry, frustrated, and used. That's what makes being cheated so painful. When you realize that you have been cheated, you feel all the worse for not having seen it coming. And yet, in this verse Paul says that is exactly what the world is doing to you with its current philosophies.

Stan believed he had to perform his work duties perfectly and compulsively. When he finally realized that he had been robbed of the productive life-style that God desired for him, he felt cheated.

Take the time today to become aware of where the world is cheating you and recognize the fact that, with God's help, you do not have to be cheated any longer.

Lord, help me recognize that You deal with me in truth and honesty.

> *Do not judge according to appearance, but judge with righteous judgment.*
> —JOHN 7:24

When my wife and I were newlyweds, we visited southern California. Among all the attractions we saw, one of my favorites was Universal Studios. The tour bus went down a street where we recognized many of the famous houses from television and movies. However, it was interesting to note these "houses" were simply fronts held up by empty shells.

It occurred to me as I was viewing this how much of my own life is a "false front" for other people to view. How often do others look at the surface or exterior of your life and feel that, because of what they see, they know you completely, yet, they do not really understand what lies behind that facade. It is important to realize that no matter what kind of front you put up for the world to see, God truly knows what is behind that front and judges your actions according to your heart. With God's help, you can concern yourself with the interior and begin to build the rest of your "house" as solidly and attractively as you have made the front.

Lord, may I trust You to begin rebuilding my life to make it into that complete edifice that You want it to be.

*There is therefore now no condemnation to
those who are in Christ Jesus, who do not walk
according to the flesh, but according to the Spirit.*
—ROM. 8:1

For those who are recovering from compulsive behaviors, this verse has to be one of the most exciting and yet most difficult verses in the Bible. It was almost inconceivable for Christine to think an all-knowing God could say that she had no condemnation when she found things wrong with her life every single day. By trying to be the perfect wife and mother, she thought she could get to the place where she did not have to be critical of herself. Yet because she could never reach that place, she was driven on and on in her compulsive cleaning, cooking, and entertaining.

This verse states exactly the opposite. Notice that this verse does not say that God chooses to look the other way because of faults as some sort of act of benevolence. According to this verse, because of what Jesus Christ did on the cross for you, the condemnation that you once might have had does not even exist anymore. If Christine's condemnation does not exist anymore in God's mind, she does not need to keep trying to "cure" herself by her compulsive behavior. Christine needs to recognize that if God no longer condemns her, then she should not condemn herself any longer either. What a liberating concept!

Father, help me recognize that the condemnation I feel is not something that comes from You.

> *They loved the praise of men more than the praise of God.*
> —JOHN 12:43

Frank was compulsive with his appearance because he had an unmet need for approval. Frank felt a tremendous need to be liked, appreciated, and praised. Any behavior that brought those responses was continued and expanded upon. What some other person might think or say became the basis for every decision or action in Frank's life. He could never get enough praise.

Yet what Frank did not realize is that there is another source of praise that is not dependent on what a person says or does. People so often focus on the idea that they can and should praise God but fail to recognize the fact that He can praise them as well. When Frank stopped and thought about the fact that the God of the universe wanted to give him praise and approval, it certainly made the praise of other men fade significantly. It also made him realize how futile his obsession with his appearance really was. As he began to understand God's praise and approval, he found all the praise and approval he could ever need.

Lord, help me accept Your praise and approval in my life.

There is a way that seems right to a man,
But its end is the way of death.
—PROV. 14:12

One of the things Drs. Robert Hemfelt, Frank Minirth, and Paul Meier point out in the book *We Are Driven* (Nashville: Thomas Nelson, 1991) is that many of the things that end up as compulsions in life start out as perfectly normal and healthy activities. People have to eat in order to live; a healthy sex life is important to a successful marriage; most people have to work to provide for their families; and everyone needs some sort of recreation to give them a break from these daily tasks. It is not the activity that creates the problem but what this activity begins to mean to the individual performing it.

That is why it is so important to look down the road to where that activity might be leading. When you begin to sense that exercise is taking up more time than it needs to, when you feel like you have to be perfect in order to gain any sense of self-worth, and when working long hours takes on more significance than anything else, you are probably in trouble. It is not the beginning of those roads that is so treacherous but rather where they end up that costs the most in your life. That is why you must allow the Lord to give you the strength to look honestly down the end of that road to see where that activity is leading. Ask for that strength today.

Give me the insight today, Lord, to look at my behaviors, not just in light of where I am now, but where I might end up if I continue to follow this path.

Whoever has no rule over his own spirit
Is like a city broken down, without walls.
—PROV. 25:28

During Bible times, the walls of the city served two important functions. The first and most obvious function was to protect the city from attacks of neighboring cities or countries. The stronger and more solid the walls, the more difficulty the attackers had in conquering the city. The second function was to provide a boundary around the city so the people inside felt secure enough to move freely and without fear. There were gates and doors to allow people to pass in and out of the city, but these were open at the discretion of the gatekeepers.

A city without walls, however, served neither purpose. Attackers easily could move in and capture people in the city, and the people had no idea where the boundaries of their protection were. This was also true of Jill's codependent life. Because she had no set boundaries, she had no protection. She had a very difficult time understanding where her life ended and someone else's began. One of the major tasks of Jill's recovery process was to begin resetting those boundaries around her life that would give her the protection and security that she needed to live as a complete and protected individual.

Father, give me the strength to repair or rebuild those boundaries around me.

To everything there is a season,
A time for every purpose under heaven.
—ECCL. 3:1

Have you ever noticed how subtly and yet consistently the seasons change from year to year? Even though you have certain dates marked on your calendar to denote the passing of time, you will not wake up one morning suddenly to find one season has changed to another. God has provided a mechanism in nature for the seasons to change at the appropriate time. Whatever is necessary for these changes is available when it is needed. There is a purpose behind the activity and rest cycle for nature to keep rejuvenating itself.

That is also the pattern that God wants for each one of us. When Luke became involved in a project at work, he felt it might be better to increase his work load or the intensity of his effort. However, he discovered by using God's creation of seasons as a pattern, there would be times when he should be very involved in his work and other times when he would need to rest. By looking at something else as being significant, important, and necessary in his life, he could remain as fresh and ever-growing as nature itself.

Help me remember, Lord, that each day is a new day, and that the tasks You would have me do today may be different from the ones I did yesterday.

> *Not that I speak in regard to need, for I have*
> *learned in whatever state I am, to be content.*
> —PHIL. 4:11

For the person involved in compulsive behavior, this verse offers one of the greatest challenges in life. Virtually all compulsive behavior is based on the feeling of discontent unless something else happens. Whether that is having more money, being thinner, doing more for the family, teaching another Sunday school class, all of these behaviors have the motivating force of discontent behind them. Where our lives are right now is simply not enough—we need more!

The encouragement found in this verse is in "learning" to be content. In my own drive toward perfectionism, I feel that whatever changes are to be made need to be made *now!* Yet I am learning that contentment is not an automatic state of mind but rather a long, slow process. It is not simply learning how to *act* content, but honestly learning to feel contentment on a day-to-day basis. So rather than focusing on what's wrong, I am learning to start each day by thanking God for one particular thing in my life and asking Him to help me be content with that thing.

Father, help me learn that wherever I am at this point in my life, I can learn to be content because I know that You are there with me.

I have seen all the works that are done under the sun; and indeed, all is vanity and grasping for the wind.

—ECCL. 1:14

One of my fondest childhood memories is taking drives with my family on cool summer evenings, when we would be able to roll down the windows and let in all the fresh country air. I remember sticking my hands out the window and feeling the wind rush past my arm as I tried to grab hold of it. I thought that if I just closed my hand quickly enough, I could capture a little bit of that wind. Yet no matter how many times I tried, I could never seem to grab hold of and bring it back into the car. It was nothing more than air blowing past my hands.

All of the success Darla tried to accomplish, all the awards and prizes she achieved over a lifetime, and all the difference she felt she was going to make in this world was simply grasping for the wind. While she was doing it, it seemed real and tangible, but the tighter she grasped, the more she felt it slipping through her fingers. Through recovery she became aware that while it is important to do the tasks to which she was called, trying to hold on to them and make them the source of worth for her life was simply grasping for the wind.

Father, help me stop grasping for the wind of my own accomplishments.

Come to Me, all you who labor and are heavy laden, and I will give you rest. —MATT. 11:28

In discussing compulsive behaviors with the people I counsel, the one thing that consistently seems to come up in the conversations is how tired they are of living that way. Irene had been keeping up her "Super Mom" routine for as long as she could remember. But all the home-cooked meals, great entertaining, and never-ending taxi service was taking its toll. "If I could just take a break from my life, I think I would be able to feel so much better," was her painful but sincere cry.

Yet this is what Jesus promises in this verse—rest from the weariness of your burden. Notice that He does not promise that He will magically take away any of those things that you are struggling with nor that He will make you give an account of why you are still struggling with them. What He promises is simple and pure rest, which is exactly what Irene needed at that point and time. Her only responsibility was that she must first come to Him, which in itself was difficult because she would have to admit that she could not do it on her own. But that wonderful rest that He promised her would make it worth any effort. He is always right there waiting for you to be willing to accept that rest He wants to give.

_____

Father, help me remember that You promised to give me rest if I would just trust You for it.

Search me, O God, and know my heart;
Try me, and know my anxieties.
—PS. 139:23

Jacob was a lawyer for one of the most successful firms in his city. He had made it his goal in life to become a great legal mind, and he was not going to let anything stand in his way of success. The late hours, the long nights, the sacrifice of relationships was all going to be worth it when he finally was made a partner in the firm. When he finally accomplished his goal, he had no one to share it with. He felt empty and frustrated, and he came to counseling seeking answers for his life.

This verse became the basis for Jacob's recovery. It helped because he could look at it from a legal perspective, something he understood very well. First, he saw that with God's help he had to begin looking for evidence in his life, evidence that indicated unmet needs or emotional trauma. Once that evidence was "searched out," it had to be "tried" or examined to see what effects it had on his life. Of course, he saw he could only do this adequately with God's help because God was the only One who could look at Jacob's life objectively and be his advocate against the guilt of addiction.

Lord, allow me to have You bring the evidence of my life to my mind so that You will be able to deal with it fairly and justly.

> *So he said, "I will do this: I will pull down my*
> *barns and build greater, and there I will store all*
> *my crops and my goods."* —LUKE 12:18

Not too long ago I had the opportunity to visit the beautiful city Rome. As I visited the various sites, one of the things that became apparent was how each new successive ruler tried to prove his greatness by the number of buildings he left behind. Today, those rulers are not known for the buildings they put up or the monuments they erected but by the quality of lives they lived here on earth. It is sobering to see how misguided they were in their ventures.

Often, in today's society, people follow that same mind-set. Dale was trying so hard to gain material possessions that would set him apart with the assumption that somehow these were going to give him worth long after he was gone. He was always competing for the most important, the biggest, the highest, and the best. And yet God says in His Word that people will not be remembered for the physical accomplishments left on earth, but rather what kind of lives they have led. No matter how big a barn Dale built, somebody would always come along and tear it down and build a bigger one. It is for the qualities of love, understanding, and honesty in your life that you will be remembered long after those barns have fallen apart.

Father, help me remember that it is not the physical barns but rather the eternal qualities of life I need to be concerned about.

*Therefore let him who thinks he stands take heed
lest he fall.*
—1 COR. 10:12

How flexible are you in your attitudes toward other people and the way they treat you? In this passage, Paul was talking about the children of Israel and how they continually trusted in their traditions and the law to be the source of their fulfillment and worth. Israel had always taken pride in their traditions, and in fact, felt quite superior to others because of the way they followed the law. Paul was bringing them in check, reminding them that a person who stands too inflexibly is more likely to tumble over the first bump along the road.

Of course, the danger of this attitude is that you will stand for nothing at all. There are times when you must take a stand on particular issues, especially when proven spiritual principles are involved. But you should also remember the firmness is not necessarily in your stance but in what you stand on. If you become too inflexible in your narrow view of things, then it is your own strength you are standing on and you are not letting the truth of what you are standing for speak for itself. You must always be careful not to let any behavior become an end in itself but rather a means to the end of letting God's truth speak through your life.

Lord, help me depend on You for strength and not rely on my own inflexible opinions.

> *There are many plans in a man's heart,*
> *Nevertheless the LORD'S counsel—that will stand.*
> —PROV. 19:21

I must confess that I am a planner. If we are taking a trip, give me the map, and weeks in advance I will have the route planned, know every rest stop along the way, how many miles it is to our destination, and the approximate time of arrival within fifteen minutes. Or tell me to plant a garden, and I can tell just how far the rows should be placed apart, what kind of fertilizer the soil needs, what plants grow best next to each other, and on what days and what time the garden should be watered. What I am not so good at is handling a situation when those plans do not go exactly the way I wanted them to.

That is the point of this verse in Proverbs. Notice that the author does not say that it is not important to make plans. Plans are helpful and productive, and they help you organize events into more manageable chunks that can be handled. The problem comes when your plans do not happen to match up with those of the Lord's. You may feel you are losing control of the situation and begin desperately to hang on. It is more important to go ahead and make plans but then allow God to work within that framework however He chooses, trusting that if He knows what's best for you, He will get the job done better than you could have.

Father, help me always to remember that my plans are subject to final approval from Your authority.

And He said to His disciples, "Therefore I say to you, do not worry about your life, what you will eat; nor about the body, what you will put on."
—LUKE 12:22

Many compulsions are related to the excesses available here in America. While there are certainly homeless people in the streets who are in desperate need, as a whole, the American people are the best fed, the best clothed, and the most indulgent society in the world today. A great many compulsions are based not on what is needed for survival but rather on accumulating enough to keep up with the Joneses. Sometimes the decisions of what to wear and what to eat can become compulsions in themselves with the almost infinite variety of choices.

Jesus was not saying that you need to go around being hungry or not having clothes to wear. What He did say is to not consume yourself with these rather unimportant details of life. He said that you need to focus on the reality of who you are, not what you look like or what you consume. The things that give meaning to your life cannot be bought or purchased, cannot be consumed or eaten. They are qualities that can only be developed from within as God brings you to the fullness of who He wants you to become.

Father, help me recognize that while I must be concerned about the physical aspects of my life, I cannot be consumed by them.

> *For there is not a just man on earth*
>   *who does good*
> *And does not sin.*   —ECCL. 7:20

Perfectionism is a common form of compulsive behavior. Renee was continually trying to prove herself by being the perfect secretary, but it was always slightly out of reach of the best of her attempts. She kept comparing herself to her coworkers, feeling if she could just out-perform that other person, she might feel good about herself. Once she accomplished some task, or thought she did, she would always compare herself with someone else and find out that she could have done just a little better. The cycle was endless, and the struggle went on and on.

We must come to the realization in life that none of us will obtain perfection. The fact is that we can do some good in our lives, and yet, as the verse says, there is not any man, no matter how much good he does, who does not sin. Therefore, everyone has imperfection in his life. Renee had to learn to deal with that imperfection the way God asked her to. It is only by admitting your imperfections to God and asking Him to forgive you that He can begin to make you perfect.

Father, help me always recognize that in my imperfections, You are made perfect.

For the good that I will to do, I do not do; but the
evil that I will not to do, that I practice.
—ROM. 7:19

Nadine sat in my office with tears in her eyes. She
had been struggling with a sexual addiction in her life.
She was finally beginning to get a sense of how valuable she was to God. That was beginning to influence
her self-worth so she was able to address some of the
issues regarding her addictions. However, she was discouraged. "I try to commit the different areas of my
life to the Lord, and I seem to do well for a while, but
every time I feel like I've made an accomplishment, it
just happens all over again. Will I ever get better?"

Dealing with compulsive behaviors is a long and difficult process. Even the apostle Paul admitted that
there were sometimes things he wished he had not
done. There were other times he had not done things
that he felt that he should have done. This is the great
challenge in life—to recognize that sin is a part of all
your nature, and as long as you live on this earth, it is
going to be part of a struggle. It is the power of Jesus
Christ working in you that gives you the hope of the
victory over these areas of your life. Nadine had to recognize that she could not do it on her own, but by letting go, God could do it through her. And that is the
hope that she clung to each day.

Father, help me recognize that those times of failure in my attempt to
break my compulsive behaviors are also part of my struggle.

He will not be afraid of evil tidings;
His heart is steadfast, trusting in the LORD.
—PS. 112:7

Art liked to give the appearance that he was confident and there were no problems in his life. Yet, underneath that exterior of confidence was a heart full of turmoil and feelings of insecurity rooted deep in his past. And when those anxieties built up, often he reached once again for his compulsive exercising as a quick anesthetic to that pain, even though he knew in the end he would just feel more painful and guilty and the cycle would repeat itself.

In this verse, however, the psalmist gives you hope that your heart can be steadfast. The basis for that is to not trust in your own strength or in the strength of those around you but to trust that the Lord will be able to handle the problems and situations in your life much better than you can. Notice that He does not say that you will never have any bad news or evil tidings; He simply provides you with a way to handle those negative inputs into your life. Art built this trust by daily reminding himself that no matter what he would hear each day to make him feel insecure, ashamed, or fearful, God would be there with him.

Lord, help me realize that there is no news today that I cannot handle if my trust is in You.

*Though I were righteous, my own mouth would
    condemn me;
Though I were blameless, it would prove
    me perverse.*
                                        —JOB 9:20

Peter had been given a particular project that he felt
would challenge and motivate him. He had worked
hard to get this project, and when he was finally
awarded it, he felt elated and excited about the prospects. Yet almost immediately, self-doubt began to nag
at him. He began to find ways to avoid the deadlines he
had set for himself. He began to feel that the task was
too great and that a mistake had been made after all in
choosing him to perform the task. He nearly destroyed
himself and the project with his self-doubt.

Often when you set high goals for yourself, you may
demand things from your own life that you would
never presume to expect from others. Even in an area
where you are successful, you tend to depreciate it and
talk it down saying, "It was just a fluke that it happened
that way." It was important for Peter to recognize that
if God gives a particular task to accomplish, He will
also provide the strength and wisdom and skills necessary to complete the task.

---

*Father, help me stop condemning myself and start trusting You for
my accomplishments.*

*Woe to those who seek deep to hide their counsel
   far from the LORD,
And their works are in the dark;
They say, "Who sees us?" and, "Who knows us?"*
                                        —ISA. 29:15

Often, it is not compulsive behaviors that prove to be the most difficult in identifying but rather the emotions behind the behaviors. Usually, a person can readily admit to the compulsive behaviors because they are on the surface. The emotions that often go with these behaviors are hidden so well and buried so deeply that oftentimes a person is quite blinded to them. Kip worked twenty hours a day, seven days a week, at the office to avoid going home. While he readily admitted he was a workaholic, he could not see how his feelings of failure as a husband and father motivated that compulsion.

It is one of the great tasks of emotional recovery to become as honest about your emotions as God is. After all, if He created you and has the hairs on your head numbered, He obviously knows what is going on within you. The more you try to hide your emotions, and the more dishonest you are, the more you are locked into repeating the compulsive behaviors. Like Kip, you need to recognize that since you cannot hide your emotions from God anyway, you need to be upfront and honest about them and get them out in the open where they can be dealt with more productively.

Lord, help me always remember that the sooner I am honest with my emotions, the sooner I can deal with them.

Let not your heart be troubled; you believe in God, believe also in Me.
                                                        —JOHN 14:1

I remember one particular high school camping trip to Colorado when I got up early one morning to watch the sun come up over the little lake that sat at the foot of the mountains. It was a breathtaking view. It appeared as if someone had simply placed a mirror at the base of that mountain to reflect everything that was around it. The lake was absolutely still, completely untroubled by any breeze or animal. It was a perfect reflection to the surrounding.

When Jesus said, "Let not your heart be troubled," He was speaking of your need to be that reflection of God's love and beauty and peace around you. When your heart is troubled, the reflection is broken. So it is in your life. Once your heart becomes troubled, all you can focus on is the problem and the fear that is consuming you at that point. But as you learn to relax in the Lord by acknowledging His control, that peaceful calm comes once again, and you are able to reflect Him to those around you.

Help my heart to be totally untroubled, Father, so that it can be a mirror image of You in my life.

> *The fear of man brings a snare,*
> *But whoever trusts in the LORD shall be safe.*
> —PROV. 29:25

I have never done much hunting in my life, so I don't know much about the sport. One thing I do know is that a snare is purposely designed to look as harmless as the surrounding area. However, it is that deception that usually allows the animal to be captured. If the trap were to look too obvious, the intended quarry would not venture anywhere near it. The less conspicuous the snare, the more easily the animal is trapped.

This is exactly what your fears do to you every day. John's fears led to his obsession with protection. He heard on the news that there had been some break-ins in his area, so he began checking the locks at night. But his fear began to consume him and he began to check them over and over each night. Soon the real danger had passed, but he was ensnared by his fears and could not seem to break them. It was only when he began to realize that he really could not control the protection of his family, that he released that responsibility to God. Rather than be ensnared by his fears, he learned to relax and allow God to do His job of protecting his family as He has promised He would.

Father, help me see my fears as snares waiting to trap me, and help me trust in Your protection for my life.

*For what is your life? It is even a vapor that
appears for a little time and then vanishes away.*
—JAMES 4:14

In her compulsive life-style, one of the things that motivated Susan was her preoccupation with what could happen in her future. She would get so concerned with trying to make sure that a particular situation turned out in a particular way, her behavior would change. Thus, she became controlled by the event.

James identifies in this verse that life is like a vapor, something that happens so quickly that it can hardly be controlled. It is visible long enough for us to recognize that it has happened; yet, by the time we see it is here, it is already gone, and we have no control over what has happened to it.

If we were to observe the vapor in slow motion, we would recognize that it cannot be controlled even while it exists, for it is ever changing and ever moving. That is part of the lesson from this passage too. Not only did Susan have little control over her future, but she had little control over what was happening right now with her life. Therefore, it was important for her to learn how to deal with what was going on in the present and let the future take care of itself. After all, we might as well enjoy the vapor while it lasts.

---

*Father, help me recognize that while I am able to enjoy the vapor of
my life, I must do so, for it is all that I have at this time.*

Woe to those who are wise in their own eyes,
And prudent in their own sight!

—ISA. 5:21

Have you ever seen a photograph of yourself and exclaimed, "I can't believe it; that doesn't look like me!"? Oftentimes you will compare a photograph with the view you have in the mirror, and it doesn't seem to match up. Have you ever listened to yourself on a tape recorder? Your voice doesn't sound anything like you expected. The picture you have of yourself may be distorted, not really the way you appear to other people.

This is often true of emotions as well. Sometimes you see your behaviors in the light of your own frame of reference, and you do not see how they affect other people. That is why it is so important in the recovery process to share your experiences with someone you can trust so that he or she may be able to show you the areas that you are not seeing. It is almost impossible to recover completely without the help of another close, trusted person, for the picture you have of yourself may not be the one that is seen by others every day. And you can only work on what you know to be a problem.

_____

Father, help me rely on those people You send into my life to help me through this recovery process.

So teach us to number our days,
That we may gain a heart of wisdom.
—PS. 90:12

I remember as a child going to the fair. As a kid, I could hardly get off one ride before I was running to the next, stopping just long enough to get money from Dad. Then came the time where he gave me an allotted amount of money, and I was responsible for how it was spent. The first few times it was amazing how quickly I used up my finances, and then I would have to spend the rest of the day walking around and watching all the other people having a good time. Eventually, I realized that if I kept track of my money and spent it wisely, I could entertain myself for most of the day.

This is the attitude that God wants you to have with your life. If you recognize how valuable your life is, it helps you to "number" your days in a more responsible manner. To spend all your energy up as fast as you can and have nothing left to give at the end of your life is as foolish and unenjoyable as the child who spends his dollars the first hour of the day at the fair. But if you learn to measure out and spend your life wisely, you can continue to be productive to the end, and your whole life will be enjoyable and prosperous.

Lord, teach me to spend each day as wisely as You would have me to.

And further, my son, be admonished by these. Of making many books there is no end, and much study is wearisome to the flesh.

—ECCL. 12:12

One of the difficult things for a counselor is trying to help individuals keep a balance between knowledge and experience. Kirk often came into my office feeling very proud that he had read the latest book on his addiction, or he had discovered a new approach to his particular problem and would think this was going to be the answer for which he had been searching. In fact, if the mental and emotional health of an individual were measured by the amount of information the person has on his problem, Kirk would have been well long ago. He seemed to think that the principles found in some of these books were automatically going to jump into his life and make the difference.

Even though the printed word is a very useful tool, there also has to be a point of practical application. Rather than spending all of his time studying, Kirk needed to spend his energy on *doing* the things he was studying about. It has been said that wisdom is applied knowledge, and that is what is needed to help you through the recovery process.

―――――――――

Help me see, Lord, that the more I know, the more I need to put into practice.

*And which of you by worrying can add one cubit to
his stature?*

—LUKE 12:25

When Jesus asked this question, He was talking with His disciples. These were the people who were close to Him, they had seen Him perform miracles, they had heard His words of hope and security, and yet obviously they still had a problem with worrying. Everyone has, at some point in his life, had difficulty worrying about something. And these questions still remain valid: What has worrying added to your life? Has it put you in control of a situation that you weren't in control of? Has it caused those imperfect people that you know to become perfect? Has it given you the strength and energy to solve an otherwise unsolvable problem?

In fact, the real issue is not what worry adds to your life, but what it takes away. Marsha thought about all the time and energy that she had spent worrying and about the positive things she could have accomplished if she had not been consumed with worry. If anything could be considered wasted time, it is time spent worrying. Marsha realized, just like the disciples, that if her life was controlled by the Creator of the universe, what did she have to worry about?

Father, help me recognize that when I worry, I am not only wasting time, but questioning Your ability to have control.

> *My friends scorn me;*
> *My eyes pour out tears to God.*
> —JOB 16:20

Have you ever dealt with a problem, and having finally come upon some realization, you went to share it with a friend only to be put down or not taken seriously? It is a very painful feeling but one that is common in the recovery process. In Celia's situation, the friends she had along the way were not comfortable with her newfound insights and reacted very negatively to her new changes, trying to keep things at *status quo* rather than be forced to make changes in their relationships with her. At the time she needed them the most, they ended up rejecting her which only added to her struggle and pain in recovery.

The comforting news is that God understands and He provides the necessary encouragement and strength. When none of his earthly friends seemed to understand what was going on, Job knew that he could always rely on God to understand and accept his tears, knowing that they were not only appropriate but often necessary in the recovery process. Celia had to remember that when she felt no one understood or cared about her, God would always be there for her.

Father, help me remember that You are there and that You understand my highs and lows in the recovery process.

But Martha was distracted with much serving, and she approached Him and said, "Lord, do You not care that my sister has left me to serve alone? Therefore tell her to help me." —LUKE 10:40

While I was growing up, whenever I heard the story of Jesus going to Mary, Martha, and Lazarus's house, I always felt sorry for Martha. Here she was, trying to do the best job that she could in making things right for Jesus' visit, and no one would help her. I kept thinking maybe if she'd had a little help from her sister, she might have eventually been able to get out there and enjoy Jesus' company as well.

However, it wasn't what Martha was *doing* that became the problem, it was how much of her this consumed. Even if everything had been done to satisfaction, Martha still would have found something else to occupy her need to have everything "perfect." It is not so much what you are doing that is the problem, but how it is affecting the rest of your life. In Martha's case, the important thing was that Jesus was there and willing to spend time with her. Where does that apply in your life today? Are the tasks you are involved in today having so much control on your life that you miss the important things of life, like spending time with the Lord?

***

Father, help me to learn how to recognize the importance of the moment.

> *And when His disciples James and John saw this,*
> *they said, "Lord, do You want us to command fire*
> *to come down from heaven and consume them, just*
> *as Elijah did?"*
> —LUKE 9:54

One of the most encouraging things that a recovering compulsive can do is to look at the lives of the disciples and see how Jesus dealt with their weaknesses. If you have ever read any of the books that the apostle John wrote, the things that come across are the strength and simplicity of his message. In reading those books, you get the impression that John is a very quiet, stable, thinking man, who never lets emotions get in the way of his message. And yet in this verse, this same John, who perhaps was very tranquil on the outside, was ready to call fire down from heaven to defend Jesus' honor.

How often are you like that in your own life? Frank outwardly portrayed a placid, controlled facade to the people around him, but when a crisis came, he emotionally went off the deep end. Jesus' response to John speaks to all of us, for in essence what He said was, "Your actions need to match up to the attitude you portray." You need to recognize if the controlled facade does not match up with the turmoil you feel, then you need to begin to face your issues so that your entire life can be in control, not just the surface.

Lord, help me recognize that You want to control my emotions and behaviors.

We should no longer be children, tossed to and fro and carried about with every wind of doctrine, by the trickery of men, in the cunning craftiness by which they lie in wait to deceive. —EPH. 4:14

In any discussion with a driven individual, the question must come up, "What are you driven by?" An object can be driven by many things—wind, steam, gasoline, manpower. All can be responsible for locomotion. A person can be driven by all types of motivation from any number of sources. One particularly destructive area of addiction is when an individual is driven to any of the latest philosophies.

Joanie was always looking for the latest fad in intellectual thinking. First, she dabbled in the Eastern religions, especially Buddhism. Bored, she switched to Humanism. And then to the New Age movement. These quests were an attempt to find some stability and calm in her life. Actually, she was like a leaf in the wind, tossed back and forth by her desperate need to find peace in her life. Stability comes from learning to trust something that has proven itself valid over time. That's exactly what God's Word has done, and that was the stability Joanie needed to accept in her life.

Father, help me increase my stabilities so that I will not be a victim of those people or those things around me that want to control me.

We grope for the wall like the blind,
And we grope as if we had no eyes;
We stumble at noonday as at twilight;
We are as dead men in desolate places.
—ISA. 59:10

Blindness is not a desirable condition. Yet today many people are choosing to be blind, especially those who are driven by compulsive behaviors. It is a self-inflicted blindness, chosen by those who would rather continue living in the darkness of their behaviors than risk the changes that sight would bring.

Helen was choosing blindness. Even though her shopping binges were about to cost her a marriage of thirty-five years, she kept blaming her financial problems on her husband's stinginess. Any time an effort was made to point out her own responsibility in the situation, she would adamantly deny it. She would then retreat back into the darkness of her compulsion and go on another unaffordable shopping spree.

Only by allowing yourself to be open to God's cure for your blindness, can you even hope to see clearly the sources of your addictions. By using His Word to help you face your needs, you can observe for the first time just how blind you were, and correct your vision so that you no longer have to stumble in darkness.

Father, remove the blindness of my emotional eyes by the clarity of Your Word.

Fight the good fight of faith, lay hold on eternal life, to which you were also called and have confessed the good confession in the presence of many witnesses.
                                        —1 TIM. 6:12

Bradley sat in my office across from me with a tired look on his face. He had been seeing me for several months regarding his compulsive workaholism, and although he had made significant progress, he was beginning to show strains. "I want to get better," he said, "and I feel I am moving in the right direction, but I never imagined the struggle would be so difficult. I feel as if I'm heading back into battle every day of my life."

And that is exactly what it is—a battle. If an individual thinks she can nonchalantly address compulsive behaviors as a minor interruption, she is in for quite a shock. It is a long, difficult war, and you will not always win every battle. But the question to ask yourself every day is how equipped are you to fight the battles that you need to? Bradley needed to simply let God do the conquering and realize that the victory had already been won.

————

Equip me each day with Your power, Father, to fight the battles I have to fight, and help me recognize that even if I lose today's battles, I can still have the victory through Your power in my life.

And not only that, but we also glory in tribulations,
knowing that tribulation produces perseverance;
and perseverance, character; and character, hope.
                                        —ROM. 5:3–4

It is often interesting to see that an individual's compulsive behavior may transfer itself over into the therapeutic process. If Nathan was driven by crippling compulsions in his life, he was also driven by the need to "hurry up and get better." He wanted results in his life, but was not excited about the idea of pacing himself and working through his pain. Yet perseverance is part of any recovery process.

Notice what this verse says is the end result of allowing perseverance to work in your life—hope. Nathan felt that there seemed to be no hope to his getting better. He had struggled so long with his drivenness that any more effort seemed impossible. Yet God said that the effort made toward recovery is different because it produces something of value rather than the emptiness of guilt and shame. And if hope is the end result, it certainly is worth the price.

_____

Lord, allow perseverance to work in my life so that the end result will certainly be worth the effort.

Who can understand his errors?
Cleanse me from secret faults.
—PS. 19:12

For a person who has experienced severe trauma in childhood, it is often very difficult and painful to look at some of the negative messages he received. Roberta discovered that her mind had been blocked of a large number of memories as a way of escaping pain. At times in the recovery process, Roberta tended to become frustrated that she could not remember some of these experiences because she recognized that the more she remembered, the more she could begin to feel whole again.

This verse gives you encouragement for those things that you have somehow blocked from your memory. You do not need to become negligent or reluctant in seeking out past issues, but in those areas that you just cannot seem to understand or grasp, God knows those areas even when you do not, and He has the ability to cleanse you and forgive you for those thoughts and behaviors you aren't even aware of. It is just one more way that God's love and forgiveness could free Roberta from her past. As she asked God to forgive her for what she didn't remember, she could move out from under the cloud of guilt that so often surrounded her.

_____

Give me the grace, Father, to face the things that I need to face, and in those places that I cannot see as clearly as I would like, cleanse me from those faults You are aware of.

But those who desire to be rich fall into temptation and a snare, and into many foolish and harmful lusts which drown men in destruction and perdition.
—1 TIM. 6:9

In today's materialistic society, the desire to be rich is a powerfully addictive agent. From every direction Clay was always made to feel that there was something else that he simply could not live without. And while what he had was not bad, there was always something else better or newer or improved that promised to improve the quality of his existence. It seems that the richer America gets, the richer the citizens of America want to become.

It is important to note, however, that being rich or having possessions is not the problem. This verse is not a judgment on the condition of being rich but rather on the individual's attitude about that condition. It is the *desire* to be rich that led Clay down a dangerous path. And notice the sequence of events: it starts as a temptation, turns into a full-blown lust, and ends up in destruction. In effect, the verse is saying that the person who has these kinds of desires ends up *not* being rich in any way. A desire like this can never be quenched.

Father, help me see that the circumstances I am in are not nearly as important as my attitude about those circumstances.

*He said to him the third time, "Simon, son of
Jonah, do you love Me?" Peter was grieved because
He said to him the third time, "Do you love Me?"
And he said to Him, "Lord, You know all things;
You know that I love You." Jesus said to him, "Feed
My sheep."*
                                                    —JOHN 21:17

Jesus was getting ready to leave His disciples and
wanted to assess where they were in terms of their relationship with Him before He left. Jesus asked Peter a
simple question, and Peter responded with a pat answer. Jesus ended up asking the question three times
before He could get an honest response from Peter. Although Peter was saying the right words, it wasn't until
his attitude was in the right place that Jesus accepted
his answer.

How often do you repeat things over and over,
knowing that you are not really meaning what you
say? It seems that if you say it often enough and with
enough force, it will be accepted as the truth, and you
can go on and live your "comfortable" life. But who are
you really trying to convince? God truly knows your
heart and motives. If you are ever to recover from the
lies you believe, you will have to face the truth as honestly as Peter did in this passage.

*Father, help me see that rather than hearing me repeat pat answers
You desire the truth and honesty needed to truly deal with my
emotions.*

For each one shall bear his own load.
—GAL. 6:5

I remember coming to gym class one day in grade school and the teacher telling us that we were going to build a human pyramid. Of course, everyone's first thought was, "I sure don't want to be on the bottom!" But as the teacher began placing us in the pyramid, we soon realized that it wasn't the total responsibility of the bottom row to bear everyone's weight. If everyone did his own job in the pyramid, no one would have to hold more weight than he was able to bear. As soon as one person decided not to support his load, the entire pyramid came toppling down.

When you look at some of the responsibilities involved in relationships with other people, you can get overwhelmed. But as you begin to build the "pyramid" of relationships, you will see as each one shoulders his own responsibilities, the relationship tends to work smoothly. However, when one person shirks his responsibility, the others around tend to suffer with the displacement of the burden. It is important for you to bear your own responsibilities in relationships—not any more or any less.

Lord, help me see that when I want to take on too much or give up too soon in relationships, I am not bearing the responsibility that I need to in the relationship.

Blessed is the man
Who walks not in the counsel of the ungodly,
Nor stands in the path of sinners,
Nor sits in the seat of the scornful.

—PS. 1:1

As a child, I had a Sunday school teacher who taught me a lesson about this verse that I will never forget. He talked about how the individual in this verse initially has no intention of getting into trouble. But as he draws closer and closer to whatever it is that these "ungodly" are involved with, he ends up becoming involved in it himself. My teacher used the illustration of a man walking by, then stopping to stand, and eventually ending up sitting in the middle of them.

Isn't this also true of compulsive behaviors? Brandon began his interest in the occult in all innocence, thinking it was relatively harmless at first. But the more it became a part of his life, the more he seemed to be controlled by it to the point where it became a driving force. It was not sudden but rather a slow progressive deception which sneaked up unaware until he was caught in the middle of it. It is so important to recognize the potential for the compulsive behaviors in life and to walk by them as quickly and as often as you can.

Give me the courage, Father, to walk by undesirable behaviors, for if I stop and stand it won't be long until I am "sitting in the midst of them."

The LORD knows the thoughts of man,
That they are futile. —PS. 94:11

Have you ever tried to build a sand castle on the beach? It can truly be an exercise in futility. As soon as you get the second wall built, the first one crumbles. About the time everything is just as you want it, a wave comes up and crashes over the castle, leveling it back to flat beach. And the worst part is trying to keep water in the "moat." You can fill it up all day and it will still run out the bottom.

Sarah's life was like that. She kept trying to build herself up, making herself available to everyone to be used as they saw fit. Each relationship would wash over her, leaving her a little more devastated, and she could never seem to fill up the "moat" of needs she felt deep inside. It all seemed so futile.

God knew about Sarah's futile behaviors. He also knew a way that she could build her life out of the granite of His power and strength instead of the sand of instability. It was up to Sarah to choose to move from the beach to the rock and begin building.

Lord, help me quit playing in the sand and start building on the Rock.

*And do not present your members as instruments
of unrighteousness to sin, but present yourselves
to God as being alive from the dead, and your
members as instruments of righteousness to God.*
—ROM. 6:13

It is amazing to think what can be done with the same tool by the hands of different people. A surgeon uses a scalpel as a tool for healing; in the hand of a murderer a scalpel can become a deadly weapon. A writer's words can stir people to great deeds of heroism or patriotism, but in the hands of an evil person those words can lead to revolution or anarchy. It is not the tool itself, but rather what one does with the tool that causes the problem.

This becomes the real heart of the issue in the life of the compulsive. Activities such as dedication to work, caring for the people around you, and wanting to do the best job you possibly can are all very positive qualities. Taken to a different level, however, these can quickly turn into compulsions that can control your every action. The issue is not the good or evil in these activities themselves but rather what is your motivation behind them. And as you begin to seek God's will for your life, you can use these tools and abilities for what they were intended for—to build yourself and others up in the love of God.

Father, help me decide today to take the unique gifts and abilities that You have given me and to present them to You for Your special use in my life.

> *And He said to them, "Take heed and beware of covetousness, for one's life does not consist in the abundance of the things he possesses."*
>
> —LUKE 12:15

In Len's compulsive life-style, there was an equation that seemed to have developed that said "money equals power." The more possessions he accumulated, the more successes he made for himself, the more others tended to idolize him and put him in a position of some type of authority. It seemed that the sole ability to accumulate things gave Len some sort of God-like quality, as if by his own material possessions, he gained the power he needed to control his life. Yet, the only real quality that accumulating things brought to Len was the need to accumulate more things.

Certainly in taking a closer look at Len's personal life, the chaos would indicate that he has no better answers to the real issues of life than anyone else does. The wealth not only did not provide solutions to his life but often added to the turmoil he was already experiencing. And when his life is over, the only thing that his money will allow others to say about him is that he was rich, and that is certainly no definition of a productive life.

—————————

Lord, help me see that if I define myself by my material possessions, that is exactly what I will be remembered for.

Will you set your eyes on that which is not?
For riches certainly make themselves wings;
They fly away like an eagle toward heaven.
—PROV. 23:5

Imagine chasing riches like chasing a butterfly. It seems that no matter how close you get, the butterfly always seems to be out of your grasp. I remember as a child spending entire mornings with my net chasing these creatures, and often had little (if anything) to show for my efforts. They always stayed out of my reach and yet just close enough to tantalize. No matter how much richer some people become, a little bit more would make them a little more powerful and a little bit more in control.

Also, in chasing butterflies, the more you chase them, the further away you get from home. By staying just far enough away, the butterfly leads you on a wild chase. Before you know it, you are in unfamiliar territory, and it may be more difficult to find your way back. This is also what riches did to Stuart. They led him on a wild goose chase. When he finally decided he had enough and wanted to give up the chase, it was very difficult to get back to the real principles of his life.

_____

Help me to see, Lord, that chasing riches is as futile and time-consuming as chasing butterflies.

> *You shall not covet your neighbor's house; you shall*
> *not covet your neighbor's wife, nor his manservant,*
> *nor his maidservant, nor his ox, nor his donkey,*
> *nor anything that is your neighbor's.*
>
> —EX. 20:17

Of course, you probably learned the Ten Commandments when you were a child. So you are aware of the commandment that tells you not to covet. While the list is not comprehensive, it gives you an idea of what you should not be coveting. However, the list names only material possessions.

Is anything said about coveting your neighbor's good attitude? How about his caring spirit or concern for others? Do you see anything mentioned about his love for God, his patient spirit, or his ability to forgive? Nothing is said about the *good* qualities your neighbor may have, and there is a reason behind this. God did not include those positive qualities in His commandments because there would be no problem with wanting these things for your life. He knows it is human nature to rarely even consider those traits as something to be desired from the people around us. Maybe that is the point of this commandment—if you want something someone else has, it should be something God can put in your life rather than what you might achieve yourself.

Help me see, Father, that if I have a problem with coveting, I am seeking after the wrong things.

Is there anything of which it may be said,
"See, this is new"?
It has already been in ancient times before us.
—ECCL. 1:10

In my profession and because I am a member of several different organizations, I am continually informed of upcoming seminars and workshops in the field of counseling. It always amazes me how each one is considered "new and improved," but in reading the fine print of what will be covered, it is just rehashing all the old ideas and presenting them in perhaps a new and creative way.

There is one thing that does not change—the truth of God's Word remains the same regardless of the time, place, or situation. While that may seem terribly unexciting to those who are always looking for a new experience in their lives, it also can be very stabilizing and comforting for one who has been driven by the instability of a compulsive addiction. After trying to find happiness through the newest philosophy, Connie found contentment in the realization that if those principles worked for all these centuries, it was encouraging to know that they could work for her the same way.

Father, help me see that no matter what else changes in my life, Your Word will always remain the same constant source of truth that it has always been.

For out of the heart proceed evil thoughts, murders, adulteries, fornications, thefts, false witness, blasphemies.

—MATT. 15:19

Have you ever noticed that when you go into a doctor's office one of the first things they do is take your pulse and listen to your heart? This is not just a simple exercise in medical ethics. The fact is that no matter what other ailment you may have, if your heart is working properly, you have a much better chance of fighting and surviving the illness. But if your heart is weak or damaged, that will not only make the situation more difficult, but in fact may contribute to the problem.

Trent could not always control the things that were said to him or the thoughts that were put into his head. But he learned that if he would take care of his spiritual heart, he was better equipped to fight the battle against those things. If he let the condition of his spiritual heart deteriorate, not only did he have less to fight back with, but often those things were allowed to fester until they became a part of him. That is why it is so important to guard your heart and to make sure that it is as spiritually sound as it can possibly be.

Father, help me allow You to control my heart so that I will be better equipped to handle the negative influences that come into my life.

*And you shall know the truth, and the truth shall
make you free.*
—JOHN 8:32

A lady once sat in my office who had been battling compulsive behaviors for years. Liz stated, "I began doing some of these things like shopping and spending as a way of gaining control of my life, a way of expressing my freedom as an individual. Now the sad reality is that I am less free than I was before. What I truly seek is real freedom—freedom from all these compulsive behaviors." It seemed like such an escape to her at first, but soon it became the thing that tied her down. These compulsive behaviors were all deceptive lies, and deception and lying never set a person free.

The only thing that can set a person free is the truth. When you are dealing with compulsive behaviors, you have to view them as things that are holding you in bondage. For even though you may want control in your life, in reality these addictions are controlling you. Until you are truthful and honest enough to see them that way, you never will be free. It is only by recognizing the bondage they hold you in and the reality of God's Word becoming your source of worth that you can truly become free—free to a life of worth and meaning in God's love.

Help me recognize that true freedom comes in realizing where my bondage lies and allowing the truth of Your Word to set me truly free.

Then Samuel said:
"Has the LORD as great delight in burnt
*   offerings and sacrifices,*
As in obeying the voice of the LORD?
Behold, to obey is better than sacrifice,
And to heed than the fat of rams."

—1 SAM. 15:22

One of the areas of the compulsive behavior that had been increasing in Cora's life was the idea of martyrdom, or continued sacrifice for the efforts of the church. She took the attitude that more was better, and she involved herself in every committee or function the church had to offer. Whenever she got tired or failed to perform all the tasks that were required of her, she felt more guilty than ever.

However, this verse in First Samuel makes it clear what God's attitude is about sacrifice. Notice that He does not say that sacrifice is unimportant; rather, He says that it takes a secondary position to obedience toward God's will in your life. If you are sacrificing to gain the approval of others, or even to gain approval of God, you are doing it for the wrong reasons and it will not be honored. It is obedience that God desires, an obedience that begins when you understand and accept your worth in Him.

Lord, may I be as willing to obey You as I am to sacrifice for You so that I will fulfill Your perfect will for my life.

Unless the LORD builds the house,
They labor in vain who build it;
Unless the LORD guards the city,
The watchman stays awake in vain.
—PS. 127:1

Have you ever worked diligently on a project, planned every detail, explored every alternative, made every part fit perfectly, and you were ready to present it only to be told that the decision was made elsewhere and the effort you expended was not even going to be considered? I can tell you it is a frustrating, empty feeling because at that point there is nothing you can do to reclaim that time. Yet that is what you are doing when you do not let the Lord be in control of your life. After all, God Himself made the blueprint so it would seem logical that He would know best how to build the house.

Also, since God designed the house, He knows where the strengths and weaknesses are. He has put in the investment, and He wants to take care of it. Because He knows your weaknesses better than you do, it is much more practical to allow Him to guard your life, rather than doing it yourself. You are so often fooled by your own denial and defenses. After all, if you truly want the best in your life, why don't you let "the best" handle it?

Lord, help me understand that only by allowing my life to be built by You will it ever meet the specifications that You have designed for it.

> *Therefore, as we have opportunity, let us do good*
> *to all, especially to those who are of the household*
> *of faith.*
> —GAL. 6:10

In dealing with compulsive behaviors, Seth began to get the idea that any act of service toward another person was somehow associated with an unmet need in his life, and therefore, he must back away from helping people at all. Yet, he was commanded in God's Word to love, to serve, and to help others along life's road. What makes the difference between a healthy desire to serve others and an unhealthy need to be totally responsible? This verse identifies the main criterion—opportunity.

Often, the basis for serving others is not what it will do for the other person but how you will feel by doing it. Wait for those special opportunities that God sends to help and serve those people around you. Not only will you recognize that it is helpful for them but it will also be fulfilling for you in that you were a part of God's will for that person's life. For Seth, becoming aware that he was at God's place and in God's time gave him a sense of satisfaction that no compulsion could ever match.

————————

Father, help me not to create my own agenda for helping people, and to be sensitive to the opportunities that You can and will provide.

But take heed to yourselves, lest your hearts be weighed down with carousing, drunkenness, and cares of this life, and that Day come on you unexpectedly.
—LUKE 21:34

Sure, I want to feel happier about my life," Cal said, "but don't ask me to give up my partying. After a boring week at the old grind, that's the only time I can cut loose and really carry on. It's a release for me. So it costs some money, and I feel lousy for two days; hey, it's the only time I can really escape. I feel free there."

It is interesting that in this verse, "drunkenness" and "carousing" are associated with being weighed down. The usual picture created is of people who are carefree, who have no concerns, who are simply grabbing for all the "gusto" they can in life. Yet, in this verse, Jesus cuts through the heart of the matter when He talks about the fact that all the "fun" part of these activities is just a cover-up for the real burden that they place on someone like Cal. They can never meet the need for which he is using them to fill. It is only when Cal begins to sense that these habits are in fact weighing him down that he can truly begin to be happier about his life, and not fool himself with the artificial "high" of a false happiness.

Father, take those things in me that would weigh me down, and make me truly free by the truth of Your Word today.

> *This is My commandment, that you love one*
> *another as I have loved you.* —JOHN 15:12

Constance was having difficulty in understanding what true love was since she had never experienced it for herself. She began studying God's Word to see what kind of love Jesus showed. Was it a demanding love that made sure people did things perfectly the first time they were asked? Was it a manipulative love that made sure His needs were met before the others involved? Was it a need-driven love that allowed others to walk all over Him and use Him for their own devices? Or was it a smothering love that gave His followers no room to develop character and personalities of their own?

No, it was none of these. The love that Jesus demonstrated was based first on the fact that He knew His Father loved Him more than anyone else in the world could. That allowed Him to give to others out of that abundance of love without demanding anything in return. And yet, because Jesus loved others so much, He treated them with the respect and the responsibility that they needed, and they were willing to love Him back. And that was the key for Constance: the way to receive love from anybody else in her life was to recognize that God loves her so much that she could afford to love another person unconditionally.

Father, help me learn that not only is it better to give than to receive but that the only way to receive is to give first.

*Who, being past feeling, have given themselves
over to licentiousness, to work all uncleanness
with greediness.* —EPH. 4:19

For people who have compulsions involving sexual
behaviors or sensual desires, one of the things that
they are seeking is the feeling of being fulfilled in a
love relationship. For Ross, what started out as a crav-
ing for an emotional need became associated with
physical satisfaction. Once that sensual experience became the goal, the quest to fill that lustful need almost
became insatiable. Ross was always looking for that
ultimate experience or new person that could bring
him the fulfillment for which he longed.

Yet, it is interesting to note in this verse, when a person falls into the patterns of sexual compulsion or "licentiousness," he or she is defined as being "past
feeling." The further Ross went into his sexual addiction, the more his senses were dulled, and the more it
took to bring any type of fulfilling response to him.
That is the trap of compulsiveness. Sex could never be
fulfilling for Ross because it would never give him
what he was longing for. That need could only be fulfilled by the recognition of who he was in the Lord and
how his compulsive behavior was destroying him.

*Lord, help me recognize that my compulsive behaviors will not ful-
fill the need but will only deaden my feelings to the needs that I
truly have.*

For this is the love of God, that we keep His commandments. And His commandments are not burdensome.
—1 JOHN 5:3

One of the first ways I could identify that Jan was addicted to the relationships in her life was when she began referring to them as "burdens." The weight of caring for all those people seemed to be making her life more difficult. Somehow she felt that if she could just be free of those people, she could find the freedom she was looking for.

That is exactly what the apostle John is talking about in this verse. God has provided in His Word the ability to live a life-style that is not only *not* burdensome but very liberating. The way of life that He provides in His Word frees you from the things that would drag you down including codependent relationships. God gives you the strength and confidence to deal with the problems you face in a way that does not have to defeat you. In fact, this passage was the yardstick which Jan used to measure her current life-style: if she felt burdened, then according to this verse, she was not following God's commandments. And that realization brought her to the point where she saw that the only way to become unburdened was to study God's Word and discover what He said about the relationships in her life.

Father, help me to find Your way of handling my problems.

For I am poor and needy,
And my heart is wounded within me.
—PS. 109:22

About a year ago, my family had the traumatic experience of rushing one of our daughters to the emergency room after she had received a pretty severe cut on her head. They shaved the wound, cleaned it, measured it, X-rayed it, viewed it, and did everything possible to determine exactly how severe the damage was. It was only then that the wound received stitches. Because they were able to see the wound, they could treat it in the best possible way.

The problem with Carla was that no one could look at her heart and see the damage that had been done. There was no way of accurately measuring the wounds that she received nor truly assessing the damage that had been done by negative messages. Even Carla did not really have an objective view of how serious the damage was. That is why it was so important for her to allow the Great Physician to examine her wounds to truly assess the damage and then allow Him to begin healing those wounds because He understands their depth and severity. No matter what kind of behavior or relationship you may try to use to treat your wounds, only the One who best can know them can heal them in the most healthy way.

Help me allow You, O Lord, to measure the true depth of my wounds and heal me as only You can.

Because "All flesh is as grass,
And all the glory of man as the flower of the grass.
The grass withers,
And its flower falls away,
But the word of the LORD endures forever."
—1 PETER 1:24–25

One of the things I enjoy doing is working in my yard in the summer. Our lawn will never be featured in *Home and Garden,* but I do get some satisfaction out of the activity. However, my neighbor's lawn is a completely different story. It looks like a golf green, with every bush perfectly trimmed, and he seems to know exactly when each leaf will fall so he can catch it before it hits the ground. But an interesting thing happens in the winter. If you were to drive by our two houses, you would not see much difference between my brown, dried lawn and his brown, dried lawn. As beautiful as his lawn is in the summer, he cannot make it last over the winter, and it eventually dies.

On the surface, you may seem to have a cluttered, unorganized life, while other lives may seem to flow meticulously together without an attitude out of place. But eventually you will no longer be here and, according to the Scripture, the things that last will be the things that you have done according to God's Word.

Lord, help me not to become so obsessed with tending to the surface details of my life that I miss the things that will last an eternity.

*Do not let your beauty be that outward adorning . . .
but let it be the hidden person of the heart, with the
incorruptible ornament of a gentle and quiet spirit,
which is very precious in the sight of God.*
—1 PETER 3:3–4

Today's society is obsessed with physical beauty. Plastic surgery is at an all-time high, and people are going in for multiple surgical procedures to help make them more physically attractive. Jodi was continually thinking that if she just had one more operation to correct that one minor flaw, it would make all the difference in her life. She believed that a face-lift, tummy tuck, or nose job could fill that empty void that she had been feeling.

This verse poses a new kind of operation—a heart lift. Just think about the kind of person you would be if you would spend the same time, money, and energy on improving your inner self as you do on trying to make your external appearance more physically attractive. The wonderful thing about the transformation of your heart is that time will not age it but it will actually improve the qualities you have gained from the Lord. When Jodi allowed God to perform that surgery on her heart and to remold it in His image, she began to realize that it was exactly what she was looking for all along.

_____

Help me be as willing to work on my inner self as I am on making my appearance more attractive.

*And they said, "Come, let us build ourselves a city,
and a tower whose top is in the heavens; let us
make a name for ourselves, lest we be scattered
abroad over the face of the whole earth."*
—GEN. 11:4

Since the beginning of the history of man, individuals
have always longed for some type of recognition in the
world. The building of the tower of Babel was only the
first in a series of attempts toward achieving that recognition, and even today that drive continues. The motivation behind this desire is for an individual to feel
that somehow he has made an accomplishment during
his life here on earth, and that will meet the need of
insignificance and low self-worth.

Drew's need for recognition was so strong and the
praise so fulfilling that he could not get enough of it.
He began to spend his life in a desperate attempt to
have that feeling as often and for as long as possible.
There was no task too large, no situation too costly if it
meant that Drew would be appreciated in some way.

What Drew did not recognize was that no amount of
self-accomplishment could ever create the worth that
he wanted to feel inside. The only One who could fill
that need in his life was the Lord, and the only way He
could do that was when Drew began to realize that he
could not do it on his own. It is important to spend your
energies productively by trusting in God.

*Lord, help me use my energies wisely by trusting You rather than
myself.*

Better is a little with the fear of the LORD,
Than great treasure with trouble.
—PROV. 15:16

I recently dealt with a couple who did not believe the saying, "Money doesn't buy happiness." Kurt and LeAnn had a successful business, lived in an estate, drove the newest foreign cars, jetted off to exotic vacations, and gave their employees five-digit bonuses. Kurt was also a recovering alcoholic, but he had transferred much of his compulsive behavior over to his work. When he did come home, he had very little emotional input to give to the family. He was in trouble with the IRS, and so in spite of his incredible salary, Kurt asked LeAnn to go back to work. She was bitter and resentful, feeling that he had cared about everyone but her. She tried to numb her pain by going on extravagant shopping trips, only to end up never wearing most of what she purchased. They couldn't have a conversation without screaming at each other, and their intimate personal life had been nonexistent for months.

Kurt and LeAnn failed to recognize the most important lesson of life—that in spite of what the outside circumstances appear to be, a person who neglects God never has everything he or she needs.

Help me see, Lord, how much You are truly worth having in my life.

Let your conduct be without covetousness, and be content with such things as you have. For He Himself has said, "I will never leave you nor forsake you."
—HEB. 13:5

Everyone has experienced some type of abandonment. Whether it has been a close friend moving away, the loss of a pet, even not having letters answered by a close friend, you understand what it is like to feel loss. However, sometimes those losses can be much greater, and the feelings of abandonment go much deeper than those experienced on a day-to-day basis. Sarah grew up in a family where her mother was emotionally unavailable to her and her father physically absent because of divorce. The feelings of abandonment led Sarah to fill that need by accumulating and holding on to as many friendships as possible. No matter how many friends she developed, Sarah never felt satisfied but was always looking for someone else to help fill that hole of abandonment.

Jesus said that He will never leave you or forsake you. As Sarah learned to go to Him first, each and every day, she began to feel His presence in her life, and she realized she could stop trying to fill that empty feeling with all the relationships she was accumulating. She simply allowed Him to be that "missing Person" in her life, and because He is always there, she never felt abandoned again.

Thank You, Lord, that You have promised always to be with us.

Indeed, You have made my days as handbreadths,
And my age is as nothing before You;
Certainly every man at his best state is but vapor.
—PS. 39:5

Because he could not comprehend eternity, Skip's limited earthly perspective began to convince him that his accomplishments here on earth were of utmost importance, and that he needed to make his presence in this world count for something. He began to convince himself that somehow if he did enough humanitarian things and made enough of an impact, that he would achieve immortality, and that even when he was gone, his name would be recognized. And so his life took on a self-importance that it was never designed to have.

In order to make your life truly count on this earth, one of the things you must always remember is how short life really is. It is true that your life has a purpose, but that purpose has its foundation in following God's plan and allowing Him to take control. God was the only One who could take Skip's short time here on earth and make it count for anything of significance, but in order for Him to do that, Skip first had to take the action of committing his life to Him. Since God looks at life through the perspective of eternity, only He can know best how to use each moment.

Help me, Father, to trust You for my brief time here on earth.

> *Let the wicked forsake his way,*
> *And the unrighteous man his thoughts;*
> *Let him return to the LORD,*
> *And He will have mercy on him;*
> *And to our God,*
> *For He will abundantly pardon.*
> —ISA. 55:7

A common misconception found in compulsive individuals is an unwillingness to turn to God. Because of all the negative things they have done in their lives and because they feel they have absolutely no worth, they are hesitant to believe He truly will forgive them. Tracy believed that she had passed a point of no return—she just had done too much to expect God to forgive her, let alone take control of her life. Hopelessness led her to more destructive and unhealthy behaviors.

The reality is that no matter where an individual is, no matter what a person has done in the past, no matter what kind of negative thinking she may have suffered, God still can and wants to forgive her. He is full of mercy and would desire nothing more than to have someone recognize her own inability to change her own life and begin to trust Him for that control. God's pardoning ability is endless, and there is nothing an individual has done that can't be forgiven. By giving up a little more of her life to Him every day, even Tracy eventually came to experience God's forgiveness.

Lord, thank You for Your unending ability to forgive me.

But godliness with contentment is great gain.
—1 TIM. 6:6

There were two negative ideas that greatly influenced Reggie's behavior. Reggie believed that he must create his own happiness. In order for him to be content, he thought he had to take charge of his own life and fulfill all of his own needs and desires as he saw fit, with no regard for anyone else. The other negative idea he had was that if he abandoned the first idea and decided to let God take control of his life, he might be doing the right thing but probably would not be happy doing it. *What God desires for my life,* he thought, *is to live a life of drudgery, always doing the* spiritual *thing and certainly never enjoying myself.*

Both of these ideas are lies that have been around for a long time. True contentment only can be found by living a life controlled by God. He knows you and understands you better than you know yourself, and so He can meet each of your needs. But beyond that, He also wants you to enjoy your life and to have it be as fulfilled as it possibly can be. God is the source of contentment. When Reggie saw he could have both, he knew he wanted nothing else.

Help me understand, Lord, that only by trusting in You can I find true contentment.

Good understanding gains favor,
But the way of the unfaithful is hard.
—PROV. 13:15

One of the driving forces behind Gail's workaholism was the need to feel important. The need for approval was so compelling that often she would push beyond her limits to get a pat on the back. In fact, the source of the approval was not nearly so important as the receipt of it because Gail felt so worthless and ashamed of her life.

God's Word talks about the source of approval in an individual's life. And it starts with an understanding of how God alone could give her life purpose. The more Gail studied God's Word, the more she realized what her purpose was. Part of that purpose was to be the person God wanted her to be, regardless of how the people at the office treated her or measured her success.

Gail learned the place to start gaining approval in her life was not through what she had done, but rather what God had done *for* her, and what He desired to do *with* her.

Lord, help me understand the approval that You give me in my life.

But all their works they do to be seen by men.
They make their phylacteries broad and enlarge
the borders of their garments. —MATT. 23:5

One group that received much of Jesus' condemnation while He was on earth was a group called the Pharisees. These were the religious leaders of the time, and Jesus spoke quite a bit about their hypocrisy. One aspect of their life-styles that He continued to disapprove of was their seemingly endless need to impress other people. Whenever these men prayed, they prayed loudly so that everyone would hear them. They competed with each other to see who could wear the finest robes and the most ornate accessories. There was no limit to what they would do to make their influence felt during those times. Even though they were supposedly the religious leaders, their motivation was entirely self-seeking.

In fact, the Pharisees were driven by many of the principles that you are driven by today. And before you become too judgmental of the Pharisees, look at your own actions. How much do you do in order to make yourself appear better in front of other people? Is love motivating you or are you motivated by the need to be loved?

Help me, O Lord, be honest enough to see Pharisaism in my own life today.

Therefore remove sorrow from your heart,
And put away evil from your flesh,
For childhood and youth are vanity.
—ECCL. 11:10

Kyle's drive for control was motivated by his need to right the wrongs done in his childhood. Because so many of his needs went unmet and so much pain was created, Kyle felt he had actually lost his childhood. There was a great deal of grief and sorrow that accompanied that feeling, and that was what led Kyle to begin using control to ease the pain. He involved himself in relationships that he used to correct those mistakes of the past. The more his pain was felt, the more intense his search became to try and resolve it.

No matter how much pain and suffering was created in childhood, it can never be relived. There are hurts and griefs that must be dealt with over the course of your life, but to try and "replace" those feelings in current relationships is an exercise in futility. The best way Kyle could begin to handle the past was to begin facing it rather than reliving it. He needed to accept it for what it was, then give it over to God and move on with his life. The only relationship that can truly help you overcome a painful past is a relationship with Someone who has been there—God.

Lord, remove the sorrow from my painful, childhood heart today.

For when he dies he shall carry nothing away;
His glory shall not descend after him.

—PS. 49:17

When the ancient Egyptians buried one of their kings, they buried his treasures along with him. The idea was that when this king went on to the afterlife, he would be able to take what he had accumulated with him to enjoy there. Of course, when those pyramids were opened, those riches that were buried with that king were found just where they were placed thousands of years ago. No matter how powerful or important those kings were, they did not possess the ability to take any of that wealth or power with them after they died.

What are you working so desperately to accomplish, perhaps in some secret hope that it will follow you after this life is over? Often you may say that you realize you cannot take anything with you. Yet you still seem to be working desperately to accumulate as much as you possibly can, as if what you get will be eternally yours. Rather than desperately attempting to accumulate things in this life that you can't take with you, begin preparing for what's going to follow you in the next life. For if God's truth is the one thing that is present both in this life and eternity, then that is the thing that you should be most interested in accumulating.

Father, help me work on accumulating Your truths in my life.

How can you believe, who receive honor from one another, and do not seek the honor that comes from the only God?
—JOHN 5:44

Most people like to receive awards and honors for the things that they have accomplished. Although at times you may pretend that these recognitions do not matter, there is something very satisfying about receiving an award for a particular job that you feel that you have done well. But often in the life of an individual who has addictive behaviors, these honors take on a new meaning. For Gerald, the reward became more important than the job or work that was done to receive it. Eventually, everything else in Gerald's life was sacrificed at the cost of gaining those precious awards.

What is far more important to those who commit their lives to God is the honor that He brings. This is true honor for it comes from the only source in the universe who truly knows your heart, and at the same time accepts you just as you are. There is no pretense here; no convincing is necessary. It is simply an act of giving your life to Him and receiving all the value and honor that He wants to give you. While the honor of others is certainly enjoyable, there is no comparison to the honor that comes from God.

Lord, help me seek after the honor You want to give me.

A man will be commended according to his wisdom,
But he who is of a perverse heart will be despised.
—PROV. 12:8

There are many things for which you can receive recognition and commendation. A war hero receives a medal for bravery. A civic-minded citizen may receive an honor for a particular project which has helped to better the town where he lives. Individuals who have had an outstanding career in a particular field are honored for their lifetime achievements. In the Olympics, the athletes receive various medals for their abilities to excel physically. All these honors and awards are certainly important because they represent a certain standard of excellence and achievement.

Consider, however, criteria for commendation. Using God's wisdom will bring spiritual commendation and merit to your life. As Bruce began to deal with the issues in his life, he learned to become aware of how his negative messages were affecting him. However, he saw mere awareness was not enough, for true wisdom is always followed by appropriate actions. Bruce began to respond to what he knew, using his wisdom to change his negative messages and work on the various areas of weakness in his life. The peace that he felt was all the commendation he needed.

Lord, help me use the wisdom that You so willingly give me if I ask.

> *Pride goes before destruction,*
> *And a haughty spirit before a fall.*
> —PROV. 16:18

It seems that there is nothing that God hates as much as He does pride. Pride can certainly be a destructive force in anyone's life, and often we are not able to recognize its presence. Laurie was surprised when I shared with her that her low self-esteem was really a form of pride. She looked shocked and questioned how that could be. "When I feel so bad about myself, how can that possibly be pride?" What I pointed out to her is that if she has low self-esteem, she believes she has no worth. When Laurie says, "Yes, I recognize that God says that I have worth, but I still have difficulty believing it," she is really saying that she knows more than God. Whenever a person thinks they know more than God, that is pride.

Low self-esteem is so deadly because it is deceptive. You must recognize that God wants you to have worth and value in your life. No matter what you might think about it, it is true because it is found in His Word. Do not let the deceptiveness of low self-esteem cause you to fall into pride. Begin to see your worth in God.

Father, help me see that low self-esteem is a form of pride and that You have overcome that by giving me worth.

*And if anyone thinks that he knows anything, he
knows nothing yet as he ought to know.*
—1 COR. 8:2

Have you ever been around a "know-it-all"? If you
have, then you will agree that they can be very irritating people. Jack was one. No matter what kind of opinion someone had, he seemed to have a better idea, a
more correct or efficient way of doing things. He
played a game of one-upmanship, always trying to
outdo someone else with his expertise and knowledge.
The more someone tried to argue with him to prove a
point, the more Jack seemed to have the last word.
Even when a person attempted to compromise with
him, he saw that as a defeat and would not give up
until his way was accepted.

This know-it-all type of behavior only indicates how
insecure Jack really was. By demanding people to see
everything as he did, he only demonstrated how desperate was his need for control. It indicated that he had
felt so little power of choice in his past that any surrender to someone else's opinion would only be viewed as
a defeat in his own life. What Jack needed to do was
recognize that he did not have all the answers. God
does, and He could provide him with the security and
stability he needed.

*Lord, help me to recognize that You are my source for all I need to
know and understand in my life.*

Those who trust in their wealth
And boast in the multitude of their riches,
None of them can by any means redeem his
brother,
Nor give to God a ransom for him.
—PS. 49:6–7

Quite a few years ago, there used to be a television show on about a wealthy man who generously gave an unsuspecting individual a million dollars and then would follow the changes that took place in the person's life. Although some shows were funny and some sad, the point always seemed to be that no matter how money changed the person's life, it did not save that individual from the consequences of his own flawed thinking. That was up to this benefactor—it was his job to teach these people the lessons they needed to learn.

Carrie found herself addicted to helping other people out of their problems. She had not learned that every individual is responsible for his own decisions. No matter how feeling or caring Carrie was, she finally learned she could not solve others' problems. No one can purchase love for anyone else, nor can anyone change the negative thinking processes of another person. In fact, Carrie was actually playing God, and it did not fulfill her because she could never live up to that role. Only God Himself could meet the needs in Carrie's life.

Lord, help me recognize that You alone can save me.

For what is a man profited if he gains the whole world, and loses his own soul? Or what will a man give in exchange for his soul? —MATT. 16:26

For what are you exchanging your life today? At first, to Brandon that seemed like a ridiculous question. He felt that he was trying everything he could to hang on to the life that he had. He would improve it and constantly make it better through his "worthy causes." In fact, the goal of his addiction was to make life as bearable as possible by bringing relief to others. The whole purpose was to give his life meaning and worth by having something to show for it when it was all over. The last thing Brandon wanted to think about was the possibility of losing whatever life he had made for himself.

But that is exactly what his addictive behaviors were doing—taking life from him. What he started out doing in an attempt to improve his life, ended up being the very thing that robbed him of any joy. He became a slave to his good works and began losing whatever control he had. God wants you to trade in your out-of-control addictions for something better. In exchange for his guilt-ridden life, He gave Brandon a life that has purpose and meaning and the power to conquer his addictive behaviors. That is the exchange that brings the greatest profit of all.

Lord, help me give You control of my life.

For the love of money is a root of all kinds of evil, for which some have strayed from the faith in their greediness, and pierced themselves through with many sorrows.
—1 TIM. 6:10

When I was growing up, I used to have a real problem with this verse. I used to feel that I was doomed to being poverty-stricken because if I had money it would get me into all kinds of trouble.

However, I was misinterpreting the verse. The Bible does not say that money is the root of all evil but rather "the love of money." The point is that money itself does not create the problem but rather the priority you place on money. The real difference between Skip and Nate was not their financial status but rather their attitudes. Skip was not very wealthy, but his financial resources were considered a blessing from God. He recognized the role his finances played in his life and used them accordingly. So there was no conflict. On the other hand, Nate's goal was to try and accumulate as much money as possible. Even though he never achieved the security he wanted, he kept looking for it. His misplaced priorities were the source of his problems. You must recognize the role that money plays in your life. If money is not used as a means to an end, but becomes an end in itself, then you are setting yourself up for future problems.

———————

Lord, help me set healthy priorities concerning money.

But we have this treasure in earthen vessels, that the excellence of the power may be of God and not of us.   —2 COR. 4:7

Luke was looking for power. Because of the inferiorities that he grew up with, he felt he needed to take command of his life. That is why he worked until all hours, driven to make just one more deal. He was searching for that feeling of being in control, of having people look up to him, of being "in charge." But it was becoming evident that the power was taking control of him. The desired effects of that power were wearing off more quickly, and that increased the drive to feel important and significant. The more he tried, the more powerless he felt.

Luke never actually found the true source of power in his life. Luke's life was like the difference between life on two, double "A" batteries and plugging into the nearest nuclear power plant. When God is in the center of a person's life, that person has at her disposal the same power that created the universe. Rather than continuing to gain that power in short bursts by the achievements of your life, God's power is available at any time. When someone like Luke truly wants power in his life, he needs to allow God to become his power source.

Lord, let me allow You to be the source of power in my life.

> *Lest I be full and deny You,*
> *And say, "Who is the LORD?"*
> *Or lest I be poor and steal,*
> *And profane the name of my God.*
> —PROV. 30:9

Colleen's life was a paradox. It seemed that when her needs were all met and when things were going her way, she began to feel that God was not important anymore. She became self-sufficient, feeling that because she had all her material needs met, nothing was lacking in her life. It was a case of "out of sight, out of mind." Since she no longer counted daily on God for His provision, she soon neglected her relationship with Him.

Yet, by not allowing God to be a part of her daily life, she became more needy than she had been in the first place. Material possessions and good feelings only lasted so long, and then they began to lose their effect. By that time, Colleen was so far away from God that she felt she could not get back so she just kept on trying to meet her needs by herself, thus perpetuating the cycle.

It is only because of God that you have anything of value or worth. The moment you begin to think that you can make it on your own, then you have forgotten who you are and to whom you belong. It is God's power in your life that makes it worth living, and it is by His grace that you are able to confront your addictions.

Lord, help me remember today how important You are in my life.

*Now he who received seed among the thorns is he
who hears the word, and the cares of this world
and the deceitfulness of riches choke the word, and
he becomes unfruitful.*
—MATT. 13:22

In the parable of the sowers, Jesus gives a lesson about
how God's Word is received by various types of people.
An individual may recognize and understand what
God's Word says but become so consumed by the
things going on in his life that the truths begin to lose
their significance. Soon the meaning of the Word in
that person's life becomes choked out by other priorities.

What kinds of behaviors in your life have taken over
the place that God's Word once used to hold? To be
even more specific, the last time you could have had
your quiet time but didn't, what was the thing that kept
you from it? The last time you could have spent time in
prayer, what were you too busy with? The last time
you could have gone to church, what need was so
pressing that it was a higher priority than spending
time with God's people? You must continually be vigi-
lant to make sure that rather than choking out the seed
of God's Word, you are cutting down and pulling out
the weeds of your addictions.

Lord, help me be sensitive to keeping Your Word in my life.

For you have said in your heart:
"I will ascend into heaven,
I will exalt my throne above the stars of God;
I will also sit on the mount of the congregation
On the farthest sides of the north;
I will ascend above the heights of the clouds,
I will be like the Most High."

—ISA. 14:13–14

For those individuals who didn't know any better, some might think that this verse is the battle cry of corporate America. In truth, this is not the slogan of the successful man, but it is the claim that Lucifer made just before God banished him from heaven forever.

The quest for power, the need for success, and the goals of achievement and ambition inundated Kevin's being. He felt that if he was not striving for success, then something was wrong with him. There was no limit on what was enough, and the more success Kevin received the more he seemed to want. It fed on itself, and it also fed on the others around him. Kevin began to feel himself invincible and developed a godlike quality in his attitudes.

God does not tolerate anyone attempting to take His place. No matter how successful Kevin was, no matter how important he thought himself to be, he was still one of God's creations and was answerable to Him for his life. True power and success can only come through Him, and if you believe anything else, you are only fooling yourself.

Lord, help me always remember that You and You alone are my God.

For if anyone thinks himself to be something, when he is nothing, he deceives himself. —GAL. 6:3

A good healthy self-esteem is important to anyone. Everyone needs to have that confidence of having value, worth, and the ability of being successful. Self-esteem is not something you can produce yourself. In order to have the kind of self-esteem you need, you must recognize the kind of individual you are apart from God.

Carrie had tried from childhood to convince herself of her goodness. She dated the right boys, went to the right college, got good grades, had a successful career. But no matter what she did "right" on the outside, it only pointed out more clearly how insignificant she felt on the inside. She began to see that nothing she herself could do would ever change that feeling.

While the individual who *thinks* he can become something by his own efforts ends up to be nothing, the person who recognizes that he is nothing *without* God can end up being the something that God wants him to be. Try it in your life and see if it doesn't work for you today. It did for Carrie.

―――――――――

Father, help me realize that on my own I am nothing so that You can make me something.

> Thus says the LORD:
> "Cursed is the man who trusts in man
> And makes flesh his strength,
> Whose heart departs from the LORD."
> —JER. 17:5

As one looks around the world today, one of the things that stands out is how fallible men truly are. As Humanism becomes more and more the belief of the day, the very things that it promises to bring about are slipping further from a person's grasp. The more that people begin to trust in themselves for answers, the more questions seem to arise. In looking to the various leaders of the country, economy, churches, and business, there are fewer individuals found who can be trusted. Scott was a pastor who always preached that a person's own abilities provided the answers for life. Yet, he himself was a sexual addict whose continual succession of affairs had cost him both his marriage and his calling.

God warns you not to trust in your capabilities and wisdom because that wisdom is flawed. You are an imperfect creature, and because of that you do not have all the answers. You cannot look into the future, nor are you often able to learn from your past. The more desperately you try to prove yourself, the more out of control your life becomes. You must recognize that in and of yourself, you do not have the answers, but that the only One who can provide the answers is the One who created you in the first place.

Lord, help me see that I cannot trust in myself.

He who trusts in his own heart is a fool,
But whoever walks wisely will be delivered.
—PROV. 28:26

Growing up, I was involved in a boy's group in our church that often went on campouts. This usually involved a hike through the woods. As the hike began, everyone was joking and pushing each other around, generally having a good time. Someone might wander off the path a little bit, but usually they never strayed too far. However, as we got deeper into the woods and the surroundings grew less familiar, our leaders continually emphasized the need to stay on the path. They pointed out that no matter how it twisted and turned, as long as we stayed on course we were assured of getting through the woods and coming out on the other end. But to get off that path and try to go our own way was inviting danger. Even though a fork might seem to be a shortcut, the woods were so dense and the undergrowth so thick, that eventually we would become disoriented and lose our way.

Christie was lost in her addictive dieting. She had wandered from the path of God's truth and tried to do things her way, but because of her confusion, she had become disoriented and lost her way. It was only through God's direction that Christie could get her life back on course. Don't try and take off on your own today, but stick to the path, and let God lead you.

Lord, help me follow Your path for my life.

For those who live according to the flesh set their minds on the things of the flesh, but those who live according to the Spirit, the things of the Spirit.
—ROM. 8:5

Are you aware of how much your thinking influences your behavior? In dealing with his workaholism, Paul tended to focus on trying to change his behavior without changing his attitude. He tried all the new programs, made promises to himself, even used hypnosis to try and rid himself of the negative behaviors. He felt that if he could just gain control over that particular area, he would be able to function more effectively.

What Paul failed to recognize was that those behaviors were merely a symptom of a deeper problem in his life. They only reflected what was going on inside where his thinking and emotions took place. Because of those negative messages regarding his performance that he had received all of his life, his thinking was altered to believe that his work would prove his value—even to his parents.

You no longer have to think negatively about yourself, but can accept God's love and worth. Before you try to correct the behaviors in your life, check your attitudes first.

_____

Father, help me see that You want to change my thoughts as well as my actions.

Here is the man who did not make God his strength,
But trusted in the abundance of his riches,
And strengthened himself in his wickedness.

—PS. 52:7

When I attended college, I was a member of a singing group that toured several weeks during the year. Often we sang in small country churches. There were local cemeteries next to these churches. It was interesting to walk through the cemeteries and read the epitaphs on the gravestones. Surprisingly, you could gather quite a bit of information about an individual from the inscription. It was a pretty good indication of what was important to that individual. As I read these epitaphs, I often wondered what my epitaph would say. I would want it to reflect what was important in my life.

Today's verse is somewhat of an epitaph. In fact, it could be the epitaph of Curtis, a doctor I counseled. Curtis had not found out how God could meet his need for recognition. He was still counting on his own worth and strength to make it through life's problems rather than allowing God to help him to do so. When his life is over, he will have nothing to show except how futile his efforts were. If someone were writing your epitaph today, could this verse describe it? Don't end up being remembered for what you couldn't do, but rather what God's power was able to do in you.

Lord, help me leave behind a legacy of Your power in my life.

For you have trusted in your wickedness;
You have said, "No one sees me";
Your wisdom and your knowledge have warped you;
And you have said in your heart,
"I am, and there is no one else besides me."
—ISA. 47:10

Have you ever left a record album out in the hot sun? Because of the intense heat of the sun, that record can become warped. If you tried to play it on a record player, it would sound nothing like the original recording. And if you brought the recording artist into your house and let him listen to that record, he would probably say that wasn't what he recorded at all. The outside elements have warped the sound into something that he did not intend.

That is what negative thinking can do to your life. It can color your perception until you are unable to recognize how distorted and warped your life has become. Jessica was in denial and would often respond, "That's not what I said." Her thinking was so distorted that she was not able to recognize what she was really saying. It is important to ask God for His objectivity, because you cannot see things clearly. You need Him to reveal the truth to help you understand and respond more honestly than you are capable of doing on your own. Only He knows the true music of your heart.

Father, take my warped mind and give it clarity.

But if you have bitter envy and self-seeking in your hearts, do not boast and lie against the truth.
—JAMES 3:14

Cheryl's devotion to the youth center certainly seemed noble, but it wasn't all it appeared to be. She tried to deceive herself into thinking that her motives were pure and her involvement was for a "good cause." But behind the mask of self-sacrifice and a giving spirit was the need to feel important and be recognized by those around her. She was so needy and desperate for the approval of others that she ended up using kind deeds as a way to get others to think better of her.

When a person does that, she is living a lie, thus creating a basis for more guilt and pain. And this guilt and pain will only lead to further addictions which is how the cycle continues. Be honest with yourself and face the truth about your behavior. By being deceptive, you are powerless to fight against the forces that are driving you. It is only when you are honest before God that you can truly begin to accept His love and forgiveness. So do not deceive yourself anymore, but become honest with the reality of your weakness so that you can start to be free from it.

Lord, help me take that first step against deceitfulness by being honest with You.

Those who are in the flesh cannot please God.
—ROM. 8:8

Whom are you trying to please in your life? Everyone is attempting to win the approval or favor of someone. Stewart needed to have the approval of his employer whose recognition would indicate success at work. Greta continued looking to her parents who never seemed to recognize her worth while she was growing up. Jeff had been seeking for years the love and adoration of his wife in an attempt to feel intimate with her. The need was so strong in Grace that approval was needed from society itself in recognition of the great accomplishments of her acting career.

Ultimately, many individuals feel a need to please God in their lives. Overinvolvement in church, legalistic life-styles, sanctimonious sermonizing, and even overzealous evangelization are ways they try and gain God's favor. God settled the matter by giving to you what you cannot give to yourself—forgiveness. By simply accepting this gift of forgiveness and allowing God to take charge of your life, He will begin working in you to help you live the life that He wants you to live. And if God dwells within you, then obviously He can please Himself, and He will do so the more you allow Him to work in your life each day.

Lord, help me continue to allow You to work in my life.

*Command those who are rich in this present age
not to be haughty, nor to trust in uncertain riches
but in the living God, who gives us richly all things
to enjoy.*
—1 TIM. 6:17

When Trevor began to seek after riches in his life, many problems occurred. First of all, he became very protective of those riches, and was concerned that somebody would take them away. Another worry which drove him to accumulate further was the realization that those riches could be gone in a moment. His wealth produced a lust for power which made him very controlling in his relationships. It seemed that the more money Trevor had and the more it became a priority in his life, the less he could enjoy his wealth. He worked so hard in obtaining it, that now he had to work to make sure that he was never without wealth again.

It is such a relief to be able to enjoy the riches that God wants to provide in your life, because you know they are from Him and you did nothing to produce them. Therefore, it is not up to you to protect your riches or to become skeptical or paranoid about them or even to begin to think that you can somehow treat people differently because of them. It is so much better to trust in the proven riches of God than the uncertain riches accumulated in this world.

Lord, thank You for the riches You provide for me in Your love.

> *Be doers of the word, and not hearers only,*
> *deceiving yourselves.*
> —JAMES 1:22

In meditating on the verses in this devotional thus far, you have probably become aware of the areas of your life that may be under the control of certain addictive behaviors. Hopefully, your awareness is growing as you begin to seek the answers to some of the questions that you have.

It is important to understand that recognition is only the first step. You now must move beyond simple realization of the problem and begin looking at some of the causes, and how to do something about them. If you don't do anything about the things you become aware of, then you truly are deceiving yourself. As you begin going around the cycle of addiction, you must learn that God will give you the strength to begin dealing with it in a very productive and practical way. He can give you the wisdom to understand the problem, and more importantly, He can give you the power to overcome it. If you will allow Him to manifest that power in your life, you will begin the long and difficult but totally rewarding process of conquering those behaviors that are driving you today.

Lord, give me the courage to face the issues and make the changes I need to make in my life.

Part 2

BREAKING THE CYCLE

1. FAMILY OF ORIGIN

TIRED OF TEARS – *April 1*

I am weary with my crying;
My throat is dry;
My eyes fail while I wait for my God.
　　　　　　　—PS. 69:3

Julia was crying once again. The product of a severely dysfunctional family, she was describing a painful memory from her childhood. "I tried to be a good girl. I tried to take care of my brothers and sisters. But it seemed there were just too many of them, and I couldn't make them be quiet enough for Daddy to sleep. I know it was all my fault," she sobbed. Even though she hadn't thought about it for years, time had not diminished the reality of these feelings.

So often I have people sit in my office and tell me that they feel that they cannot shed one more tear for their past, only to cry fresh tears of pain as they recall a particular incident in their childhood. It seems that the crying will never stop; the hurt will never go away.

That is why it is so important to begin the recovery process right now. Certainly it may be difficult and at times very painful, but can anything match the anguish you have felt over the years? It is time to begin to deal with those hurts, like Julia did. As she was able to list her unmet needs one by one and find verses that showed how God could meet each of those needs, she was finally able to stop the pain that stopped the crying.

Lord, help me see that now is the time to begin dealing with my hurts.

> *When my father and my mother forsake me,*
> *Then the LORD will take care of me.*
> —PS. 27:10

One of the most significant factors leading to compulsive behavior is the feeling of being rejected by parents. Abandonment is always difficult to handle, but when it occurs in childhood, the results can be exceptionally painful and long-lasting. When Tom was six years old, his father decided that he no longer wanted anything to do with the family, so he packed up and left. Tom's mother tried to support the family, but she just couldn't make ends meet, so Tom was sent away to live with his aunt and uncle. They were nice to Tom, but he couldn't help feeling that he had been rejected— that no one really cared about him. Although in his mind he tried to make excuses for his parents' actions, it still did not remove the pain of feeling abandoned.

It is wonderful to have this promise in the Scripture! When you are forsaken by those whom you love, God will take care of you. The knowledge that you have a heavenly Father can give you the security to live with the rejection of earthly parents. So whenever you feel abandoned by someone today, remind yourself that God still cares for you.

Lord, help me remember that You are the one parent who will never forsake me.

O LORD of hosts,
Blessed is the man who trusts in You!
—PS. 84:12

As Kevin was growing up, he got the idea that no matter what he did, he would never be appreciated. So he strove on and on, driven by that need to have just one kind word spoken to him about his accomplishments. The harder he tried, the more frustrated he became, but he couldn't stop because he never felt the feeling of success. It was like the proverbial carrot dangling in front of the horse's mouth—it was always just one step away.

How wonderful it is to have a heavenly Father who recognizes your efforts. This verse doesn't say, "Blessed are you if you just do one more thing" or "Blessed are you if you just try a little harder." God recognizes your limitations and weaknesses, since He created you. Your efforts are important to Him, and He recognizes and appreciates what you do for Him, even if it's not done perfectly. You can learn to accept His approval in your life by recognizing your accomplishments each day, and choosing to accept yourself just as God does.

Help me be encouraged, Lord, by the appreciation and approval that You give to me in my life.

He will feed His flock like a shepherd;
He will gather the lambs with His arm,
And carry them in His bosom,
And gently lead those who are with young.
—ISA. 40:11

Joan was describing the unmet need she had as a child to be physically touched by her parents. "So many times, when I was hurt or disappointed, I just wanted my parents to put their arms around me and comfort me. I wanted some indication that they cared. But it never happened. I still long for that loving touch. Is there anywhere I can find it?"

What Joan needed to realize was that God provides that loving touch for His children. Often in the Bible, God's love is compared to a shepherd's love for his sheep. A shepherd becomes personally involved in their lives, he holds them in his arms, close to his heart.

That example describes God's tenderness and care which will minister to you when you feel that no one around you is concerned about you. God takes you into His arms, holds you close to Himself so that you can begin to feel the warmth of His love.

So the next time you are hurting like Joan and need to experience the care of someone holding you, meditate on God's Word so He can hold you close to Himself.

_____

Thank You for holding me today, Gentle Shepherd.

Take heed that you do not despise one of these little ones, for I say to you that in heaven their angels always see the face of My Father who is in heaven.
—MATT. 18:10

Sometimes a child in a dysfunctional family feels defenseless against the world in which he lives. Every time Jesse tried to stand up for himself, he was knocked down by evil words and hateful attitudes. "Shut up and get out of here or I'll kick you out myself" was his father's favorite refrain whenever Jesse made a comment. He looked for someone whom he could count on, someone who would stick up for him when the going got tough, someone who would at least see his point.

Think how important you would feel if someone came to you and said, "I would like to represent you and your needs to the President of the United States. The issues in your life will have top priority with him, and he will be apprised at all times of how things are going for you." You would certainly feel important and special, wouldn't you? That is exactly how important you are to God. And while knowing this doesn't make all the hurts and pains of your childhood go away, it should bring some consolation in those times when you thought nobody knew or cared how you felt.

Help me realize, Lord, that there was Someone who knew and cared about me all along.

> *O Lord my God, in You I put my trust;*
> *Save me from all those who persecute me;*
> *And deliver me.*
> —PS. 7:1

While growing up, Craig often felt persecuted by his dysfunctional family. He never knew what mood his father would be in when he got home from work, but it usually would end up in some type of physical abuse. Because his father constantly hit him even when he had done nothing wrong, Craig developed a lack of trust in others. Everyone became viewed as a potential abuser, and it was better to keep his distance than make a mistake trusting someone. It even made it very difficult for him to trust God.

Developing trust in God can be difficult for those who grew up in these kinds of situations. The abuse and persecution leave emotional scars that are difficult to erase. However, when all human relationships fail, God can still be trusted.

By identifying the specific ways his father abused him, Craig was able to see where he had lost trust. When he turned those areas one by one over to God and used the promises in His Word, Craig slowly was able to build that trust into his life again.

Lord, help me see that trust in You is the basis for trust in anyone else.

Be of good courage,
And He shall strengthen your heart,
All you who hope in the LORD.
—PS. 31:24

I am so frightened of my past, I don't know if I have the strength and courage to deal with it." Have you ever said these words before? Dealing with past hurts that occurred in your family can be a very painful experience, but many people don't realize that they can be very frightening as well. And if those childhood fears have not been dealt with, they can continue to be as real today as they were years ago. Time does not make the fear go away.

It often takes a great deal of courage to face the issues of your past. By expressing your emotions in the safe environment of group counseling or with a trusted friend, you begin to see that they don't have to be as frightening as they first might seem. And by realizing that others have gone through many of those same experiences, you gain the courage to face the next one, and the next one, until all those hidden fears are finally out in the open.

Father, give me the courage to face the issues in my past.

> *But I say to you, love your enemies, bless those who*
> *curse you, do good to those who hate you, and*
> *pray for those who spitefully use you and persecute*
> *you, that you may be sons of your Father in*
> *heaven.*
> —MATT. 5:44–45

Whenever I heard this verse in Sunday school, I always pictured the bully at school who tried to intimidate me into giving him lunch money. When I thought about being nice to him, I realized, *I can do that.* My contact with this boy was so limited that I could do *anything* for that short five-minute period.

In all the years Maria lived at home, not once did her parents ever tell her they loved her. In fact, they often put her down in public and told her she was no good and would never amount to anything. She knew they hated her, and she felt she had a right to hate them too.

Even if family members continue to reject you and treat you this way, you can still have a family relationship with God. He is the one family member who will never reject you. Once you know He accepts you as you are, you will want to show your love for Him by loving those who hurt you as He suggests in this Scripture. By recognizing God's acceptance and unconditional love, Maria began to see that it was possible not only to forgive her parents but actually begin to love them as well.

———————

Father, help me see that it is just as important to forgive my family members as it is my enemies.

For your Father knows the things you have need of
before you ask Him.   —MATT. 6:8

A child in a dysfunctional family learns that sometimes it is better to go without than to suffer the hurt
and abuse that might go along with his request. Gwen's
mother would always forget to give her money for
lunch, usually because she was still asleep with a hang-
over when Gwen left for school. The few times Gwen
did muster up the courage to ask, she was screamed at
and told to get out of the house, so she soon learned to
not ask and just go hungry.

As an adult, Gwen was still "going hungry." Rather
than express any emotional need she might have, such
as a shoulder to cry on or just a supporting word, she
quietly moved through her life, never asking or expecting anything from anyone, yet desperately hurting.

In counseling, Gwen was confronted with her need
to begin asking for the things she needed. In the beginning, this simply involved her asking God to help her
make it through another day. But as she saw how God
met her needs, not only for survival, but for friendship,
acceptance, and comfort as well, she was able to learn
to ask others for things when she needed them. And
she discovered that the more she asked, the more she
was able to receive.

Lord, help me remember that You see the needs in my life and are
always ready with Your perfect answer to those needs.

Even so it is not the will of your Father who is in heaven that one of these little ones should perish.
—MATT. 18:14

Within the distorted dynamics of the dysfunctional family, some individuals begin to perceive themselves as responsible for the problems found within that family. Rachel always believed that she was responsible for the problems at home. When her father stayed out late and often never came home, she knew it was because she couldn't make him happy. When her mother complained that no one ever came to visit, Rachel felt it was because she hadn't kept the house clean enough. When her brother sexually abused her at night, Rachel believed it was because she was an evil person who deserved such treatment.

While everyone has done things that would deserve correction and even consequences, no one deserves to be abused. *No one!* Rachel eventually was able to take each of these relationships and slowly, painfully write down exactly what should have been expected from her as a child, compare it to what actually was expected, and begin to see that the problems of her family were not her fault or her responsibility to change. She was able to realize that she didn't deserve the treatment she received as a child, no matter how much her family made her feel that way.

Lord, give me the grace to recognize that I did not deserve to be mistreated.

*Blessed be the God and Father of our Lord
Jesus Christ, the Father of mercies and God
of all comfort.*
                                    —2 COR. 1:3

I remember in school when our teacher used to have us play a particular game that involved associating one word with another. She would say a word, and then we were supposed to say the first thing that popped into our minds. If she said, "House," we might respond with, "Garage," or if she said, "Sky," someone might say, "Blue." How would you respond to the word, *father?* Would you think of words like *hurt, demanding,* or *angry?* Or perhaps words like *absent, abandon,* or *rejected?* Would you think of the word *mercy?*

It took Danielle a long time to discover the meaning of the word *mercy.* Her own father left home when she was six, and though her mother was often sick and there were four other mouths to feed, her father never sent any money to support them. The few times she saw him in town, he totally ignored her. She grew up with anger and bitterness, never giving anyone a break. It was only after she saw from God's Word how empty her own life was and how much God wanted to forgive her that she began to understand what mercy was all about. It finally allowed her to be merciful enough to forgive her own father.

Help me learn to associate mercy with You, O heavenly Father.

Every good gift and every perfect gift is from above,
and comes down from the Father of lights, with
whom there is no variation or shadow of turning.
—JAMES 1:17

Many people share with me their memories of uncelebrated birthdays, forgotten Christmases or other holidays. Usually these occasions become more hurtful because of the happiness that is supposed to be associated with them.

Even at those rare times when these events were celebrated and perhaps gifts were given, they were accompanied by so much rejection and so little love, it was more painful to receive the gift than to ignore the event.

In his entire childhood, Bruce never received one gift that he didn't have to pay for. A birthday present was always presented with "you really don't deserve this, but . . ." And his graduation gift was a packed suitcase with a note telling him to be out of the house before evening.

Isn't it precious to know that you have a heavenly Father who loves to give good and perfect gifts to His children? Bruce realized that God's love was free and unconditional, that he never had to do anything to earn it, and that God would never take it away. His gifts are never accompanied by the demands that other people may have made on you. Knowing that allowed Bruce to stop being so demanding on himself and accept himself as God does.

Thank You, Lord, for Your good and perfect gifts to me.

*Behold what manner of love the Father has
bestowed on us, that we should be called children
of God!*
—1 JOHN 3:1

I remember hearing the beautiful old spiritual, "Sometimes I Feel Like a Motherless Child," for the first time and trying to imagine what that would feel like. Now I understand it to be a very empty, lonely feeling, a place of utter rejection and abandonment. It is a feeling of having very little direction, of having no one to put their arms around you and comfort you when you're hurt, and feeling that you are virtually alone in this world. No matter what the emotion, there is no one to share it with—no one who seems to care.

Margie had a weight problem and the kids at school would make fun of her. Every day she would come home and tell her mother what they said, hoping to find the comfort she desperately needed. Instead, her mother would laugh and say, "You'll get over it one day." The less comfort she received, the more lonely she felt.

When Margie was able to identify that loneliness and write it down to God in a prayer, she began to experience His love that comforted her no matter what the circumstance.

Father, help me to accept the love that You so freely give.

But let him ask in faith, with no doubting, for he who doubts is like a wave of the sea driven and tossed by the wind.
—JAMES 1:6

Have you ever stood at the shore of an ocean and watched the waves as they roll in? Sometimes they lap up on the shore quietly. Other times they come crashing in, spewing water in every direction. The waves are at the mercy of the elements surrounding them—wind, the tides, and natural disasters like hurricanes. The waves are totally at the mercy of these other forces and can only react, rather than act.

That is how James described the doubting of the insecure individual. If the outside stresses are calm, then the individual remains in control. Whenever the circumstances of life churn up, however, the individual becomes totally controlled by those outside forces, with no mind or will of his own. Yet, if you can have the childlike faith to "be guided by a hand we cannot hold," as Michael Card suggests in his song, "That's What Faith Must Be," you will have a rudder to keep you steady despite the wind and rain.

Father, help me increase my faith so that I will not be a victim of those people or things around me.

Because you say, "I am rich, have become wealthy, and have need of nothing"—and do not know that you are wretched, miserable, poor, blind, and naked.
                                                    —REV. 3:17

Jack's life would be considered a success story. Growing up in severe poverty, often with little to eat, Jack determined one day to never be in need again. So he worked and struggled, obtaining possessions, climbing the corporate ladder to the point where there was nothing else to be desired. It was important for people to see how much Jack had materially, for that is what gave him value and worth in life.

However, those people in the verse, like Jack, were defining themselves by what they had and not by who they were. In terms of eternal worth and value in God's economy, they were bankrupt. And perhaps the saddest part of this verse is that these people did not even recognize it. Yet that remains the challenge to you today. When Jack finally took the time from his busy life to read and meditate on God's Word, he was able to receive from God that worth that he was looking for. Do you continue to define your worth by the world's standards? Or are you willing to take a good look with eyes of honesty, like Jack, and begin to see that you don't need to work for anything, but accept what God has already done for us?

Father, instead of accumulating the riches of this world, help me desire the riches of Your grace in my life.

> *But I see another law in my members, warring against the law of my mind, and bringing me into captivity to the law of sin which is in my members.*
> —ROM. 7:23

Richard, a young man in his thirties, sat across from me with a tired look on his face. Although he had made significant progress in overcoming his workaholism, he was beginning to show the strain of the recovery process. "I want to get better," he said, "and I feel I am moving in the right direction, but I never imagined the struggle would be so difficult. Whenever I conquer one issue, another one pops up somewhere. I feel as if I'm heading back into battle every day of my life."

The following are key strategies to help you face each new struggle:

1. Spend time each day on the recovery process, including time in prayer and meditation to ask for God's help.

2. Remind yourself of previous battles that have already been fought and won. Nothing breeds success like success.

3. Share the battles with a friend. Letting someone know of your progress will not only give you the courage to continue the struggle, but can be a source of new techniques as well.

4. Celebrate each new victory by writing it down.

Equip me each day with Your power, Father, to fight my battles.

> *But let patience have its perfect work, that you*
> *may be perfect and complete, lacking nothing.*
> —JAMES 1:4

Patience is part of the recovery process. But for Grant, patience certainly was not his virtue. All his life he had been told to hurry up by others. His mother said, "Hurry up and take out the trash." His father said, "Hurry up and get the yard done." His teachers said, "Hurry up with that paper." His baseball teammates said, "Hurry up and throw the ball." So Grant learned to hurry up—no matter what he did in life, he did it the quickest, easiest way. By the time he came into my office, he was on the edge of burnout. His opening statement was, "You've got to hurry up and make me better!"

Through the counseling process, Grant began to see that often, to do things in a hurry is not to get them done well. By taking the time to make a complete inventory of relationships, patiently looking at all the sources of his compulsive behavior, carefully considering how all the "hurry ups" had driven him to his frenzied life, he was able to break the tyranny of the urgent. And in the process he realized he could enjoy life at a much more patient pace.

Lord, allow patience to work in my life and help me see that the end result will certainly be worth the wait.

> *For I am poor and needy,*
> *And my heart is wounded within me.*
> —PS. 109:22

A few years ago my grandmother had bypass surgery. Since the heart is a very delicate instrument, no cut was made without first considering all the options. Even then it took my grandmother many months to recover from that surgery. Doctors treat the physical heart so carefully in an operation, yet people often speak and act without regard for the damage they may be doing to a person's inner heart.

What kinds of wounds does your heart carry today? Have you carried those pains around so long that it seems to be taking forever for them to heal? Just like a medical procedure, all the sources of pain and injury must be considered and examined before healing can take place. Take time today to examine those sources. Begin looking back and identify each hurt you can remember, where it came from, what was said, how you felt, and how you reacted. Once all of these have been identified, write them down. Then you can begin developing a plan to deal with each of those hurts specifically. This initial process of discovery may be long and painful, but only then can the direction of recovery be known.

Father, help me understand that the recovery process may be long and difficult, but You are there to comfort me when I need it.

All my bones shall say,
"LORD, who is like You,
Delivering the poor from him who is too strong
*   for him,*
Yes, the poor and the needy from him who
*   plunders him?"*
                                        —PS. 35:10

Sometimes patients ask, "Why wasn't I able to recognize what was happening to me? Why didn't I do something to protect myself?" I often reply by asking them if they've ever seen an old movie about war or read history books about battles. Sooner or later a conquering army comes to a small village and plunders the town. It's not that the people do not fight back, but the army is just so strong that the village eventually succumbs.

In your own childlike way you tried to fight back, but the strength of your parent (or parents) was too overwhelming so you really had no alternative but to learn to live with the abuse the best way you could.

Yet, now as an adult, you no longer have to live that way. By actually confronting those sources of abuse, you can once again begin to rebuild the "plundered cities" of your life. The confrontation could involve a face-to-face discussion or a letter expressing how you felt. However it is done, it will help you begin to see that however you handled it in the past, you're going to do something positive about it today.

_____

Help me realize, O Father, that whether I recognize it or not, I did the best I could.

> *Reproach has broken my heart,*
> *And I am full of heaviness;*
> *I looked for someone to take pity, but*
> *there was none;*
> *And for comforters, but I found none.*
> —PS. 69:20

Judi came into my office just after her fourth marriage had broken up. She seemed drained and cried as if her heart would break. "I feel so alone. I keep trying to be the perfect wife, but all men ever do is reject me. I just want someone to take care of me, to give me some sense of security. I just want to feel like I am needed. Yet no matter what I gave my husband, he still kept drinking. I just want someone to love me, who understands me. Is that too much to ask?"

There is Someone who understands your needs. He comes and speaks in His still, small voice and says, "I am the one who can meet all those needs you are so desperately seeking to fill."

What Judi needed to realize was that she was looking for the right thing but in the wrong place. Judi was still trying to "rescue" her alcoholic father through her marriages, and just like her father, all those men kept rejecting her. When Judi was able to identify that experience from her past and realize that it was only through God's love that she could ever get that need fulfilled, she was able to give her need for love to Him and through His acceptance finally feel cared for.

Lord, help me see that when no one listens or understands me, You always will.

By You I have been upheld from my birth;
You are He who took me out of my mother's womb.
My praise shall be continually of You. —PS. 71:6

Many patients have asked me, "Why was I even born?" "After all," they go on, "is that what God really intended for me? Did He really expect me to experience all that hurt in my childhood?"

I certainly don't have the answers to all those questions. However I tell them, "There is a purpose for your existence." And then I tell them about Brad.

Brad was abandoned by his parents at birth. He grew up never knowing what it was like to be cradled in a mother's arms, to be able to toss a football with a father. His few experiences in foster homes only created more sense of abandonment, as each time he was returned to the orphanage. No one ever said "I love you" to Brad.

Finally, Brad came in contact with a counselor who helped him see that God loved him and could use those hurts for good if Brad would let Him. By choosing to believe in God's love, each time a hurt arose he was able to see value in others. Brad started a "big brother" program for orphaned boys in his community to show other boys that they also can find value and worth in their lives.

Lord, help me always remember that no matter what happens to me, You have a purpose and plan for my life.

When you pass through the waters, I will be with
*   you;*
And through the rivers, they shall not overflow you.
When you walk through the fire, you shall not be
*   burned,*
Nor shall the flame scorch you.   —ISA. 43:2

Many times my patients describe a feeling of being
drowned by their past—fearing that they may be going
under for the final time. It is almost as if the dam has
burst and the emotions so tightly held in check for all
these years will sweep them away. Or all the fire of
their pent-up anger suddenly bursts forth and seems to
ignite everything they do. These patients feel so much
at the mercy of their emotions that they think they will
not survive the impact.

Notice that this verse does not promise that the flood
will be stopped or that the fire will necessarily be put
out right away. Instead, God promises to be there with
you right in the middle of those terrible, emotional
times. He says, "I will not allow those emotions to consume you." When I talk to patients about this verse, I
often think of the poem, "Footprints." The writer asks
God, "Why is there only one set of footprints during
the difficult times?" God replies, "My precious, precious child, I would never leave you . . . When you see
only one set of footprints, it was then that I carried
you."

Help me today, Lord, to recognize that You are carrying me through
the fire so I can relax in Your arms.

And God will wipe away every tear from their eyes;
there shall be no more death, nor sorrow, nor
crying; and there shall be no more pain, for the
former things have passed away. —REV. 21:4

Isn't it great to know that there is coming a day when you will never have to worry about the pain of your past any longer? And if the victories of this lifetime don't give you enough hope for recovery, you can always look toward that time when the past will be gone for good.

Sheila finally had the courage to confront her past. Through all her successes at work, moving from mailroom clerk to secretary to sales rep to vice president of merchandising, she had been running from her childhood by proving her worth as a businesswoman. But she could always hear the voices of her teachers saying, "You won't make it—you just don't have what it takes. You'll never amount to anything." Now, facing burnout, she could not run from those messages anymore.

By taking the time to turn around and face that past, she discovered that she did not have to believe those messages any longer. And also, by writing each and every one of those teachers and telling them that she was successful, she freed herself to face the future without the pain from her past.

Father, help me get a glimpse of my future life in my present-day recovery here on earth.

> *Hope deferred makes the heart sick,*
> *But when the desire comes, it is a tree of life.*
> —PROV. 13:12

Matt kept trying to have hope that he could do things right, but it got harder and harder. He kept hoping that a better grade or a cleaner room or making the football squad would finally meet his parents' approval. But the only response he got from his mother was, "That's nice, dear," and his father would barely grunt behind his newspaper. So he grew up believing that he was a second-rate individual, that he was incapable of getting people to like him, and he spent years hidden behind a wall of self-hate and depression.

The prospect of recovery is exactly like the tree of life that the writer of Proverbs talks about. By making an inventory of his relationship with his parents and through that, recognizing how they had not met his emotional needs, he came to the conclusion that he in fact did have worth, and that God had already given him the approval he so desperately sought. When he finally realized he could recover, it was a life-giving experience, and he found hope once again.

Lord, help me no longer to defer my hope but to make it happen in the prospect of recovery.

And now, Lord, what do I wait for?
My hope is in You.   —PS. 39:7

Many times patients feel as if the struggle of the recovery process is not worth all the pain. Yet whenever discouragement and self-doubt set in, you must recognize that another step needs to be taken. Your hope in God will give you the courage to take that step.

What is the next step? Pause a moment and take a brief self-inventory.

1. What abuse or hurt have I still not faced?

2. What emotional need can I identify that is still not being met by my addiction?

3. To whom do I need to tell my story?

4. Is there someone from my past whom I need to confront regarding the way I was mistreated by them?

Whatever the next task is, it is encouraging to know that your hope is in the almighty God who is sufficient enough to bring you through whatever is necessary to deal with your past. With that kind of hope and assurance, what are you waiting for? Take the next step and trust the God who can move mountains.

Lord, help me realize that whatever the next step is, You will be there with me.

2. NEGATIVE MESSAGES

April 26 – NOT GOOD ENOUGH

> *Let no corrupt communication proceed out of your*
> *mouth, but what is good for necessary edification,*
> *that it may impart grace to the hearers.*
>
> —EPH. 4:29

Kirk was fighting the urge to explode in rage. His boss had just informed him that his project was good, but it just wasn't good enough, and so the job had been awarded to someone else. All Kirk heard was "not good enough." That was just like his dad who continually met every accomplishment Kirk made with, "It's OK, but it could have been better." He was told he could have done better with his career, his education—even his wife wasn't "good enough" for his father.

So often in dysfunctional families, people say negative things to one another like "It's not good enough." People begin to believe things about themselves and their families that are not necessarily true. Often it takes many years of replacing those negative messages with positive ones for a person to really begin to be free from those impressions they have.

Kirk had to begin telling himself that just because a particular project was not good enough, it did not mean that *he* was not good enough. He had personal worth and value from God that would surpass any project he could ever accomplish.

Lord, help me build up people in Your love.

But, speaking the truth in love, may grow up in all things into Him who is the head—Christ.

—EPH. 4:15

Sometimes accusations about your weaknesses and your faults are not untrue. You may have a hard time recognizing or understanding why you hurt so bad when those things actually were true and therefore should be accepted as part of you. After all, if you are ever going to accept yourself for exactly who you are, you should be able to deal with the truth of your life, positive or negative, in a realistic way.

If you were in a dysfunctional family, the messages you heard were spoken in a harsh negative way. To recover from the pain of the negative impact of those messages, you must learn to speak the truth in love to yourself. You don't need to criticize your weaknesses but rather learn to accept them as part of the *whole* you that God is concerned with. By identifying a weakness and telling yourself one way that God has used that weakness in your life, it will begin to free you from the negative impact of those early messages.

Father, help me not to just simply speak the truth, but to speak the truth in love.

> *Let this mind be in you which was also in*
> *Christ Jesus.*
> —PHIL. 2:5

When I was attending Bible school, "May the mind of Christ, my Savior, live in me from day to day" was a line from my favorite hymn. Yet it wasn't until much later that I recognized the true meaning of those words. Jesus was subject to more negative messages than anyone has ever been. Everywhere He turned, His identity was questioned, and the validity of His message and mission was always subject to intense ridicule. Even in His childhood, His parents questioned His actions and the motives behind them.

Yet how did Jesus respond to these negative messages? Did He develop a "poor me" complex, which caused Him to withdraw from people? Did He develop a need to continually prove Himself to others and compulsively do miracle after miracle to get people to like Him? Or did He get angry and curse them all, exploding with rage every time someone questioned Him? No. He could deal with the negative messages because He knew who He was. He knew God was in control of His life, and He would not be swayed from God's direction. He purposely chose to accept God's view of His worth rather than man's view, just as you need to do each day. Does the mind of your Savior live in you from day to day?

Father, may I sincerely ask that my mind may begin to be changed.

Finally, brethren, whatever things are true,
whatever things are noble, whatever things are
just, whatever things are pure, whatever things
are lovely, whatever things are of good report,
if there is any virtue and if there is anything
praiseworthy—meditate on these things.
—PHIL. 4:8

I don't know about anybody else, but if I allow my mind to be put on automatic pilot, I find myself reflecting on past failures. I seem to focus on the way I mishandled my last counseling session or perhaps an article I am writing that I just can't seem to find the right words for—anything that focuses on what I haven't done right or what I could do better.

Notice, however, that the things you are to think about in this passage of Scripture do not involve "doing" but "being." You are challenged to think about things that are praiseworthy or noble or true like the incredible value you have in God's eyes or the fact that you have had the courage to begin recovery. You may even think about one quality you have that you especially like. You are not even asked to manifest these characteristics, just to meditate on them. The implication is that if you keep these ideas in your mind, your thoughts will develop your character. So today, whenever a negative message comes to your mind, stop and think of one noble or true experience in your life today.

Father, help me focus on "being" instead of on "doing."

Let the words of my mouth and the
meditation of my heart
Be acceptable in Your sight,
O LORD, my strength and my redeemer.
—PS. 19:14

One way to identify how someone thinks about himself is to hear what he has to say about himself. If he continually puts himself down, always apologizes for something he has done, or is always trying to prove his worth to everyone, it is clear that what he thinks about himself is not very healthy.

Laura was always putting herself down. No matter how well she performed at her piano recitals, she always felt like a failure. Each tiny mistake she made was always accompanied by the voice of her mother in her mind saying, "Why do you even try to play that thing? Quit now and stop wasting your time." Laura eventually learned to repeat those messages to herself and those around her.

In counseling, Laura was challenged to stand in front of a mirror and repeat those messages to herself, watching how painful it was to both give and receive those messages. By viewing this experience, Laura was able to come to recognize just how damaging those messages were and begin to stop saying and believing them.

Father, help me see that my words are a reflection of what I believe.

May my meditation be sweet to Him;
I will be glad in the LORD.
—PS. 104:34

If ever there was a sad person, it was Mark. The product of a broken home, Mark never felt he really belonged in either of his parents' homes. When he was with his mother, she was always questioning him: What had his father said about her? Was he dating? Did Mark love him more than her? When he went to visit his father, he would continually hear him say, "Go back to your mother, you sissy! You always were a momma's boy." The confusion of those messages led him to eventually adopt a homosexual life-style. But Mark felt like he didn't really belong anywhere—that no one cared about him. Thinking about that all the time only increased his sadness.

What Mark needed to learn was that God did care for him and by accepting God's love, his whole outlook on life could change. He began to write down every negative message about himself he had ever heard or believed. And he began to identify the source of each message, why it wasn't true, and identify what God felt about him. Once he realized how differently he could think about himself, his sadness was changed to gladness.

_____

Help me experience the true gladness only Your love can bring, O Father.

My eyes are awake through the night watches,
That I may meditate on Your word.
—PS. 119:148

Slowly the clock ticks away. You really don't want to know the time, but something deep within you forces you to look at the clock once again. 2:07 A.M. Another night spent lying awake, thinking about all the *things* you have to get done tomorrow. In just a few hours, you will be faced with another day of uncompleted projects and myriad new crises that you can't even imagine, only to come home tomorrow night and again fall exhausted in your bed. Except that you won't sleep.

Try meditating on the truths as found in God's Word:

- God so loved the world. (John 3:16)

- I come to give you abundant life. (John 10:10)

- He cares for you. (1 Peter 5:7)

- When you pass through the waters, I will be with you. (Isa. 43:2)

- With God all things are possible. (Matt. 19:26)

Maybe, just maybe, if you focus on those positive truths, you will not spend so many hours lying awake at night. Rather than repeating the negative messages, begin to memorize the Scriptures.

Or, you could stare at the clock again. 2:09 . . .

Lord, in those sleepless hours, help me focus on You and Your care for me.

I love the LORD, because He has heard
My voice and my supplications.
Because He has inclined His ear to me,
Therefore I will call upon Him as long
as I live.   —PS. 116:1–2

Les was always being ignored. Being the youngest of ten children, it seemed that his voice was never heard. Maybe he was too quiet, or maybe he was simply lost in the shuffle. Either way, his requests always seemed to fall on deaf ears. No one would help him with his schoolwork, no one responded when he told them he was sick. It was as if he somehow was invisible, and he began to believe that it must be something about himself that made others treat him that way. So the negative message Les received was that he really was not worth enough for anyone to hear what he had to say.

Through the recovery process, Les finally found someone who would listen. First, he talked to his counselor who quietly listened as Les poured out his story. Then he became involved in a group where people not only listened but also identified with his experiences. And through the process of others listening to him, Les was then able to turn to God and tell Him his story. He discovered that if other humans never listened again, the fact that God thought him important enough to listen to was validation enough for a lifetime.

Lord, help me see beyond the negative messages in my life and recognize that You are always at work.

> *This persuasion does not come from Him who calls you.*
>
> —GAL. 5:8

Have you ever tried to get someone to do something she did not want to do? You don't just walk up to a person and say, "This is what I want you to do" or "This is what I want you to believe" and automatically expect to change that person's mind. If you take children, who are very susceptible, and give them the same message time and time again, sooner or later they end up believing it. The sheer quantity of the message is sometimes too overwhelming to fight. Pete could not begin to count the number of times he had been told "You're so stupid" by his smart sister. He certainly had proved it by his life choices—his marriage had failed, his business went bankrupt, and his own kids thought the same thing his sister did.

When he entered counseling and took some tests, he discovered he was not stupid at all. But the test results alone could not change his thinking. By writing "I am not stupid. I am an intelligent person. I have worth in God's eyes" on a three-by-five card, carrying it permanently in his pocket, and pulling it out and looking at it whenever he had negative thoughts, he finally began to stop the tide of those messages.

Help me understand that as persuasive as negative messages are, Father, they are not from You and therefore are not to be believed.

Be still, and know that I am God;
I will be exalted among the nations,
I will be exalted in the earth!
—PS. 46:10

One of the most difficult tasks in dealing with the negative messages in life is to get them to stop long enough so you can consider the truth. The more you try to focus on them, the more strength they gain and the louder they become. The less confident you are about yourself, the more you are driven to prove your worth. And the more you realize that a promotion at work or a new car does not fulfill that need, the louder those negative messages become. The cycle repeats, and the frenzy builds. You need to hear God's voice saying, "Be still and know that I am God."

Denise was a victim of negative messages from childhood, and she kept drowning them out by building up enormous credit card balances. Denise needed to have the courage to face those messages by reminding herself that they were not true and that she had been able to rise above her childhood. Once those messages were stilled, she could then begin to accept the messages of love and worth that God had for her in His Word.

Lord, give me the strength to still my mind long enough to let Your voice of assurance speak to me.

> *A merry heart makes a cheerful countenance,*
> *But by sorrow of the heart the spirit is broken.*
> —PROV. 15:13

You can't judge a book by its cover." While there is some truth to that old saying, the cover of a book does give some indication of what's inside. You often can get an indication of how someone is feeling on the inside by what is portrayed on the outside. Nancy had not smiled for years, but then, she had no reason to. She grew up in a strict pastor's home and basically was told that to enjoy life was sin—hard work and unqualified dedication was the only source of true happiness. So she became a missionary teacher and spent the first thirty years of her life living up to those axioms. But she still wasn't happy.

In counseling, Nancy came to realize that those principles her father preached were his attempt to fight off his own problem with lust. When Nancy saw that she no longer had to live by those messages and that they were her father's problem, she could begin enjoying the wonderful life that God had in store for her. Her outward appearance was even affected—Nancy learned how to smile again.

_____

Father, help me be sensitive to my countenance.

Even so the tongue is a little member and boasts great things. See how great a forest a little fire kindles!
—JAMES 3:5

Every year during the summer and fall months, destructive forest fires consume huge portions of forest land. Once these fires get started, it may take days or even weeks of the work of hundreds of men and machines to finally stop them. Often these fires are started by the carelessness of one individual, perhaps by throwing down a lighted match or leaving a campfire unattended.

The careless remark of one person can set off a chain reaction that ends up spreading throughout your emotional life. If your life is emotionally dry and barren anyway because of years of neglect, the sparks of those words literally can cause a fire-storm of emotions. Did negative messages rage in your life? If so, it is time to allow the quenching waters of recovery to begin putting out those fires. As those negative messages come to mind, identify who gave you that message and what that message really said about the sender. Then verbally relinquish that message back to the sender, refusing any longer to claim it as your own. The more you give up the old messages, the more you'll be able to replace them with new, positive truths about yourself.

_____

Lord, please allow the water of Your Word to quench those burning emotional fires within me.

*The words of his mouth were smoother
   than butter,
But war was in his heart;
His words were softer than oil,
Yet they were drawn swords.*
—PS. 55:21

Negative messages like harsh words and strong accusations are easy to identify. But so often it is not necessarily what is said but what is *not* said or the way something *is* said, that can harm us. Whenever Christine's mother told her older sister how pretty and attractive she was, she would always turn to Christine and say, "And you're a nice girl too, Christine." Then she would turn back to her sister and begin primping her hair or fussing with her dress. Though the words were never spoken, Christine got the message loud and clear: "You're not pretty like your sister."

After her tenth plastic surgery, Christine finally began to see the destruction she was causing herself. But in counseling, Christine needed to go beyond the actual words spoken and identify the message behind the words. Once she realized how that minimized her worth and recognized that she was indeed worthy in God's eyes, she saw she could begin to make healthy choices for her life.

Lord, give me the wisdom to understand when I am hearing negative messages.

O LORD, You have searched me and known me.
—PS. 139:1

One of the ways a person gains validity in his life is to be able to have what he says understood by another person. Often, in a dysfunctional family, the parents have their own agenda for what they wish to hear from their children, and no matter what is said, it will be twisted to fit their way of thinking. Whenever Carrie's perfectionist mother asked her to clean the house, Carrie tried her best to do a perfect job. But sure enough, her mother would find something wrong. When Carrie tried to explain that she had done the best she could, her mother would go off on a tirade, accusing Carrie of deliberately trying to ruin her life and then would blame her for her high blood pressure.

Carrie grew up feeling responsible for her mother's illness and began questioning her own motives. When she finally made the decision to deal with her past, the first thing she had to do was see that she was not responsible for her mother's illness. She then wrote her mother a letter, relinquishing that responsibility. By validating her own opinions and realizing that God knew her worth whether anyone else did, she was able to make positive decisions for her life.

Father, help me see that when people twist my words that it is their problem, not mine.

There is one who speaks like the piercings
of a sword,
But the tongue of the wise promotes health.
—PROV. 12:18

Pick up any daily newspaper and you will quickly become aware that stories of stabbings and shootings are as commonplace as the weather report. Interestingly, what you won't see printed are the wounds and hurts people receive from the painful words that are spoken in their lives. Oftentimes nobody sees those wounds or is even aware of them, but these individuals have to deal with this pain alone.

Toby was like that. He had loved his father so much and wanted that love to be returned. But work was his father's love, and Toby was always informed that he was in the way—that his father was simply too busy to be bothered. Toby saw himself as an inconvenience, and though he remained compliant on the surface, inside the thought that he wasn't worth his father's love cut him like a sword. Toby remained in that hidden pain until he began to understand that it was his father who had the problem, not he. As God worked in his life, he began to choose to accept that God loved him. This became more important than acceptance from his father. Toby's wounds finally began to heal.

Lord, help me realize that I need to care for the wounds of my heart as much as the wounds of my body.

> *How precious also are Your thoughts*
> *to me, O God!*
> *How great is the sum of them!*
> —PS. 139:17

For an individual who is the recipient of negative messages from her family on a consistent basis, one of the most refreshing things is to find a source of positive input in her life. Rona was part of a local theater company, and several of her performances had been covered in the newspaper. "When I was a child in dance class," she said, "I would always want to practice in front of my parents. But they never had time to watch me because they were so busy with their own lives. They didn't even come to my performances. The only thing that gave me any reinforcement was the applause of the crowd so that's what I began to live for."

What Rona was still looking for was that parental approval and affirmation, but part of her recovery process was taking the painful step of admitting once and for all she was never going to get that. Then she had to understand that, while the approval from others was important, it couldn't be the source of her worth. She took on the task of realigning her priorities with God's affirmation being first and foremost, then giving herself positive messages, so she could once again enjoy the applause from others.

Father, help me see how precious Your affirmation is to me.

Set your mind on things above, not on things on the earth.
—COL. 3:2

Troy knew he exercised too much. But he couldn't figure out why. He always felt he was running from something, that his life was missing something he desperately needed. The fact he was healthy gave him some relief from the memory that his childhood friends always called him a "wimp." But he needed to look beyond that to a more permanent source of relief from the past.

That's what God wants you to do with the negative messages in your life. He challenges you to take a break from your compulsive behavior and to begin to focus on His love and His worth for you so that the negative messages you feel today don't have the effect on you that they could. How can you do this? The next time you become aware that you are exercising at midnight or buying your twenty-fifth pair of shoes, stop and ask yourself, "From what negative message in my past am I trying to escape?" Then focus on what that message says about your worth. Once you do that, repeat these words over in your mind: "The fact that God made me proves I have value, so I don't need to use this behavior to prove it." Then, like Troy, you can stop running from the past.

Father, help me diminish the power of negative messages in my life by focusing on Your love for me today.

And be renewed in the spirit of your mind.
—EPH. 4:23

About a decade ago, many of the downtowns of cities had decayed to the point where the damage was too widespread to correct. The leaders of these cities decided to tear down the old, outdated edifices and build new sparkling buildings in their places. In fact, because of urban renewal many forgotten cities were virtually reborn.

There is no point in trying to salvage the worn-out foundations of negative messages in your life which you have spent so much time and effort trying to repair. Instead God wants you to replace them with the wholesome attitudes and healthy outlooks that He can provide. The best way to do that is to face them head-on. On a sheet of paper, list the negative messages you received as a child in a column. On the other side of the paper, opposite each message, write a sentence that states the truth about yourself as God sees you. For example, a negative message such as "I am fat and ugly" might have as its corresponding truth "God made me exactly the way I am." Each time you recall a negative message and replace it with God's truth, your spirit truly will be renewed within you.

Father, help me allow You to construct the life that You want me to have.

> *Buy the truth, and do not sell it,*
> *Also wisdom and instruction and understanding.*
> —PROV. 23:23

One of the difficult realities for anyone to recognize is that learning to appropriate God's truth is going to cost something. For Wayne, it meant looking back on a past that he felt he had left far behind. No one would guess from his million-dollar home, his designer clothes, or his foreign cars that he grew up in total poverty. As a child, he always was teased about his shabby clothes and ramshackle house. The negative message that screamed in his head was, "You're poor, and you're a loser." Once Wayne broke away from that situation, he vowed never to be poor again. So he spent his life working to accumulate as many material possessions as he could, but throughout his life he could never buy enough to escape the pain of that message.

Wayne's possessions could never remove that negative message from his mind. What Wayne needed to do was accept the truth of his life—that growing up in poverty had nothing to do with his worth as a person. When he began choosing to believe that truth and saw that those others in his past were wrong, he realized that he no longer had to "buy" his worth. Rather, he began to see that buying the truth at the price of giving up the negative messages was the best investment he could ever make.

Help me, Lord, see the value of buying the truth in my life.

Let no one deceive you with empty words, for because of these things the wrath of God comes upon the sons of disobedience.   —EPH. 5:6

One of the best ways for a person to recover from negative messages is to learn how to receive honest, positive affirmation from other people. The first night Vera came into group therapy, she was full of mistrust and skepticism. She told the group that the only time her father said anything kind to her was when he wanted her to do something, like get a drink for him or rub his back. Eventually this led to sexual abuse by using "sweet words" of persuasion. Afterwards, he would tell her that she was a tramp and no good. She grew up so desperately wanting to hear kind words that she would do anything to hear them and eventually turned to a life of prostitution.

As the individuals in the group began to go around the circle and share their positive affirmations toward Vera, she slowly began to see that perhaps she did have some value in her life after all. It did not happen immediately the first night, but she slowly came to see the deception behind the empty words of her father. She realized, through others' feedback, that she could begin believing in herself as a person of worth.

Father, help me see that Your truth can replace the deception of the empty words of those people in my life.

*Consider what I say, and may the Lord give you
understanding in all things.*   —2 TIM. 2:7

How can what I experienced in my childhood have a
negative influence on me now?" Scott asked. "I've gotten over all that now." Scott was fully convinced, like
so many people, that his current need to be in control
had nothing to do with any negative messages from his
past.

In order to see the impact of childhood experiences,
I asked him to pick just one to talk about. The only
stipulation I gave him was that he not only relate what
had been said but what he felt at that time. He began
confidently enough, stating that his grandfather would
never allow him to work in the garden because it was
his garden and he didn't want any little pip-squeak
spoiling it. As he began to express his anger, the tears
started to flow, and the rage exploded from him. "He
knew how much it meant to me," he cried. "But he
always had to be in control . . ." After several seconds
of quiet, he looked up and quietly said, "Just like me."

As you begin to look at the negative messages from
your past, don't dismiss them casually. Ask God to give
you the courage to face them completely so you can
see how they are affecting you today.

*Lord, help me not minimize anything from my past, so I may know it
as You do.*

Pleasant words are like a honeycomb,
Sweetness to the soul and health to the bones.
                                        —PROV. 16:24

Mariann had spent most of the counseling session describing negative messages she had received throughout her life and how they had affected her. Although most of her life seemed to be in shambles, she had made a couple of good decisions in one or two situations. When I reminded her of this, she looked up at me, and said in a quiet voice, "Thank you, thank you for saying that." Her simple response took me back for a moment, then I responded, "You're welcome."

Afterwards, I realized how important it is to speak kind words to others whenever the opportunity presents itself. So many people receive negative messages from the world that they need positive messages just to help them make it through a particular day.

In Mariann's case, it was the first time she had received affirmation from someone else. By acknowledging that positive impact, she was able to identify other situations when she had made good decisions. "I finally feel like I have the ability to do something right." And that knowledge continued to help her make right decisions for herself.

In a world of negative messages, O Lord, help me speak positive words to others.

But those things which proceed out of the mouth
come from the heart, and they defile a man.
—MATT. 15:18

As a child, when someone hurt my feelings, I would come home and tell my parents. Often their response would be "Well, just consider the source." What they meant by that, of course, was that it really wasn't anything that I had done that was making that person respond that way, but rather his own feelings about himself and others.

When Allen began his recovery, all he could see was the pain his father had caused him by continually disapproving of his friends, his clothes, his music, his dates—any choice that he made was wrong. But when Allen began to look back into his past and see the perfectionistic household that his father had come from, it made him realize that his father was only repeating messages he had heard all his life. He couldn't give Allen anything else because he didn't know anything else—it wasn't because of Allen. When Allen accepted this, he courageously confronted his father with it. It helped his father look at the source of his own demanding nature. But most of all, it helped Allen see that he no longer had to accept those messages as truth.

Father, help me always to "consider the source."

*This is the covenant that I will make with them
after those days, says the LORD: I will put My laws
into their hearts, and in their minds I will write
them.*

—HEB. 10:16

I have learned from experience that if I truly want to remember something, I need to write it down. Whether it is an address, a phone number, even a joke I want to tell, if I don't write it down, I won't remember it.

God said He will write His laws on your mind. This is part of God's plan for getting rid of the negative messages in your life. By studying John 10, you can begin to see a few of those messages.

- I came to give you abundant life. (v. 10)
- I love you enough to die for you. (v. 11)
- I know you specifically. (v. 14)
- I will protect you. (v. 15)
- I can give you eternal life. (v. 28)

As you learn to replace the old messages with God's Word, you can begin to see that there is hope to heal the past, hope to live in the present, and hope to look forward to the future.

Lord, help me open my mind to truths.

> *And immediately, when Jesus perceived in His spirit that they reasoned thus within themselves, He said to them, "Why do you reason about these things in your hearts?"*
> —MARK 2:8

Negative messages can be so strong in your life that even when you know and recognize the truth, you still fall back on those old ideas from the past. Connie had this struggle almost daily. Her mother had always told her, "When the chips are down, I know I can count on you." As the years wore on, Connie came to realize that this was just her mother's way of controlling her. Even though she knew it wasn't healthy and she so desperately wanted a life of her own, her view of her own worth was clouded by the messages that if she let her mom down, she would not be a good daughter.

The point of this verse is that rather than arguing with yourself as to what needs to be done, you should spend your energy doing what you know to be the truth. Connie had to realize that no matter how much she sought her mother's approval, she wasn't going to get it. She had to leave those messages of worthlessness behind and begin spending her energy on choosing daily to accept her worth in God.

Help me realize, Lord, that I have nothing to lose and everything to gain by trusting in Your Word.

3. SHAME BASE

But we have renounced the hidden things of shame, not walking in craftiness nor handling the word of God deceitfully, but by manifestation of the truth commending ourselves to every man's conscience in the sight of God.
—2 COR. 4:2

Joanna had become an expert at hiding. In her childhood, she always tried to keep the secret that her mother used to be a stripper for a club in the shady part of town. No one ever talked about it, and on those few occasions where Joanna's father brought it up against her mother, it created such a tirade of screaming and slapping that Joanna would run to her room and hide. In fact, she developed such a need to hide this buried secret that she decided to become a missionary in order to somehow compensate for that terrible past.

What Joanna had to do was stop running from the past. Only by acknowledging the shame and the damage it had done, could she be free from it. She began to do an inventory of the guilt she felt in her life, and as she looked at her guilt from her mother's past, she was able to realize that she had no part in that past, that she was not responsible for it, and she was going to give it back to her mother. By "renouncing" her shame she could put it behind her forever and finally stop hiding.

Lord, help me begin the process of allowing You to bring those hidden things out so I may be done with them forever.

> *For it is shameful even to speak of those things*
> *which are done by them in secret.*
>
> —EPH. 5:12

One of my patients is a little boy named Cory who has had some difficulty adjusting to his parents' divorce. Whenever Cory comes for his session he is usually very talkative and will fill me in on all the activities that have been happening until I mention the divorce. Then he will change the subject or begin answering questions in a baby voice and then giggle. He has even gone so far as to start dancing around the room. When he finally calms down, he will speak in the softest voice he can and often look down at the floor. Even though he has not been responsible for any of the issues he feels bad about, that deep shame base has infiltrated his whole life.

How many people are just like Cory when it comes to talking about the things of their past? They may not actually go through the physical maneuverings he does but emotionally dodge and dart around discussing the issues. As Cory began to identify what happened and who was responsible for those behaviors, the weight of the shame began to lift. He could begin to see that he hadn't caused his parents' divorce. By sharing his story with someone, he was able to release the grip of shame.

Help me, Father, begin speaking about things I have hidden so long.

Would not God search this out?
For He knows the secrets of the heart.
—PS. 44:21

Brian was a world-class charmer. Whenever he was asked a question, he would always smile his big toothy smile, and begin telling you how nice your tie was or ask what you had done over the weekend. He always seemed to divert the attention from talking about himself. Finally, one day, in desperation I asked him, "Brian, if God knew *everything* about your life and could sum it up in one word, what would He say?" The grin dropped, he swallowed hard, and after about a minute of silence he said, "Pervert." He then spent the next hour telling me of a secret he had never told anyone—his older brother had molested him when he was six.

People often try to hide issues from their past from God as if He is not aware of them. Yet God knows *everything* about you—your past, your present, and your future. He is already aware of those things, He still loves you as much as He ever did, and He wants to begin the healing process in your life. Brian wrote a letter to his brother, telling him how angry he had been and that he no longer claimed responsibility. He wrote a second letter to God, telling Him how he had been hiding all these years. He also asked God to continue helping him with all the other secrets he had been hiding for so long. Now the smile on Brian's face is genuine for there are no more secrets.

Help me remember that there is nothing I can hide from You, God.

*And they heard the sound of the LORD God walking
in the garden in the cool of the day, and Adam and
his wife hid themselves from the presence of the
LORD God among the trees of the garden.*
—GEN. 3:8

Carlos believed he was alone in his shame. His
father's drinking became the family secret. Everyone
else thought he was a loving family man, always at the
sporting events and church services. But Carlos knew
the truth, especially on those nights when he would
come home drunk, hitting everyone that got in his
way. Carlos soon learned that it was not something to
be discussed, so he suffered alone, sure that no one
else had ever gone through such shame.

The reality is that this shame base has a very long
history. When Adam and Eve ate of the fruit, their first
response was to try to hide what they had done.

Once Carlos took the time to look further into the
past, he discovered that his father also had shame—
shame from the fact that he was an illegitimate child.
Carlos then wrote a "last will and testament" from his
father's perspective, one that identified all the unmet
needs and unfinished business his father had passed
down to him. That helped him realize that he was not
alone in the legacy of shame.

Help me, Father, see how impossible it is to hide my past from You.

He who covers his sins will not prosper,
But whoever confesses and forsakes
them will have mercy.
—PROV. 28:13

The shame base has been the groundwork for so many individuals' attempts at wealth and fame. The trauma of her parents' painful divorce and the ensuing poverty from her father's missed child support payments was a terrible scar from Lindsey's past. She was determined to keep it a secret, and the way she determined to do that was to get as far from her past as possible. She decided to become a model. Her natural beauty combined with her determination to be free from her past made her an international cover girl. Yet no matter how "popular" and "respectable" she became, she never felt like it was enough.

For a person to feel truly prosperous and successful, he must deal with his past and recognize that God has worth and love for him regardless of what he is trying to keep covered from his family of origin. Lindsey needed to face that child within her who was still a victim of that divorce. She imagined that she was sitting down with that child, told her the divorce was not her fault, and that she knew and understood her pain. When Lindsey saw that she actually could care for herself, she was able to finally enjoy all of her accomplishments.

Lord, help me recognize where the source of true prosperity lies.

You have set our iniquities before You,
Our secret sins in the light of Your countenance.
—PS. 90:8

A familiar sequence occurs in many of the movies and TV shows that involve courtroom scenes. A defendant will vehemently deny his guilt in a particular crime. No matter how much badgering the prosecution does, he so unequivocally denies any wrongdoing that even the audience begins to believe him. Then the prosecutor turns around, walks to his desk, and brings back a piece of evidence that irrefutably implicates the defendant. A look of shocked horror appears on the face of the defendant, and then finally he shouts "I did it!" and pours out the whole sordid story.

This must happen to you in your healing process. As God begins to bring forth the evidence, you must be willing to recognize its truth and the effect it has had on your life. Meditation is a technique that involves taking one event from your past, closing your eyes, and using all five senses to recall the event. What do you see? What sounds can you hear? What particular smells do you remember? What type of physical touch was experienced? Is there anything you can taste? As you begin to flush out those experiences, you can also begin to see them in a more realistic way and break out of denial into the truth.

Help me, Lord, to recognize the evidence that You have brought before me.

For the Holy Spirit will teach you in that very hour what you ought to say. —LUKE 12:12

One of the difficult things in dealing with the shame base in your life is that sometimes you don't even really understand how it has affected you or what you need to identify about it. Perhaps you see your family of origin as relatively healthy with a few minor flaws that seem to have had little impact on you. Hal had come into counseling to deal with his drive toward perfectionism, but looking back at his family only made him feel worse. They always did things right and they never failed to point out when he did something wrong. Hal was spending his life trying to live beyond the shame that he felt by being so imperfect.

The Holy Spirit needs to work in a person's life to help him recognize what exactly he needs to say and do regarding the past. Hal was asked to make a list of everything that he felt he had not lived up to at home. Then, prayerfully, he was to look at that list and identify the actual problems which were reasonable for a child to solve. The majority of issues were problems no child could be expected to live with, let alone solve. He was able with God's help to recognize the false guilt that he had been living with all these years, give it back to his parents, and begin to recover from his perfectionism.

Lord, bring to mind those things that I need to know about my past and teach me how to handle them in the best possible way.

> *"Can anyone hide himself in secret places,*
> *So I shall not see him?" says the LORD;*
> *"Do I not fill heaven and earth?" says the LORD.*
> —JER. 23:24

The question has often been asked, "How big is your God?" In fact, it is so relevant as to have been the title of tracts, books, and songs. The question is certainly a valid one, especially for the individual dealing with the secret things from the past. When you begin to look back and deal with the issues that have developed your base of shame, do you recognize that God is big enough to help you deal with those situations?

When Lisa finally began to uncover the memory that her father had physically abused her as a child, she wanted to leave it buried. "No," she said. "This is too painful to face. I can't do it alone." Lisa was encouraged to remember God would be there with her to help her face that pain. That knowledge finally gave Lisa the courage to face her father, tell him that she knew what he had done, that she would no longer take responsibility for it, that it was now his to live with. Then she calmly turned around and walked away. She later commented to me, "If God could help me through that, then He truly is big enough to trust."

Help me understand, Father, that You are big enough to handle my past, present, and future.

My enemies would hound me all day,
For there are many who fight against
me, O Most High. —PS. 56:2

As the vice president of a large corporation, Grace was trying to stop her compulsion to put in twenty-hour days and expect her staff to be at her every beck and call. "Everyone in my family had something to hide—Dad's rages, Mom's affairs, Grandma's bottle, Grandpa's girlie magazines, my brother's drug habit, my sister's smoking, even my best friend's sexual relationship with her boyfriend. Everyone made me responsible for their secrets, and I was always caught in the middle. I have enough shame to last for two lifetimes—how can I ever begin sorting it out?"

It was true. Grace was bearing the past of a multitude of people in her life, and she needed to begin giving it back. To help her sort it out, she wrote the name of each significant person in her life on separate envelopes. Then she took a page for each person, listed all the things she had falsely felt responsible for, folded up the paper, put it in the appropriate envelope, and sealed it. When she had sorted out all the shame and identified all that she was not responsible for, she could stop running and begin her recovery.

Lord, give me the courage to begin sorting out my past.

And do not hide Your face
from Your servant,
For I am in trouble;
Hear me speedily.
—PS. 69:17

Sometimes the shame a child feels growing up is due to the emotional unavailability of a parent. This is especially true if the parent has an addiction that takes up much of his or her time. Perry's mother had a consuming passion with her community organizations. Whenever he came to her with some question or problem he had or when he just wanted to talk, she put him off with, "Not now, dear, you're interrupting my work." The emptiness of her loveless marriage and her need to feel accepted by the socially elite crowd drove her on. But all Perry could see was that he wasn't important enough to spend time with, so he began hiding his own emotional pain.

It is important to understand that no matter how unavailable people were in your past, God is always available. By making Himself open to you, He teaches you how to be open with yourself and others. Once Perry began to realize that through prayer God was available to him anytime, he came out from hiding. The burden of shame was lifted even more when he found the courage to share his story with a trusted friend. Finally, Perry was able to stop hiding once and for all because Someone was always there to listen.

Because You do not hide from me, O Lord, teach me how to no longer hide from myself.

When pride comes, then comes shame;
But with the humble is wisdom.
—PROV. 11:2

A person's pride is usually based on his accomplishments. The positive, successful image he is projecting is so important that he cannot tolerate any negativity in his past. That would indicate weakness which is certainly not part of a "self-made man."

Families tend to react in the same way. In order to save face with those who give them the approval they need, everyone in the family buries the things from their past. But they see themselves as frauds living a lie. Before you can escape from the shame, you also have to get rid of the pride. The way to do this is to face the past head-on and begin to see what family secrets are creating the shame base.

Take a sheet of paper and make three columns. At the top of one column, write: "The Little Secrets My Parents Kept from Me." Title the second column: "Secrets I Kept from My Parents," and the third: "Secrets Our Family Kept from the World." Now list the secrets from your past, putting them in the proper columns. By identifying the secrets, and getting them out in the open, you can begin facing each one and removing each one once and for all from your past.

Help me, Lord, begin to deal with the pride as well as the shame in my life.

Then I would not be ashamed,
When I look into all Your commandments.
—PS. 119:6

To be honest," said Dana, "I'm a little scared of recovery." Although this feeling is not unusual, I assured him, I was interested in why he felt this way. "Well," he said, "I've always had to live up to expectations from my family, and I feel like I've failed them. I couldn't get the grades Mom wanted, I wasn't the football player Dad wanted, and I know I've made them ashamed of me because I didn't grow up to be the lawyer they both wanted. Since they are that demanding, I can't imagine trying to live up to God's standards. I'm sure I would only be a disappointment to Him too."

When considering recovery according to God's Word, that feeling often will spring up as you begin to see what God expects of you. However, God is there to provide help every step of the way. When Dana began to compare his parents' expectations to their assistance, he realized that his mother never helped with homework, Dad never tossed a football, and neither ever encouraged his college education. He saw his shame had been based on *their* inadequacies, not his. He also recognized that by giving him unconditional love, unmerited grace, and promises in His Word, God provided the means by which to never feel ashamed.

Help me recognize that You provide the way, Father, for me to never feel ashamed.

For the Lord GOD will help Me;
Therefore I will not be disgraced;
Therefore I have set My face like a flint,
And I know that I will not be ashamed.
—ISA. 50:7

In Tony's opinion, he was a disgrace in the eyes of his father. As far back as he could remember, his father wanted him to be a doctor. Tony had interest and a great deal of natural ability in music. But when it came time to go to college, Tony's father told him, "Either go to med school, or I won't pay for your college." Tony tried to convince him that he would do well in music, but his father didn't budge. So Tony had to put himself through school, paying for all his own lessons, all without any help or support from his father. In fact, even after becoming a concert musician, his father never came to hear him play. He always felt he had disappointed his father.

No matter what kind of situation you find yourself in, your heavenly Father never lets you down. By developing his own "Bill of Rights," Tony began to realize that he was not responsible for his father's disappointment. He also began to see that his own feelings were valid. By itemizing his basic rights, including his right to pursue whatever career he chose, he saw he did not have to make any excuses for his life anymore.

Thank You, O Lord, for being the Father who never lets me down.

> *You shall eat in plenty and be satisfied,*
> *And praise the name of the LORD your God,*
> *Who has dealt wondrously with you;*
> *And My people shall never be put to shame.*
> —JOEL 2:26

My wife and I often invite people for dinner or for a snack after church. I can always count on my wife serving something delicious to our guests—people always compliment her on her cooking. That knowledge makes it easy for me to trust her ability as a hostess. Her reputation as a good cook and great hostess can always be counted on.

God has the same kind of reputation with His children. When Cliff looked back over his own life, he was amazed at the way God had worked. His father had the reputation of being "Mr. Tightwad" because of his frugal business practices. Cliff finally left home, and spent years donating his time and energy to charitable organizations, hoping to erase his past. He came in contact with a counselor who was able in a loving, supportive way to confront Cliff with the reality of his addiction. When he finally accepted that God didn't care about his reputation, he was not only freed from his past but found hope to be able to confront his father in the future. God proved His reputation in Cliff's life.

Help me realize, Lord, that You will never make me ashamed but that I will always be satisfied in You.

*According to my earnest expectation and hope that
in nothing I shall be ashamed, but that with all
boldness, as always, so now also Christ will be
magnified in my body, whether by life or by death.*
—PHIL. 1:20

One of the most difficult things for the person recovering from compulsive behaviors to understand is the totality of recovery that is possible in the Lord. Larry believed that recovery from the intensity of the physical abuse from his childhood was impossible. He had gone through the process of recognizing that the abuse had taken place and could even recall some of the instances. Recovery might be possible in some areas of his life, but not where the abuse was concerned. So for a long time, that part of his life remained buried, and he could not experience full recovery.

What is that particular area in your life that you still have covered and buried? Is there something that you feel is so deep, so secret, so shameful that you will never be able to recover? As Larry continued to identify all of the things causing his feelings of false guilt, he slowly began to see that if he wasn't responsible for the other actions of his father, like his drunkenness and laziness, then he wasn't responsible for his abusiveness either. Only then was Larry able to take it out of his life, give it back to his father where it belonged, and be completely free of that shame forever.

*Help me, Father, settle for nothing less than the total recovery that
You promised.*

> *And now, little children, abide in Him, that when*
> *He appears, we may have confidence and not be*
> *ashamed before Him at His coming.*
> —1 JOHN 2:28

One of the signs of a shame-laden past is a lack of confidence. Although on the surface it may seem that a person is successful and has the world by a string, deep within there is a nagging sense of inadequacy. The achievements, the accolades, the praise never seem to shake that feeling of lack of confidence that the pain of the past has brought. So how does one overcome this feeling?

The answer is found in this Scripture—"abide in Him." In order to begin trusting God completely for your life, you must say good-bye to the negative relationships from the past. This is not an easy task because they have such a strong hold on you. But once you begin to see you no longer have to be bound by this shame, you can start to let go. By realizing that you are not responsible for that shame, you can give it back to its rightful owner and walk away. Letting go forces you to turn to God to meet those needs. If He is all you have left, you must depend on Him. So today, begin releasing yourself from your crippling past and begin to have the confidence that God can give.

Lord, help me learn what abiding in You truly means.

He dams up the streams from trickling;
What is hidden he brings forth to light.
—JOB 28:11

People who deal with shame often have dark corners of their past that they sometimes have difficulty facing. The door of denial has been shut firmly on those experiences, both to protect what's inside from coming out, and to make sure what's outside never discovers what's behind that door. Jordan felt shame from his past, but his memory was blocked on his first six years of life—he couldn't remember a thing. Yet, every time he started to get close to anyone in a relationship, he would pull away, often with a feeling close to terror.

In counseling, Jordan was encouraged to visualize the part of his life that was locked behind a closet door. He was able to approach the door, stand in front of it, unlock it, turn the knob, and open it. Then he visualized slowly walking into the room. He identified and felt each experience in that room, then handed it to God to be removed forever. Eventually he was able to face everything in that closet, even the long forgotten memory of his uncle's sexual abuse that was behind his inability to get close to people. Jordan found that God's light was powerful enough to clean that closet. Is there a closet in your life that God's light can help you face today?

Lord, let Your light as well as Your love work in my life.

He reveals deep and secret things;
He knows what is in the darkness,
And light dwells with Him.
—DAN. 2:22

Were you ever afraid of the dark? I must confess that I was. I especially remember those times when I would go on camping trips. Once all the lights were put out for the night the incredible darkness of the surrounding woods would almost seem overwhelming. As soon as the campfire died down and all the flashlights were turned off, I heard strange sounds and rustlings. I was sure some evil monster was lurking just on the edge of the clearing. I was too frightened to turn my flashlight on for fear the light would confirm my worst suspicions. Yet with dawn's first light, I was able to see that my fears were unfounded.

Are you still afraid of the dark emotionally? Are there still hidden corners that have grown so ominous over the years you feel they could reach out and destroy you at any moment? Why not allow the light of God's Word to reveal those things to you so that you no longer have to live with the fear and shame from those past influences?

_____

Lord, let Your light reveal the "monsters" in my life.

Therefore do not fear them. For there is nothing covered that will not be revealed, and hidden that will not be known. —MATT. 10:26

Jesus warned His disciples about the persecutions that following Him would bring. He told them that they were not to fear the people who persecuted them. Even though these men might say things about them that could cause great shame in their lives, He assured them that in the end, the truth would be known.

Are you like the disciples? Do you have people in your life who make you feel ashamed because of the secrets of your past or your lack of accomplishment today? Carla had a great fear of her brother bringing up her past weight problem. He would always tease her and call her names like "Roly-Poly" or "Carla the Car," so that even today she was afraid to be with him. Through her recovery, Carla was able to acknowledge her worth in God and was able to see that just because he said those things didn't mean they were true. By facing her past rather than fearing it, she was able to walk away when he began to tease her. This allowed her to start protecting that worth she had discovered.

Lord, help me recognize that the truth will never allow me to be ashamed.

For He will deliver the needy when he cries,
The poor also, and him who has no helper.
—PS. 72:12

Kelly sat in my office, telling me all the secrets that she was made to keep and how responsible she felt for the actions of the family. "The most horrible part of my childhood experience was the fact that even though I had so many needs and even though I hurt so much, I wasn't able to share that with anyone because of the shame I felt for my family. I felt totally and helplessly alone."

The sad news of that particular situation is that it is repeated countless times and by countless individuals every day of the year. It is so important in the recovery process to begin sharing the pain of shame with someone else. Kelly had a trusted friend to whom she finally began telling her story. As the words poured out, so did the emotions, and the burden of shame finally began lifting. By telling it to her friend, she also realized that she could tell it to God as well. And just like with her friend, each time she cried out a hurt to the Lord, the burden became lighter as well. It gave hope to Kelly to find out that she no longer had to feel alone.

Father, help me recognize that only by sharing the story of my shame can I ever be free of it.

Then the man said, "The woman whom You gave to be with me, she gave me of the tree, and I ate."
—GEN. 3:12

People have been making excuses since the beginning of history, and they can usually find someone to blame for their actions. Greg became everyone's excuse in his family. Being the youngest, he seemed the easiest target for blame, since everyone else was bigger or older than he was. And by accepting that blame from everyone else, he learned how to make excuses for himself as well. In fact, he had never held a job for more than six months because he would get fired for being late or be asked to resign for not getting his work done on time. But if asked, he would always have an excuse for his behavior. It was never his fault.

Rather than trying to excuse or defend his actions, Greg needed to look at himself honestly. He came to realize that he could never face the truth about himself because he hadn't faced the truth about his past. By blaming others for his own shortcomings, he was doing exactly what he had resented his family members doing to him—not taking responsibility for their actions. When he gave those issues back to them, he could finally stop making excuses and start working on his own real issues.

Lord, help me see that my excuses are only ways to hide from my past.

*Therefore you are inexcusable, O man, whoever
you are who judge, for in whatever you judge
another you condemn yourself; for you who
judge practice the same things.* —ROM. 2:1

A constant revelation to people is to discover that
their base of shame can be traced back several generations where individuals, unable to face the shame of
their past, pass it on to the next generation. Barbara
felt anger and resentment from always having to protect the family secret—her mother and father had a
sham marriage, and that they had done little more
than speak to each other for fifteen years. Yet, Barbara
kept the secret, pretending to the world that they had
the perfect family, even though she wanted to scream
the truth out loud. Finally, Barbara took the courage to
face her mother and give back all the shame she felt all
those years. She confronted her with her anger, waiting for a response. Finally, Barbara's mother spoke in a
broken voice and told Barbara of her shame from her
own family. She asked Barbara for forgiveness, and determined to begin facing the shame in her own life.
Barbara not only forgave her but was able to gain
more strength to continue her own recovery, so that
the legacy would not be passed on to another generation.

*Lord, help me see that the shame I feel is not all my own, but is
something passed down to me.*

The secret things belong to the LORD our God, but those things which are revealed belong to us and to our children forever, that we may do all the words of this law.
—DEUT. 29:29

Don't you wish there was a place where you could take those awful things from your childhood and dispose of them forever, put them someplace safe and far away where they wouldn't be able to harm anyone else? It would be a toxic chemical disposal plant for your secret emotions, which would remove them from your own "house" where they cause so much damage.

Believe it or not, there is such a place. In fact it is not so much a place, as a Person. God wants you to turn these toxic emotions that are destroying you over to Him so He can take care of them and dispose of them. Then you will be free to focus on the positive things in your life and pass those on to future generations. Why not close your eyes and tell God about your pain and anger and hurt. Use *all* your senses in describing what you remember and don't leave out any detail. Once you have told your story to Him, picture yourself putting all those hurts in a box, shutting the lid, and handing it over to Him to take care of once and for all.

Lord, help me realize that in You my past is gone once and for all.

*So then each of us shall give account of himself
to God.*
                                        —ROM. 14:12

The old saying, "Pay me now or pay me later," applies
to actions as well as money. The consequences of any
action or behavior in life must be dealt with sooner or
later. They can't be postponed indefinitely. Unfortu-
nately, if you postpone these results and think you have
avoided them, they only tend to grow and multiply to
a point where they become much more difficult to
handle.

You must begin dealing now with the shame from
your past. Think how long you have been involved
with the compulsive behaviors you have been using to
avoid it. Marla was spending all of her energy being
the perfect wife and mother, trying to escape the
shame of a mother who left her when she was six. But
even with all her best efforts, she still could not live up
to the standards she had set for herself and she was
beginning to feel she was a failure at motherhood just
like her mother. Marla finally took the time to stop and
see her perfectionism as a way to escape the shame
from her past. She needed to begin dealing directly
with that shame. She found out that the sooner she
dealt with it, the sooner she would stop having to pay
for it.

---

*Lord, help me begin now in dealing with my past, rather than putting
it off until later.*

Now hope does not disappoint, because the love of God has been poured out in our hearts by the Holy Spirit who was given to us. —ROM. 5:5

One of the things that contributes greatly to the shame a person feels about his past is the continual disappointment of unmet expectations in his life. Justin always felt a desire to try just one more time to make his parents listen to him. Yet each time Justin went away unfulfilled and dejected and the shame of disappointment overwhelmed him. "It was like I had some kind of thirst, and I was looking for just one drop of water to quench that thirst. But the more that thirst wasn't quenched, the more pronounced it was to the point that it was all I could think about."

However, when Justin finally came to the place in his life where he realized that he could go to God to quench his thirst, he did not come away disappointed. In fact, during his family inventory, each time an unmet need came to Justin's mind, such as his need to be listened to, he pictured himself going to a cool stream full of God's love and drinking from that stream until he was no longer thirsty. In that way, he allowed God's love to be "poured out" in his heart and fill each of those needs.

Lord, quench my desolate spirit of disappointment with Your unquenchable resource of love.

4. LOW SELF-ESTEEM

June 15 – SOMETHING TO BE PLEASED WITH

*Then God saw everything that He had made, and
indeed it was very good. So the evening and the
morning were the sixth day.* —GEN. 1:31

Have you ever made something you were pleased
with? That was God's feeling after He created man. But
often, you don't see yourself the same way God does.
Jenny found it almost impossible to see anything good
about her life. As early in her childhood as she could
remember, she felt inferior. Of course, her mother reminded her daily of her lack of worth by telling her
what a burden she was to the family—if she hadn't
come along, her mother could have pursued her career
as an actress. Jenny worked hard in school to try to be
important somewhere, but she still couldn't get any
love from her mother. Now in college, Jenny had made
the dean's list and become a cheerleader, yet she still
saw herself as a failure.

What Jenny was doing was trying to find her value
in things that don't last. Jenny needed to go to the One
who made her in the first place to see what He had to
say about her worth. When she read in this passage
that God thought she was important and of value, she
realized that she was a creation pleasing to God.

Help me recognize that I am one of Your special creations, Father.

So God created man in His own image; in the image of God He created him; male and female He created them.
                                                    —GEN. 1:27

Peter's one wish in life was to grow up to be like his father. The problem was, he could never seem to measure up. He tried to be tough and strong, but his dad always said he was being "macho" and punished him. He tried to be smart, but his dad always said his ideas were "stupid." He tried to be brave, but somehow his dad always found a way to make him cry. He just wanted to be like his dad, but the more he tried, the more discouraged he became because as far as he could see, his dad was great, and no matter how hard he tried, he was nothing like that.

Peter was trying to live up to the image of his father, but that wasn't who Peter needed to be. Anytime you start measuring your value by someone else's standard, you set yourself up for failure. Peter was created in God's image, and the only way Peter would find self-esteem was to start focusing on the positive qualities he had. When he started to look at the characteristics of God such as mercy, love, and trust, he realized that those were the qualities God could develop in his own life and that was where his focus should be.

Lord, help me remember that the image You used to create me was Your very own.

Let not mercy and truth forsake you;
Bind them around your neck,
Write them on the tablet of your heart,
And so find favor and high esteem
In the sight of God and man.

—PROV. 3:3–4

Why is it that so many people can give someone else a compliment or encouraging word, but it is so difficult to believe those same things about themselves? Carolyn was always the most supportive in the group, having an uplifting word for everyone else who was struggling with self-esteem. But whenever she shared an experience in her own life, she would put herself down, always making excuses like, "I don't deserve to be happy," or, "See the mess I got myself into." She was making sure they were emotionally indebted to her by making them feel good at her expense.

One day, Carolyn was confronted by another member that she had not been kind or honest with the group. She was stunned and speechless. Then the other group member told her that she was being unkind and dishonest with herself, and she was as important as any of the other group members. She sat quietly as each of them pointed out her good points and how she had helped them. By receiving their affirmation, Carolyn was able to see that she did have good qualities and that it was healthier to be nice to herself than to put herself down. By being merciful and truthful with herself, she could be more so with those around her.

Help me apply Your truth and mercy to my life.

He who diligently seeks good finds favor,
But trouble will come to him who seeks evil.
—PROV. 11:27

Bill was considered a "great guy" by all the men in the office. He was always the one to pick up the tab for lunch. Whenever anyone needed assistance, Bill was always right there. He was always the one to turn to in a bind. But Bill began to see that what was once a good quality had now begun to destroy him. It was taking money out of his pocket that he needed to pay bills, and the time he spent with his "needy" friends was eating more and more into family time.

As Bill did those "good" things he began to receive praise along with them. Because he was so starved for praise from childhood, he began to crave it, and so his motivation changed from doing good to receiving praise. Rather than doing good for its own sake, he was using it as a means to an end—to gain the approval he wanted so badly. What Bill needed to do was distinguish between those things he did for approval and the things he did because he truly cared. When he made the two lists, he could see that many of his activities needed to be removed from his life. That gave him freedom to enjoy the ones he chose to do.

Lord, help me focus more on doing good rather than the favor it brings.

> *He has shown you, O man, what is good;*
> *And what does the LORD require of you*
> *But to do justly,*
> *To love mercy,*
> *And to walk humbly with your God?*
> —MIC. 6:8

Glenn sat in my office describing his childhood to me. "No matter how much I tried to live up to the requirements my father set for me, it always seemed to be just out of reach. The rules kept changing. As soon as I would accomplish one type of behavior, another would immediately take its place. I felt as if I was on a treadmill, and he was continuously pushing up the speed."

The feeling of never fulfilling the requirements of your parents can be a devastating thing to a child's self-esteem. That is why it is so important to recognize the need to gain your self-esteem from the Lord. His requirements are simple, and they never change. Basically they just involve recognizing who you are in your relationship to God, how much love He has for you, and to therefore pattern your life after that kind of love. When Glenn compared what his father's requirements were with God's requirements, he saw that it would actually be possible to please God. That was all the incentive Glenn needed to overhaul his goals, and once he began to seek God's never-changing priorities for his life, he was finally able to feel acceptance.

Lord, help me seek Your requirements for my life today.

A good man out of the good treasure of his heart brings forth good things, and an evil man out of the evil treasure brings forth evil things.
—MATT. 12:35

It was hard for Barry to understand why he wasn't making it at college. He had gone with every intention of doing well, and he initially studied very hard. His parents had always told him he would never make it because he was so irresponsible. His greatest desire was to prove them wrong and he had signed up for the most difficult courses, and joined every possible organization. Yet, he was failing his classes and dropping out of his clubs. What was going wrong?

Actually, in a dysfunctional way, everything was really right on schedule. Barry felt the need to prove his worth, but he also had been programmed to doubt his abilities, so he took on so much that he made it impossible for him to succeed. The buried treasure of his heart, his low self-esteem, was influencing all of his choices. Barry had to dig up that old treasure by identifying all his parents' expectations that were really not his own. Then he had to replace it with the treasure of God's love in his heart. With that treasure in his life, his life took a whole new direction.

Lord, help me understand that You must put the treasure of Your love in my heart before I can begin to feel good about myself.

His lord said to him, "Well done, good and faithful
servant; you were faithful over a few things, I will
make you ruler over many things. Enter into the joy
of your lord."
—MATT. 25:21

One of the biggest lies that low self-esteem causes a person to believe is that she has to be completely successful at every task. Carmen always felt that as soon as she had mastered one thing, there was something else she could improve on. If she threw a party, the house had to be spotless, the lawn immaculate, the food outstanding—then she would spend hours after the party criticizing herself for the small flaws. It was the ghost of her mother's voice saying, "Yes, your room is clean, but there is a wrinkle on your bed." The only way to try and still that voice was to keep doing more and doing it better.

God does have specific tasks for you to do, but God recognizes your limitations. He never asks you to attempt something that, with His power, you cannot handle. If you simply attend to the tasks He has called you to and do your best, then you will feel that sense of accomplishment because He will bless you in those particular areas of your life. To help herself realize this, Carmen started keeping a daily diary, and each day she would remind herself of one thing she did well that day. By seeing that she could do something well, she stopped feeling the need to prove it.

Lord, help me simply be faithful to what You have called me to do.

And God is able to make all grace abound toward you, that you, always having all sufficiency in all things, have an abundance for every good work.
—2 COR. 9:8

I just don't see myself as a capable person," Sara said. "I can't seem to get past the belief that my life will never be in control." Far from being out of control, her life was controlled to the extreme. Sara had her days planned down to the minute, her house was immaculate, even her clothes were hung in her closet according to color and fabric. Because of the chaos of growing up in a broken home, she never saw herself as being capable of controlling her life.

Sara used the technique of "taking off the old glasses" to see her life and her worth from a different point of view than the one influenced by her past. She was encouraged to view her life through the eyes of a close friend and describe what that friend would see. This helped Sara not only identify the areas where she was too controlled but also admit the ways she demonstrated her capabilities in a positive way. By recognizing that she did have capabilities, she could develop the self-esteem that would release her from her need to control.

Help me, Father, recognize the full extent of my capabilities in You.

And let us not grow weary while doing good, for in due season we shall reap if we do not lose heart.

—GAL. 6:9

When Lori considered all the negative messages of her past that caused her to question her worth, it was difficult. Just remembering the abuse, how her friends treated her because of her bruises, how she always felt the shame of her daddy's drinking, made her feel unworthy. As she came to see the devastation of those old messages and began to let go of them, she was still receiving negative input from her family who kept telling her, "You'll never get well," "You're just imagining these things," and "Who do you think you are anyway?"

It takes time and effort to overcome the bad habits of the past, and it is important to develop new and healthy habits to replace the old. Lori identified one positive strength each morning to remember that day and then that evening, one positive thing that she had accomplished. By giving herself positive affirmation, she would in time reap the harvest of a positive outlook and a healthy life-style.

When I grow weary, Lord, help me recognize that in the end it will be worth the effort.

For we are His workmanship, created in Christ Jesus for good works, which God prepared beforehand that we should walk in them.
—EPH. 2:10

If I were to place before you a block of unmolded clay and a beautiful, hand-painted vase, which would you tell me has more worth? You probably would respond that the vase has more value. Both objects are made of the same thing, and one doesn't weigh any more than the other one. The difference is that one has been the subject of someone's work and effort, and the quality of craftsmanship that has been placed upon it begins to increase its value.

God talks about you being His "workmanship" or the product of His efforts. Your value is not increased by all the things you achieve in your life any more than that block of clay could add any value to itself. What gives you worth is the fact that God has specifically and especially designed you. To help you recognize this, sit back for a moment and think about the qualities in your life. Ask yourself this question: "If I were in charge of remaking me, what five qualities would I not change but include in the new and improved model?" Write those qualities down, and each day pick one of those qualities, thank God for it, and ask Him to use it in your life that day. Then you can truly begin to see His workmanship in your life.

Help me begin to recognize Your hand at work in my life, Father.

*That you may have a walk worthy of the Lord, fully
pleasing Him, being fruitful in every good work
and increasing in the knowledge of God.*
—COL. 1:10

Have you ever noticed how sometimes people's attitudes change when their positions change? For example, as unpolished commoners marry into a royal
family and become more aware of who they are and
what they represent, their actions seem to more
closely correspond to their position. Even in an elec-
tive office in high school, a person can rise to their
calling and become a much more poised individual.

As a youth, Juan was the brunt of every ethnic joke
about his race, and he couldn't walk down the hall at
school without someone yelling, "Hey, Spic" or "Mr.
Greaseball." That low self-esteem became hidden behind a wall of rage. Because of his temper he could
never hold a job for more than a few weeks which only
deepened his sense of worthlessness. But through
counseling, Juan began to see that God didn't disqual-
ify him as a worthwhile human being because of his
race. To reinforce that, he wrote "I am worthy" on a
three-by-five card, and whenever he was put down at
work, he would pull out his card, and it would help him
control his temper. He soon was able not only to keep
his jobs but became foreman as well. He learned to live
up to the person he was all along.

Lord, help me begin to live up to my position in You.

For I, the LORD your God, will hold your right hand,
Saying to you, "Fear not, I will help you."
—ISA. 41:13

Fear is a very real part of low self-esteem. It may be fear of rejection—you feel that no matter what you've done it will not be accepted. It might be fear of abandonment—you believe that everyone you love has pulled away from you because of something you have done. Or your fear may be of the unknown, of never knowing what to expect because life has been so mixed up and dysfunctional. Whatever its source, fear plays right into the feelings of low self-esteem and can be totally debilitating. Jana's fears led her from one meaningless relationship to another. Every time she got close to someone, one of her fears would kick in, she would panic, and pull out of the relationship.

God recognizes and understands each of those fears. He also gives you one thing that people with low self-esteem need most—companionship. He lets you know that He will be with you through all those fearful places in your life, holding your hand in protection and comfort. As Jana learned to trust God, she found that whenever the fear arose, she could visualize God holding her hand, and that helped her in learning to trust others.

Remind me in those fearful times that You are here with me, O Lord.

Therefore you are no longer a slave but a son, and if a son, then an heir of God through Christ.
—GAL. 4:7

Are you a slave? Even though slavery ended in this country with the Civil War, people can still be slaves to many things. Lance was a slave to his clubs. Growing up on the wrong side of the tracks, he never felt like part of the "in" group. Whenever he tried to make friends, he was ridiculed and reminded of his poverty. That feeling of being nobody drove him to the determination that he would someday be one of "them." So he climbed socially to the place where he was asked to join the clubs. But the need to always be seen at the right time with the right people began to take its toll, and soon he felt trapped by his friends' expectations for him always to be there. He became a slave.

God will take you out of the slavery of your compulsive behaviors and will give you a new identity by making you His child. In order to break that slavery, Lance had to see that his value to his friends was obtained by what he could do, but his worth to God was simply his for the taking.

Now it's up to you—which will you be, a slave or a child of God?

Lord, remove me from the slavery of my compulsions and help me live as Your child today.

Let love be without hypocrisy. Abhor what is evil.
Cling to what is good. —ROM. 12:9

Kyle was addicted to many things, but one of the most significant was negativism. Kyle always saw things in a negative light because that was the way he thought about himself. He was never given praise as a child, and so rather than continuing to try and expect it, he chose to believe the worst so that he would never be disappointed. Whenever he criticized some performance he saw or someone's decision, it was with the hope that it would make him feel superior, more significant. But usually, when he saw the hurt feelings in someone else, it only made him feel more negative about himself and his life.

Everyone has the ability to choose how to look at life. It is the same concept as looking at the glass half empty or half full. Kyle always had the choice; he just didn't see it. When he began to realize he did not have to see things negatively he focused on the positive aspects of his life such as his sense of humor or his giving spirit. He could then find the good in others and give up on his negativity.

Help us, Father, to look for the good in our daily circumstances.

Have I not commanded you? Be strong and of good courage; do not be afraid, nor be dismayed, for the LORD your God is with you wherever you go.
—JOSH. 1:9

In struggling with self-esteem issues, you often get the feeling that you are virtually alone in whatever tasks you have to face. Receiving so little support from family and friends in childhood, Curtis began to rely totally on himself and his own abilities in facing his problems. Yet, even though he saw himself as the only one he could count on, he still did not see himself as being capable of handling situations. Each time he worked hard to prove himself right and failed, his low self-esteem was reinforced. His perception of himself as being the only one he could trust, yet being a failure, made him feel totally helpless.

That's why God *commands* you in His Word to trust in Him for help through those difficult times. He knows your weaknesses and failures, and He wants you to acknowledge them to Him so He can begin to help you. Curtis had to learn that he never could "go it alone," but that in being responsible for his choices, he had the ability to *choose* to let God handle his problems. For it is only by turning your problems over to God that you begin to see how He can solve them. The choice was Curtis's—the choice is yours.

————

Father, help me recognize that to choose to be strong in You is the best choice I can possibly make.

"Not by might nor by power, but by My Spirit,"
Says the LORD of hosts. —ZECH. 4:6

When you think about trying to overcome the low self-esteem in your life, often you feel the need to accomplish some great task or achieve some momentous honor in order to stop those negative feelings. You may look around at the accomplishments of others and say, "If I could just do something great like that person, I would feel better about myself." Although his dad paid no attention to him at home, Cody saw how much time his dad spent at his work. He began to believe if he was ever going to get his father's attention, he would have to do it through his successes. But the higher the corporate ladder Cody climbed, the higher his father climbed, so Cody never felt he had accomplished what he set out to do.

Cody had to realize that he had made his father his "mini-god." When he took time to compare what God required of him versus what his father did, he could see that it was no wonder he had never achieved his father's approval. Cody also found that not only were God's standards more attainable, but He provides the means to achieve them through His Spirit.

Lord, help me rely on Your Spirit to give me what I need in my life.

> *Now I myself am confident concerning you, my brethren, that you also are full of goodness, filled with all knowledge, able also to admonish one another.*
> —ROM. 15:14

One thing low self-esteem takes away from an individual is the ability to confront another person. Rather than confront her issues of hating men, Luann hid behind her addiction of one-night stands. For a brief time, she could feel needed and loved, but when the anger and hurt from childhood abuse reared its head, she would always cut the cord and move on to a new relationship rather than face the hurt.

If Luann was ever going to have healthy relationships in her life, she was going to have to confront her past and the individuals involved. In order to gain the self-esteem she needed, she had to begin trusting God, but even that was difficult and she couldn't understand why.

By listing all the emotions she felt toward God, then replacing God's name with her father's, she was able to see that she was placing the feelings she had toward her father who molested her on God who loved her. When she saw that she actually could trust God, she became confident enough to confront her father, the real cause of her mistrust of men.

Lord, give me the self-confidence to be able to confront those situations I need to in my life.

For though He was crucified in weakness, yet He lives by the power of God. For we also are weak in Him, but we shall live with Him by the power of God toward you.
—2 COR. 13:4

In helping Sherry deal with self-esteem, I suggested to her that if she did not understand that she is weak and helpless, she would never begin to develop a healthy self-esteem. This seemed to be a contradiction to her because she saw her weaknesses as something that could never be corrected or changed and something that she might fight against in order to become healthy. To identify and accept weakness was seen as a last defeat for her.

Admission of your weaknesses does not defeat your self-esteem but rather your sense of self-sufficiency. It is only when you begin to realize how little your own capabilities can achieve for you that God can begin to work in your life. If you still cling to the belief that you can accomplish all these things by yourself, then you are not allowing God to take control of your life and make you into the person He wants you to be. Sherry identified her weaknesses one by one and acknowledged them as a part of her life. She then handed them over to God. By recognizing how powerless she was, she had to begin to trust God to be that "higher power" in her life and allow Him to build her self-confidence in the way that only He could.

Lord, help me realize that only by admitting my weaknesses can I be strong in You.

> *But we have this treasure in earthen vessels, that*
> *the excellence of the power may be of God and*
> *not of us.*
> —2 COR. 4:7

One thing that people with low self-esteem are seeking in their lives is power. Having so little control early in life creates a void that can only be filled by grabbing all the power they can get. When Darrell was seven, he was suddenly sent to live with his domineering grandmother who controlled every area of his life. He was told what to wear, what to eat, how to speak—he made no decisions on his own. That led to the determination that whenever he gained control, he would never give it up. But it became a compulsion, and eventually he realized that as wealthy and powerful as he had become, no amount of money, no number of corporations, no collection of artwork was ever going to fill that need. In fact, the more control he got the more he realized he had to have.

Darrell finally learned to recognize that to have control in his life, he had to give that control to Someone who could handle it better than he could. By allowing God to control his life, he did not have to feel the burden of proving himself anymore. So, one by one, he named every one of his possessions to God and asked Him to take responsibility for them. And for the first time in his life, Darrell felt in control.

Lord, help me tap the resources of Your power and let them begin to work in my life.

Are not two sparrows sold for a copper coin? And not one of them falls to the ground apart from your Father's will. . . . Do not fear therefore; you are of more value than many sparrows.
—MATT. 10:29, 31

Marcia was having a difficult time accepting the fact that God cared enough to help her through emotional pain. All Marcia could feel when she thought about her father was resentment and hurt. She was unable to accept care from anyone, much less God. She had longed for her father's attention and had tried everything— excellent grades, awards, good behavior—to get him to pay attention to her, but he never would. So how could she trust God to care about her?

Then Marcia came across this verse in her recovery. She began to envision God's hand reaching down and lifting up a tiny bird that had fallen from its perch and placing it safely back up in the tree. She began to understand that if God cared that much for a tiny bird, He could care for her as well. In fact, each time she came across a painful memory or negative message that caused her to fall from her recovery, she imagined herself to be the tiny bird that God was holding in His hand, lifting her back to the place of health and safety.

Help me see, Father, that if You care that much about the sparrow, how much more You will care for me.

For you were bought at a price; therefore glorify
God in your body and in your spirit, which are
God's.
—1 COR. 6:20

How do you determine the value of a particular object? One way to determine something's value is to see what someone will pay for it. It is certainly true that one man's junk is another man's treasure! At a flea market, something I might find particularly valuable, another person might not care for at all. The more valuable an item is to someone, the more he or she is willing to pay.

"I'm just junk," said Chris. "You look at the designer suit and you may think you see someone who's very important—very significant. But it's all a sham, a cover. I've been trying to 'impress' my way to the top for years. But it doesn't change how I feel on the inside. My mom always said I would never amount to much, and I guess she's right."

So often in a dysfunctional family, a person begins to feel that according to other family members, he or she has no worth. The way to determine your worth is by what your Creator was willing to pay for you. When Chris considered the great price paid by God's Son on the cross, he began to understand that he must be worth quite a bit to Him. Even though his family considered him "junk," God considered him a very special treasure to be willing to pay that much.

Father, help me see by the price You paid how much I am worth to You.

I can do all things through Christ who strengthens me.
                                        —PHIL. 4:13

In looking at your past, how many times were you told, "You can't do that"? Each time Gina heard that, it took another chunk out of her self-esteem until soon she really believed that she couldn't do anything, and so she stopped trying. This created a vicious cycle. The only thing she felt successful at was her ability to kill the pain by eating. Then she felt guilty about the amount of time she spent eating, and that created negative self-esteem. Her guilt became such a burden that it began to zap all of her strength and resources until she truly felt she was incapable of doing anything that would be healthy.

When Gina came into counseling, the first thing she was asked to do was make a list of her positive qualities. Once she made this list, she was able to thank God for each of those qualities. Then she was asked to list one thing each night that she accomplished that day, no matter how insignificant it seemed. Then she was to thank God for giving her the power to do it. As she affirmed herself by recognizing her good qualities and acknowledging what God could do with those qualities, she was able to learn that she *could* become healthy.

Father, help me recognize that in Your strength I am capable of anything.

That He would grant you, according to the riches of
His glory, to be strengthened with might through
His Spirit in the inner man.   —EPH. 3:16

It has been said that a person's checkbook is the barometer of what he or she feels to be important in life. If that is the case, then Wendy's life was dedicated to her appearance. She spent hundreds of dollars each month buying clothes, going to the health club, getting facials, having her hair and nails done—all to make sure she looked great, believing that if she looked great she would feel great. But she didn't. The more she tried to build herself up through her appearance, the more the "real" Wendy inside reminded her of how bad she felt about herself. She was spending more to keep from feeling less, but it only pointed out how truly empty she felt.

For Wendy, the problem was an issue of refocusing her goals. Rather than work on her outward appearance, every time she felt the need to go out and make herself look better, she began to stop and ask, "What need in my life am I trying to obtain by doing this?" Once she identified that need, she would remind herself of a way God could develop that quality in her, such as reading His Word or sharing with a friend. By focusing on the inner person, the outer person became healthy as well.

Help me realize, Father, that You truly are stronger than all the negative doubts in my mind.

*Now to Him who is able to do exceedingly
abundantly above all that we ask or think,
according to the power that works in us.*
—EPH. 3:20

One of my favorite movies is *Willie Wonka and the Chocolate Factory*. One interesting scene is when young Charlie is told by Willie Wonka that he has won the contest. When Charlie replies, "You mean I get the chocolate?" Willie Wonka laughs. The chocolate is only the tip of the iceberg, for what Charlie wins by his honesty is the privilege of becoming the owner of the chocolate factory. Not only does he win all the chocolate he will ever want, but he gains the ability to provide for himself and his impoverished family far above his wildest dreams.

That is exactly what God has in store for you. You initially may come to Him with low self-esteem and simply ask for strength for another day. I think there is such love in His eyes when He responds, "Is that *all* you want? Look at what else I have to offer you." For in dealing with your low self-esteem, not only will He give you that strength but also the courage to face your past, unlimited access to Him through prayer, unconditional acceptance of your weaknesses, and the privilege of having a Friend who understands your emotions. Take the time today to let your imagination go and begin thinking of all the things He can provide for you!

Help me, Father, recognize the tremendous resource I have at my disposal through Your love.

> *But God has chosen the foolish things of the world
> to put to shame the wise, and God has chosen the
> weak things of the world to put to shame the things
> which are mighty.*
> —1 COR. 1:27

An interesting thing to consider is that God some-times has a usefulness for your low self-esteem. You may think that you have nothing of value to offer Him, but He can use your weakness for His own glory. How does He use it?

Rachel had spent most of her adult life trying to hide the fact that she was afraid of speaking in public be-cause she stuttered when she was young. That fear drove her to avoid public speaking at all costs, even though she was in danger of losing her position at work, since her job involved making presentations to the board. When she finally had the courage to admit she was afraid to speak and turn it over to God, she found that the pressure was finally off. She was freed to begin feeling confident enough to speak in public and actually became a spokesperson for children with speech problems.

The next time you feel reluctant to come to the Lord with issues of low self-esteem, remember that He has a way of turning your weaknesses into strengths.

Lord, help me see that You have a way of using my weaknesses.

5. EMOTIONAL PAIN

LOOK UP – *July 10*

Terrors frighten him on every side,
And drive him to his feet.
—JOB 18:11

Have you ever been to one of those house of mirrors at a carnival? As you walk in, it seems innocent enough, but soon you are surrounded by different images of yourself. There are reflections of reflections, and false entrances and exits all around. And if you lose your bearings, you soon can become terrified that you are trapped. Before I went in, someone who had had the experience before told me the secret—"Look up." If you look up, you can see which walls are attached to the ceiling and follow your way all the way through to the end without further problems. Believe it or not, it works.

Your emotional pain is like that house of mirrors. Once you begin to really deal with the pain, it seems like it becomes magnified over and over in your life, and just when you think you have turned a corner, there is another set of mirrors reflecting that pain back to you. Instead, try looking up. When you look up and focus on God, you begin to realize that He can give you the perfect directions for getting out of that pain. And when you are looking to Him, you are not as afraid by what is around you anymore.

Lord, when I am caught in the terror of my own pain, help me remember to look up.

For God has not given us a spirit of fear, but of
power and of love and of a sound mind.
—2 TIM. 1:7

After feeling helpless for so long, Jacob had some serious doubts about how effective God could actually be in his life. In looking at this verse, Jacob discovered some of the tools that God had promised to help with his emotional pain.

First, He has given Jacob the spirit of power. When his fear seemed overwhelming, he needed to remember that God is the source of power in his life. That does not mean that he would not experience some pain as he worked through recovery, but he needed to believe that God was stronger than that pain.

The second thing He had given Jacob was the spirit of unconditional love. So often the pain that Jacob felt was created by the belief that he could never be loved or that love had to be earned. There was nothing that Jacob could do to lose it.

The third thing that He promised was a sound mind. Jacob felt like the pain was chipping away at his sanity, bit by bit, but God promised a sound mind. Jacob could begin to trust Him to help him think clearly in dealing with his emotional pain.

Help me, Lord, begin to use the tools You have already given me to deal with my pain.

He who is slow to wrath has great understanding,
But he who is impulsive exalts folly.

—PROV. 14:29

Emotional pain sometimes can manifest itself in explosive anger. As the pain of rejection and abuse builds over the years, it becomes more and more difficult to hold down.

Brett had spent his life trying to hold down his rage. A victim of child abuse, he was determined to keep that part of his life buried. He tried to be in control of his life, but that rage would come to the surface when things went wrong. His controls weren't working anymore, and that pain from his past was making itself known.

While it is certainly important to express your pain and anger, you must also learn to do that in a healthy way. By striking out at someone else, you are simply perpetuating the cycle of pain. Brett had to realize that, in order to control his anger, he had to confront it directly. He imagined his father was sitting across from him in a chair and expressed all the rage and anger that had built up over the years. Once he finally expressed all that pain and anger, he could respond in healthy ways to the frustrations of his life.

Help me, Father, not take out my pain on others in angry ways.

*"Be angry and do not sin": do not let the sun go
down on your wrath.*
                                    —EPH. 4:26

In dealing with the anger that emotional pain almost
inevitably produces, you must learn how to handle it in
the proper way. As you begin to explore your emotional pain and begin to grieve your past, the recognition of how the abuse affected your perception of
yourself and your view of those around you is bound to
produce a response in which anger is a part.

Brad had learned how to identify his anger but did
not know how to begin dealing with it. To turn it back
on himself only created more low self-esteem. To turn
it out on others only passed it along to the next generation or to another family situation. Even to place blame
on those people in his past who perhaps helped create
some of the emotional pain didn't get rid of it. He
needed to take it to the source of all forgiveness—God
Himself. One way that helped Brad do that was to set
aside his "anger time" each day. He would jot down
each angry episode; then during his anger time, he
could allow himself to feel the emotion, then forgive
the other person and release the anger to God, remembering that God had also forgiven him. By doing that
each day, the sun never went down on Brad's anger.

*Help me, O Lord, to come to You with my anger, so that I may learn
how to deal with it in the best way possible.*

For it is better, if it is the will of God, to suffer for doing good than for doing evil.

—1 PETER 3:17

There is often a great deal of suffering experienced in the childhood of the driven individual. In fact, escaping that pain is usually what leads to addictive behaviors. Doug turned to body-building in an effort to build up his self-esteem and stop the pain of being called a "wimp" in childhood. The stronger he became, the more he felt he could improve, and the tougher he became on himself. This "toughness" spilled over into his personal life, and soon he found himself right back where he had started—angry and alone. His attempts to run from the pain only created more pain.

Each time Doug decided to try and deal with his past, it began to hurt, and he would return to his weight-lifting to stop the pain. What he had to learn was that healing involves some suffering. Each time he began to feel that pain from the past, he would recall the "Serenity Prayer" and focus on the phrase, "Courage to change the things I can." By imagining each incident as an exercise that would build his emotional strength just like the weights built his body, he was able to "lift" each one and emerge an emotionally stronger person.

Help me recognize, Lord, that it is better to suffer in getting healthy than to suffer in staying driven.

> *Happy is he who has the God of Jacob for his help,*
> *Whose hope is in the LORD his God.* —PS. 146:5

The more I see how much pain I have inside me, the more I'm starting to believe I will never be happy again." I had been seeing Gayle for several months. Because of an abusive past and a loveless marriage, she had developed compulsive behaviors in almost every area of her life to escape her pain. While she was having some limited success in beginning to control the addictions, she realized how much pain she really had in her life. "That is starting to frustrate me," she said. "Now that I'm trying to do the right thing, I hurt more than I did before. Is this what recovery is all about?"

As a person begins to remove the upper levels of denial, the levels of buried pain make themselves known. That can be a source of discouragement but, however overwhelming the current situation may be, you must never forget the fact that God has promised to be with you. Each time Gayle experienced fresh pain in her life, she began to share that pain—both with God in prayer and with a trusted friend. By sharing that pain, she could experience God's healing, the source of real happiness.

Father, help me see that when my circumstances bring me no happiness, my trust in You can make me happy.

My mouth shall speak wisdom,
And the meditation of my heart shall
bring understanding. —PS. 49:3

One of the best ways to understand emotional pain is to begin practicing meditation. So often, the initial response to the pain is to avoid thinking about it at all costs. "If I can just put it out of my mind," Joel said, "I can be done with it." Denial became his way of life, and soon he began to close off more and more parts of his life as he tried to escape the effects of the pain. But shutting it off had a boomerang effect on Joel because the more he tried to avoid thinking about it, the more it popped up unexpectedly in his emotions. He began to be more condemning of others in an effort to protect himself.

Throughout God's Word, meditation is specifically mentioned as a way to gain understanding. Joel began to meditate on his relationship with his mother and recalled unpleasant encounters with her. He saw that whenever he got in an argument with her, she would always end up saying, "I'm done talking" and walk away before Joel could express his point. He also thought about what he would tell her now if she were still alive, and that allowed him to release his anger so it wouldn't boomerang back.

———————

Lord, through my meditation bring me more understanding of You and Your work in my life.

> *I will also meditate on all Your work,*
> *And talk of Your deeds.*
>
> —PS. 77:12

One technique that I often use in helping my patients deal with emotional pain, is to have them list the ways God has shown His power in history and specifically identify how those can apply to their lives today. The same God who knocked down the walls of Jericho can help you knock down the walls of denial and hurt you built to protect yourself from abuse. The same God who protected David from all of his enemies can protect you from the negative messages concerning your self-worth. The same God that was with Jonah when the fish swallowed him can be with you in the darkest depths of loneliness caused by shame. The same God who freed the Israelites from slavery can free you from an alcoholic father or a neglectful mother. The same God who guided the children of Israel through the wilderness for forty years can guide you through the process of doing your inventory of past relationships. And probably most significant, the same God who was victorious over the power of death can help you be victorious over any part of your life that would threaten to consume you. It is so important to consider the works of God from old and choose to apply them when they would be most helpful in your life today.

Help me remember, Lord, just how powerful You can be in my life today.

Meditate on these things; give yourself entirely to them, that your progress may be evident to all.
—1 TIM. 4:15

So often in counseling, people complain that they feel that they are getting nowhere. "If I could just see some results," Candy said, "then maybe that would help me feel a little more hope." Candy had done a remarkable job of identifying experiences from the past, coming to terms with them, and turning them over to God to let Him take care of her from now on. But because of the extent of worthlessness she felt in her life, she was still having difficulty identifying as progress what she had accomplished. I pointed out to Candy that change *was* taking place in her life whether she felt it or not.

Sometimes you need to stop and remind yourself of those changes in a direct way. Candy began to talk about her behaviors over the past week and identify specifically what she was doing this week that she was not doing a month ago. Perhaps it took a little more to upset her at her office, or maybe she didn't yell at her kids quite so quickly. She also began to recognize that people were responding differently to her and she was better able to handle herself in tense situations. Seeing the specific progress she was making gave Candy the encouragement to have a more positive outlook.

Help me remember, Father, that a change on the outside often reflects a change on the inside.

> *Fearfulness and trembling have come upon me,*
> *And horror has overwhelmed me.* —PS. 55:5

Delores was trembling again. "I've had another set-back" she told me. "My friend Sharon and I were out shopping, and I was trying on a dress I liked. I came out to show Sharon and she looked at me and said, 'It seems a little snug, don't you think?' Well, all those self-doubts from my past about my size flooded back. It hurt so bad to feel that pain all over again." She broke down in fresh sobs.

What happened is not unusual in the recovery process. Setbacks are part of the process, and the fresh pain needs to be dealt with just as courageously and honestly as the earlier hurts. Delores once again needed to talk to that child within her and reassure her that the adult part was with her. She didn't need to worry about anyone putting her down or making fun of her anymore because she had set boundaries and would always protect that child. Then she needed to ask for God's help in keeping those boundaries. As she was able to do this with confidence, she was able to release more and more of the pain.

Help me remember, Father, that You do understand all the aspects of the emotional pain that I am going through.

The spirit of a man will sustain him in sickness,
But who can bear a broken spirit?
—PROV. 18:14

Lee wanted to tell someone how badly he hurt, but he never trusted anyone. After he finally mustered up the courage to let his mother know that his brother was always beating up on him, not only did his mother not believe him, but she asked his brother if this was true. This only created more abuse for Lee, so he learned that to share his hurts with someone was simply to ask for more trouble. Yet, the more he isolated himself and the more he worked, the more lonely he felt until he could bear it no more.

During those times of loneliness, you need to find the support of a trusted friend. By sharing your pain with someone else, it helps lift the burden and gives positive feedback. For Lee, it was a courageous step, but once he began trusting one friend enough to share his pain, he found not only did it lighten his load, but he was able to experience acceptance from another person for the first time.

Lord, in those times when I feel I cannot bear emotions alone, help me find someone to share with.

We are hard pressed on every side, yet not crushed;
we are perplexed, but not in despair; persecuted,
but not forsaken; struck down, but not destroyed.
—2 COR. 4:8–9

In looking back at his emotional pain, Norman sometimes felt that everyone and everything was out to get
him. No matter which direction he turned, there was
another new issue to be faced, another abuse threatening his personal safety, another negative message reinforcing his already low self-esteem. It seemed that he
had tried to depend on people all his life, but they
always ended up failing him. This only made him feel
more isolated and lonely. Norman thought he couldn't
trust anyone and that sooner or later he would have
nothing left in his life.

Norman needed to find a source to trust in that
would be greater than his pain. Through the process of
recovery, he discovered that God was that source.
Rather than burying the pain when he felt someone
had hurt him, he simply acknowledged it to God, and
left it there. Norman's circumstances did not change,
but by applying God's power in his life, his attitude did.
And that made all the difference.

Help me see, Lord, that the pain may be great but You are greater.

The Lord also will be a refuge for the oppressed,
A refuge in times of trouble.
—PS. 9:9

If you have ever watched the devastation that a hurricane can bring, you understand what a terrible time it must be for those people who are involved. Although many of them try to weather out the storm in their own homes, one of the things the local authorities always do is encourage people to "seek refuge." They suggest that the people go to a safe place that has been designated by the local authorities to be protection from the ravages of the storm—a place of safety and escape from the fury of the storm even though it is pounding around them. Once the storm is over, they can leave the refuge and begin to build their lives once again.

The next time you have to deal with some experience that creates a "hurricane" of emotional pain, picture in your mind God as a refuge—a storm shelter. As those pounding waves of negative messages and winds of self-doubt crash around you, remind yourself that you are in the safety and protection of His care. Then as that storm subsides and you see you have survived, it can give you the confidence to go on, knowing He is always there to provide that shelter for you.

Help me use the refuge that You provide in Yourself, Lord.

> *I sought the LORD, and He heard me,*
> *And delivered me from all my fears.*
> —PS. 34:4

In dealing with emotional pain, it is important to find someone who will simply listen to your story. Being able to express your pain and talk about it freely after carrying it around for so long is part of the healing process. Most people who deal with the emotional pain in their past have never experienced adequate listening. No one at home had ever paid much attention to Pat. Because of that feeling of never being heard she was influenced to become a stage actress. However, after the lights went down and the crowds went home, there was still no one to listen to her, to hear the things she really wanted to say.

It was important for Pat to know that there is Someone who listens regardless of the time and circumstance, Someone who cares for her and understands emotional pain. Pat had always believed in God, but she never really took the time to develop a personal relationship with Him. What Pat did initially was to sit down one evening and pour her heart out to God, asking Him to help her put her life together again. Then she daily set aside time to spend with Him, so that the hurt and pain would never have the chance to build up again.

————————

Thank You, Father, for being available to hear me when I cry out to You.

Many are the afflictions of the righteous,
But the LORD delivers him out of them all.
—PS. 34:19

How many times have you been hurt in your life? To help people understand the scope and intensity of their emotional pain, I suggest to them to consider whether they have been hurt in some way at least one time a day. Most of them would agree with this. I then point out to them (if they are somewhere in their early thirties) that this would mean that they had been hurt somewhere between ten and twelve thousand times in their lives. And this is only considering one time a day—imagine the amount of hurt in a very abusive or dysfunctional family! Though the actual numbers really don't mean anything, they begin to see how much hurt they are carrying.

One way to avoid the risk of all that emotional pain building up over time is to do a daily inventory of what's right and what's wrong in your life. For example, if the way your boss spoke to you has hurt you and you feel the need to revert to your old addictive "rageaholism," you can identify it immediately and turn it over to God right away. This way you prevent the problem from building up in your life, and keep it in good working order.

No matter how much pain I have, Father, help me remember that You can heal it all.

This is my comfort in my affliction,
For Your word has given me life.
—PS. 119:50

Sticks and stones may break my bones, but words will never hurt me." But words can hurt. Tracy knew how much words hurt because her mother had used them in hurtful ways. Every time she yelled an obscenity at Tracy or called her an "ingrate" or a "tramp," those words cut deep to the point where she would gladly have taken the sticks and stones over the pain of the words. Now, every time someone criticizes her, even if it was meant to be helpful, all Tracy feels is the pain.

Words can also be healing, helpful things. As abusive as the words of those people in your past have been, God's words of love, care, and power can begin healing those wounds from your past. By spending time in His Word every day and allowing Him to speak His message of peace and hope to her heart, Tracy began to feel its life-giving power. She found that whatever pain she experienced in her past life, whatever circumstances she had endured, God's Word had something to say about it. As she discovered those words, she could begin to experience life at its fullest.

Father, help me experience the life-giving power of Your Word today.

He heals the brokenhearted
And binds up their wounds.
—PS. 147:3

Usually in a movie or television show battle scene, there are scores of men lying around, some mangled beyond repair. Among all the noise and smoke, you can also see the medics going around, attempting to bind up the wounds of the soldiers. They are really not concerned with who the individual is or how he got the wound; their interest at that point is saving that person's life by stopping the bleeding.

Jake felt like he was "bleeding to death" emotionally. It was strange, because everyone that knew Jake liked him. No matter what the need, he always would be there to give love and support. Because of the lack of love he received as a child, Jake had little left to give. His own emotional "love tank" was running on empty, but Jake felt he had to support his friends. Finally, he could stand the pain no longer and in desperation poured out his story to God. When he finally had the courage to share his pain, he found the Lord was able to stop his emotional "bleeding" so his wounds could heal.

Lord, begin binding up my emotional wounds with Your love.

Then He said to them, "My soul is exceedingly sorrowful, even to death. Stay here and watch with Me."

—MATT. 26:38

Sometimes people get the idea that because Jesus was God and that He lived the perfect life here on earth, that He never experienced the emotions or feelings that they do. But that is simply not true. In this scene in the garden as He approaches His death, He expresses the hurt and anguish that His soul is going through. You see Him at His most vulnerable, where simple words and pat answers won't ease the pain. He wants human companionship but even His closest friends let Him down in the hour that He needed them the most. You understand what it is like to be let down by those you are counting on, especially in the times when you are hurting badly and you need them to be there.

The question is, what did Jesus do at that point? First, He was honest enough to admit that He hurt, that He was really suffering—He cried out, "Take this away from Me." Second, He turned to His Father, the only One who could help Him. Third, He reaffirmed God's will in His life, acknowledging that He did know best. Last, and most important, He left it there for God to take care of. That is the best example you can find to show you how to deal with your own emotional pain.

―――――――――

Help me always remember, Lord, that You do understand the emotional experiences I go through.

*My loved ones and my friends stand
    aloof from my plague,
And my kinsmen stand afar off.*
        —PS. 38:11

One of the most profound feelings that a person dealing with emotional pain can experience is the feeling
of being utterly and totally alone. Blake's feeling of
aloneness started in his childhood when he felt rejected by parents who were too busy with their own
problems to bother with him. Blake went through life
with the negative message that he wasn't worth having
attention paid to him. He struggled with the conflict of
wanting someone to get close enough to care, while at
the same time alienating anyone who got that close.
This created resentment toward others and only continued to feed his emotional pain.

Do you feel alone today? Has your emotional pain
taken you to the place where you feel alienated from
everyone around you? When others do offer some concern, do you lash out at them in an attempt to prevent
them from getting close to you? Blake eventually
learned that the only way he could ever open himself
up to others was to be a friend to himself. When he
finally confronted the child within him and began caring for that part of him, those protective walls he had
built began to come down. When the walls finally
came down, then he could afford to let others in.

Help me, Father, remember that I never have to be alone.

The heart knows its own bitterness,
And a stranger does not share its joy.
—PROV. 14:10

There is nothing so personal as emotional pain. Although you may be able to find people who can understand the issue that you are dealing with, it is not possible for anyone to know the pain that you personally are going through. I recall an incident several years ago involving the death of my brother's first wife. While all of us were trying to deal with the trauma in our inept way, the loss was especially hard for my father. He had lost his first wife at the same age that my brother had, and so he could understand the pain my brother was going through. "This hurts me so badly," he said, "because I know he has to deal with his pain by himself. I would do anything to take that pain for him. But I can't. No one can experience someone else's pain, and no one but the Lord can see him through it."

Although it hurt desperately at times, my brother never denied the reality of what he was feeling. I also saw how he was able to turn to God, hand the hurt over to Him, and leave it there in those times when he felt he could not bear it.

Help me see, O Lord, that only You can understand the very personal pain I go through.

*Let all bitterness, wrath, anger, clamor, and evil
speaking be put away from you, with all malice.*
—EPH. 4:31

Emotional pain can manifest itself in many different
ways. Nancy had always gotten along with other people in her life. Sometimes she was *too* nice, sacrificing
her own feelings at the expense of making everyone
else happy. But as she went through the initial stages of
her recovery, many of the emotional experiences of
the past began to surface, and she felt those emotions
in a strong and powerful way. And often, without any
warning, they would come out toward others, to the
extent that it was starting to alienate some of her
friends.

While emotional pain can certainly stir up strong
feelings, there are healthy and unhealthy ways of dealing with it. This verse encourages you actively to
choose to handle your negative emotions in the correct
way. One way Nancy learned to handle these feelings
was to take the time each evening to look back over
her day and identify what words or statements had
caused her negative feelings. Through this exercise
she could remind herself of the invalidity of these messages and of her worth, then once again turn them
back over to the Lord. By doing this each day, she
never gave the feelings the opportunity to build up and
become destructive.

*Help me, Lord, learn the proper way of dealing with my emotional
pain.*

For my life is spent with grief,
And my years with sighing;
My strength fails because of my iniquity,
And my bones waste away.

—PS. 31:10

The grief that is associated with emotional pain can be a difficult experience. Not only does it take its toll in terms of the energy spent dealing with it, but it also can be a very time-consuming process. Certainly, going into the grieving process is not something someone would choose. There are no hard and fast rules as to exactly what a person should feel or how long it should take or when she is supposed to be "well."

That was why the grieving process was particularly difficult for Amanda. Her way of avoiding emotional pain was to meticulously plot out her life so that she was in absolute control and there were no surprises. But when her meticulous plan began to fall apart through a divorce and job termination, the emotional pain began to surface. In her recovery, Amanda found that she could not control all the circumstances of her life, so she had to let the grieving process take its own course as well. The best she could do was take each hurt as it came, face it, grieve it, then give it up to God. For while grief is not limited by time or circumstance, neither is God.

Help me remember, Lord, that wherever my grief takes me, You are there with me.

Yea, though I walk through the valley of
the shadow of death,
I will fear no evil;
For You are with me;
Your rod and Your staff, they comfort me.
—PS. 23:4

The Twenty-third Psalm is often used to help people who are going through a difficult time. Wesley could identify with it, for he felt he was in a valley that seemed impassable. After spending years of his life trying to avoid facing his feelings of inadequacy by building up his company to a Fortune 500 corporation, he found that being on top only made him more insecure and alone.

In this psalm, David is talking about the horrible experience of the "valley of the shadow of death" that he is going through. He doesn't say "*if* I make it," or "*suppose* I get to the other side." He knew he had to go *through* it, and he was not looking forward to it, but he also had every expectation of coming out on the other side alive and well. He knew God would be right there before him, comforting him and directing him all the way. Wesley realized that he could begin turning to God instead of his drive to achieve. By doing that he could face the insecurity directly instead of avoiding it. He began to see that the deep dark valley did have another side.

Help me remember, Father, that there will be the "other side" to emotional pain.

> *Call upon Me in the day of trouble;*
> *I will deliver you, and you shall glorify Me.*
> —PS. 50:15

When emotional pain starts welling up within you, where do you turn? Do you turn to your work, hoping that by keeping yourself busy you won't have time to think about that pain? Do you turn to your money, thinking that by giving yourself the pleasure and indulging your cravings, it will quiet the voice inside you? Do you turn to exercise, pushing and punishing your body with the driving force to "become perfect" enough to answer the doubts in your mind? Or perhaps you turn to the people around you, trying desperately to meet their every need so that your own unmet needs won't seem quite as important?

There is one resource to which you have been given complete access that can truly help you deal with the pain. As stated in the Twelve Step Program, you have the choice of turning to that "higher Power" that promises to help. He won't allow you to avoid the pain, as your addictions do. Rather, as you go to Him in prayer and identify the abuse or neglect or unmet needs that you have, you can become free not only from the pain but from those addictions as well. Can those other things give that kind of guarantee? If not, why not go to the Source that promises it—and delivers.

_____

Lord, remind me to call on You in my time of trouble.

*Therefore, my beloved brethren, let every man be
swift to hear, slow to speak, slow to wrath.*
—JAMES 1:19

How good a listener are you? In my professional life I
have learned to be a good listener, but I confess that in
my personal life sometimes I have more to say about
things than I need to. This is especially true when
someone has hurt me. Rather than attempting to understand the situation and to perhaps see an expla-
nation for it, I lash out with my own anger and
resentment in an attempt to "fix" the pain I am feeling
inside. Even when God may be trying to speak to me, I
want to tell Him what is going on and how I have been
hurt without waiting to listen for what He might be
trying to teach me.

It is important to understand that God may want to
teach you something through your pain. When you are
hurting inside, the last thing you want to do is sit and
listen to someone—even God. Yet, as you allow Him to
minister to you and to speak to you through His Word
and prayer, you can begin to see His purpose for your
life and gain a much better understanding and appreciation of who God is and who you are as well. As you
deal with your pain today, don't just tell God how you
feel. Take the time to listen to what He may be saying
back to you.

Lord, make me as willing to listen to You as I am to talk to You.

6. ADDICTION

August 4 – MEETING OUR NEEDS

And my God shall supply all your need according to His riches in glory by Christ Jesus.
—PHIL. 4:19

Human beings have certain needs in life. These needs can range from the most basic, like the need for food and shelter, to the most complex of emotional and spiritual needs. By most people's standard of living, Luke had everything he possibly could want. Everything, that is, except love and attention from his parents. Sure, they always bought him things, but that was their attempt to buy him off so they could go on ignoring his emotional needs. So to meet his needs, Luke turned to the thing that his parents had best trained him in—materialism. He soon realized even he couldn't buy the love he needed.

Luke needed to realize that there is Someone capable of meeting all the needs of his life. It is only through a relationship with God that those needs can be met. Initially, Luke had a hard time accepting that because he had learned that if you couldn't calculate the material value of an object it wasn't valid. But slowly, surely, as Luke opened up his closed-off emotions to God a little at a time, he saw how God could meet those needs with riches beyond even Luke's imagination.

Lord, help me see that You are the true answer I am seeking to meet my needs.

Commit your way to the LORD,
Trust also in Him,
And He shall bring it to pass.
—PS. 37:5

One way to assess what is important to someone is to look at what they are committed to. The thing a person will sacrifice everything else for is the thing he is using to meet his needs in his life. James is a workaholic. He arrives early in the morning, takes no break for lunch, and usually doesn't arrive home until late in the evening. When he does have time off, his discussion usually centers on some aspect of the job. He is always trying to make a deal; always trying to find out some new bit of information that will advance his career. Birthdays, anniversaries, holidays, and special events all take a backseat to that work situation. Even his health is suffering because of the time and energy spent on the job. He is committed to nothing else in his life but work—that one thing that seems to meet the need of blocking out his emotional pain.

The truth is that James is looking at the wrong source to bring happiness to his life. God desires control of your life because He knows what's best for you and has designed a program for your life that will fulfill your needs. It is simply a choice of whether to commit your life to things or to the Creator of all things.

Help me trust You and commit my life to You today, O Lord.

Trust in the LORD with all your heart,
And lean not on your own understanding.
—PROV. 3:5

In dealing with the addictive agents in your life, one of the things you have to come to terms with is how limited your understanding of your problems can be. So often a person who comes from a dysfunctional family sees particular events and situations from a limited perspective. Because her parents never gave any words of encouragement, Connie grew up with a distorted view of herself and her relationships. She had no one to let her know that her beliefs might be inaccurate, so she took them into adulthood and continued to make decisions based on the faulty premise of low self-esteem and shame. The longer she believed these ideas, the more negative her self-concept became.

It is important to trust your life to God because you have a less than perfect way of looking at things. By going to a source outside of herself, a source who sees things truthfully, Connie could begin to see how her perfectionism was really a futile attempt to try to make her own life right. She realized that reliance on God rather than on her own faulty wisdom was the only way to finally be free from her compulsive behaviors.

Help me see, Father, that through You I can gain the understanding I need in my life.

You shall have no other gods before Me.
—EX. 20:3

Jeremy certainly did not think he was practicing idolatry. After all, he considered himself to be civilized, and idolatry was usually associated with pagans. Even the mention of the word conjured up images of scantily clad natives with masks and headdresses dancing around a fire, falling prostrate before some type of stone or wood image. That was not Jeremy, the successful stockbroker.

There is another form of idolatry, however, that is equally unacceptable. Jeremy practiced the idolatry of addiction, trying to find his worth and the answer to his emotional needs by giving himself over to his facts, figures, and predictions with the belief it would somehow remove the pain and give him control over his life. By meaningless repetition of these behaviors, just like the incantations of those natives mentioned above, he believed he could somehow appease his conscience and gain the peace for which he so desperately longed. This was replacing what God desired to do in his life. When other things or people take the place of the role that God desires, that, indeed, is idolatry. Jeremy needed to begin the task of clearing out the idols and making room for God in his life.

Lord, show me the idols I need to clean from my life today.

> *Will a man make gods for himself,*
> *Which are not gods?*
>
> —JER. 16:20

It is interesting to recognize how the most innocent behavior has the potential of becoming an addictive agent. Lena came into counseling two years after joining the health club. She began the activity with good intentions, but as time moved on, exercising developed a life of its own. She did not intend for it to control her, but as she gained more satisfaction and control from the results, she began to count on it. Eventually, exercise was no longer something she wanted to do; it became something she couldn't live without.

Anything can become a god in your life when it is given prominence. Even something that would be healthy under normal circumstances can become overwhelming. It was important for Lena to see just how much control this exercising had taken over her. She was put on a program of limiting her time at the gym to two hours a week and spending the other time she would have been at the gym developing her relationship with the Lord. The stronger the relationship with God is, the less likely other things will take His position in your life.

Lord, help me allow You to meet those needs in my life.

Knowing this, that our old man was crucified with
Him, that the body of sin might be done away with,
that we should no longer be slaves of sin.
—ROM. 6:6

The idea of slavery has always had a negative connotation. It means that a person is being controlled and has no choice in any matter. Usually the "master" has very little consideration for the slave, so the more service the slave performs and the more the master provides his needs, the more indebted the slave actually becomes.

Trent was a slave to his addiction for writing. It had taken charge of his life to the point where he had very little ability to control it. The more his writing seemed to be meeting his need for immortality, as he lived on in his readers' minds, the more inclined he was to go back to it again and again. He felt like a slave.

He needed to understand the freedom that Christ gives from those addictive behaviors. Because of His concern for your worth and His unconditional love for you, He paid the price for you to be free from the slavery of those addictions. What Trent needed was to accept that freedom and become more acquainted with the Provider of that freedom on a personal level.

Lord, help me allow You to free me from the slavery of my addictions.

Take heed to yourselves, lest your heart be deceived, and you turn aside and serve other gods and worship them. —DEUT. 11:16

Humans have an uncanny ability to deceive themselves. This is especially true when it comes to compulsive behaviors. Charlotte seemed to be able to convince herself that because what she was doing was not necessarily a negative thing, it was not bad for her to do it. She began to believe that if a little of her volunteer work was OK, more was even better. Soon she became so involved, she was gaining her worth from it. By the time she realized how much it had taken over her life and thought about stopping, it was out of control. The appetite had been created, and she continually had to feed it or else be consumed by it.

How could she stop this negative cycle? The answer was in allowing her heart to experience the truth of God's Word, and not allow her deceptions to control her any longer. She had to honestly face her addictions in the light of God's love and realize that they were only poor substitutes for the way God could meet her needs. She also recognized how susceptible she was to that deception in her heart and began daily to turn her volunteer work over to Him so that His truth could lead her into the health she desired.

Help me, Father, no longer be deceived by my own heart.

*Not with eyeservice, as men-pleasers, but as
servants of Christ, doing the will of God from
the heart.* —EPH. 6:6

Consider how many of your addictive behaviors involve pleasing someone else. In your vocation, do you work harder to please your boss? Are you obsessed with beauty and fitness in order to please your spouse? Have you become addicted to material things to keep up with the people in your neighborhood so that they will give you their approval and acceptance? Are you unable or unwilling to say no in your church to gain the praises of the pastor or other leaders? Do you use any or all of these addictions to please yourself, to make you feel that you have the worth that you desire?

No matter what kind of behavior you use to try to please other people, sooner or later there will come a time when you will not succeed. Instead, consider your worth in God's eyes. When He asks you to commit your life to Him, He requires nothing of you other than your faith and love. There are no stringent demands, no unrealistic expectations. When you make that choice, then you can see that there is no need to try to please everyone else, because you are already pleasing God.

Help me, Father, find my worth in You and not in the eyes of those around me.

> *I drew them with gentle cords,*
> *With bands of love,*
> *And I was to them as those who take*
> *the yoke from their neck.*
> *I stooped and fed them.*
>
> —HOS. 11:4

In counseling Ken, I told him that sometimes God uses compulsive behaviors to lead a person to Him. Ken's look was incredulous. "You mean to tell me that the fact that I spend too much money is leading me toward God? How can that possibly be, especially when I feel so guilty?" I pointed out to him that by involving himself in that compulsive spending, he was looking for something to meet those deep needs of approval. The more involved in that spending he became, the more desperate he was to have that need met.

God wants to meet every need in his life no matter how desperate it is. When Ken was able to realize that it was God he had been searching for all along, he began to see the futility of his compulsive behaviors and was able to give Him control of those needs.

In what kind of compulsive ways are you searching for God today? How desperate are you to have someone or something meet the needs in your life? Then it is time that you got to know the one Person who can meet those needs. Meet Him today.

In my desperate hours, Lord, help me turn to You to meet my needs.

Every way of a man is right in his own eyes,
But the LORD weighs the hearts.

—PROV. 21:2

Whenever the pain of the past was bearing down on April's life, taking care of her animals seemed to be the right thing to do. It eased that pain, and she was able to justify the cost of all the food and vet bills for the warm feelings they brought. After all, caring for these creatures wasn't a "bad" thing; she just was doing it for the wrong purpose.

But that is exactly the point. Whatever action you involve yourself in, it is the motivation of your heart that makes the difference. If you involve yourself in an activity because you choose to and you enjoy it, then your motive is genuine. But if you feel that you *have* to do something, that you are driven to do it in an attempt to take care of some unmet emotional need or stop some negative message from playing in your mind, you are substituting this behavior for God's grace and power. Any time you prohibit God from working in your life, then you are being disobedient.

The next time you choose some activity to meet some deeper need or stop some pain, ask yourself this question: Could this be taking the place of God in my life?

Lord, help me not substitute my compulsive behavior for Your power in my life.

*Having their understanding darkened, being
alienated from the life of God, because of
the ignorance that is in them, because of
the hardening of their heart.*   —EPH. 4:18

As you live day to day, you must continually evaluate
the direction that your life is taking. Terry's need for
superficial relationships involved a denial of his problems, an unwillingness to face his emotional pain, and
an attempt to try to "fix" his life through maintaining
his independence. The more he tried to run away from
the pain in his life, the more it seemed to control his
behavior.

There is, however, another direction that would allow Terry to face his past and learn how to deal with it
in a healthy and wholesome way. This direction would
allow him to experience unconditional love. This direction would also move him beyond temporary, superficial relationships to deep, meaningful, trusting
relationships with God and with others.

Choose your direction today—the path towards continued addiction and alienation from God or the path
toward emotional health as you rely on God's power in
your life.

_____

*Lord, help me choose the path that would bring healing to my
life today.*

Oh, taste and see that the LORD is good;
Blessed is the man who trusts in Him!
—PS. 34:8

Several years ago, there was a commercial on TV that captured the attention of America. Three little boys sat at the breakfast table, and the two older ones were arguing about not wanting to try the new cereal. Each kept refusing to try it with the assumption that since Mom wanted them to eat it, it must taste awful. Finally they decided to get their little brother, Mikey, to try the cereal. They put the bowl in front of him, expecting him to reject it. However, Mikey began eating the cereal with a vengeance. Soon the other two boys realized that it might not be as bad as they thought and began eating as well.

You may have laughed at that commercial, but is that the way you view a relationship with God? Your assumption may be that because of negative relationships with other authority figures, whatever God has for your life, it will be distasteful to you. God is willing to put Himself on the line, to show you that what He wants for you is the best. One way to build that trust is to take the time to listen to the experiences of those who have already allowed Him to direct their lives. If He has "tasted" that good to so many others maybe it is time you tried Him today.

Lord, I have tasted of You and I know You are good.

Or do you despise the riches of His goodness, forbearance, and longsuffering, not knowing that the goodness of God leads you to repentance?
—ROM. 2:4

One of the things that continually amazes me about God is how long He is willing to wait for us to come to Him. This is often difficult for someone like Toni, who came from a dysfunctional family, to understand. Growing up, she could never do anything fast enough or soon enough to satisfy the demands of her parents. There was no waiting for anything, and if it wasn't done right the first time, it was of no value—there was no use trying again. Growing up in that kind of atmosphere, Toni got the idea that change was impossible, doing something right an unachievable goal, and having someone accept her unconditionally was a fantasy that would never be realized.

God provides a completely different kind of attitude for us. Toni had to learn that God would be longsuffering with her weaknesses and that He wanted to take the time to change her if she would just let Him. Then she would feel freedom from her emotional pain. Through studying God's Word, Toni changed her picture of God from a perfectionistic parent to Someone she could love and trust with her pain.

Father, help me not reject Your willingness to work with me any longer.

The LORD is good,
A stronghold in the day of trouble;
And He knows those who trust in Him.
—NAH. 1:7

Individuals who are battling addictive behaviors often believe that no one else knows what they are going through. Jerry, who was addicted to pornography, felt alone and isolated, and thought he was the only one struggling with that issue. He was unable to share his feelings with family members because he blamed them for the dysfunction. He felt that if his friends knew about his life, they would reject him. That would only create more of a need to be involved in the pornography.

But notice what this verse says. It says that God Himself knows those who trust in Him. Wouldn't it be great if your life was known by Someone who could give you an occasional kind word, by Someone who could help you actually change the very direction and course of your life? Someone who could give you all the worth you ever desired? Someone who could provide the answers you are looking for in all of your addictive behaviors? One way Jerry began to develop that trust in God was to get involved in a recovery group for persons with sexual addictions. As he learned to trust the others in the group with his feelings, that gave him the courage to begin trusting God. And the more he trusted, the more he knew he was no longer alone.

Help me trust today, Father, that You may be able to begin knowing me in a way that only You can.

*But God demonstrates His own love toward us, in
that while we were still sinners, Christ died for us.*
—ROM. 5:8

One of the negative beliefs behind Janell's addiction
to cleanliness was the idea that she had to be perfect in
order for people to accept her. She developed the idea
that if people knew she was flawed or could not live up
to the expectations that she or others set for her, then
she would not be accepted and she would be considered of little value. So she immersed herself in perfectionism, and used her "clean" addiction to push her to
that point where she felt she would be finally acceptable to herself and others.

God will accept you exactly as you are. In fact, in His
perfection, He was so willing to accept imperfections,
He sent His Son to die on the cross in order to forgive
imperfections. It was hard for Janell to believe someone would accept her even if she was perfect, but she
could hardly imagine what kind of love God must have
had for her that He was willing to accept her in her
imperfect state. The least God deserved was her commitment to Him. She found that since He could accept
those weaknesses, she could too. She was imperfect,
but finally that was OK.

Lord, help me realize the incredible love You have for me.

For God so loved the world that He gave His only begotten Son, that whoever believes in Him should not perish but have everlasting life.

—JOHN 3:16

In trying to replace the false gods of his addictions with the true God, Steve was asked to write down the attributes God would have, based on the unmet needs of his past. Steve identified four things that God must provide:

1. The love that I have never felt;
2. The ability to give instead of just take;
3. Release from emotional pain;
4. A promise of better things to come.

This verse says that God loved the world with an unconditional love. It simply was based on the fact that God chose to love. Second, God was willing to give first before anyone gave to Him. And He gave the most valuable thing He had—His Son, Jesus Christ. Third, through this gift, He provided a way for each individual to escape the emotional pain and trauma of his life by turning over control of his life to Him. Fourth, He provided a way in which anyone could live on through eternity.

Steve discovered there is no addictive behavior in the world that could match up to what God has provided for him.

———

Help me recognize, Father, that you can meet every one of my emotional needs through Your Son.

And Jesus said to them, "I am the bread of life. He who comes to Me shall never hunger, and he who believes in Me shall never thirst."

—JOHN 6:35

Have you ever been thirsty? I mean, *really* thirsty? I can only remember a couple of instances in my life when I was that thirsty. Water was all I could think about. In fact, the more I tried to divert my attention to other things, the more my thoughts always came back to the fact that there was only one thing that could quench that thirst. I was not able to satisfy that thirst until I finally got what I needed.

Pete tried to quench the thirst in his emotional life by acquiring material possessions. Yet it seemed that no matter how much he owned, no matter what he obtained, the thirst only grew stronger, which led him to buy more things. Eventually he recognized that there was only one thing that would quench the thirst of those unmet emotional needs—a relationship with God. He saw that God created that thirst within him, and so nothing else but Him would fully quench that thirst. By learning to come to God daily with his needs, and "drink" of the love and acceptance He had to offer, Pete saw he never needed to be thirsty again.

Lord, help me go to You, the source of living water, to quench the thirst of my life.

Now acquaint yourself with Him, and be at peace;
Thereby good will come to you.   —JOB 22:21

Once Crystal recognized the need for God in her life and came to the decision to accept Him, she began the process of becoming acquainted with Him. First, the most important way to get to know God was to spend time with Him. She made it a priority in her life to begin reading His Word and discover the positive messages for her life. She also spent time responding to Him in prayer, letting Him know how she felt. The more communication involved in a relationship, the stronger that relationship will be. Second, she involved herself in a local church that taught His Word where individuals who had a longer acquaintance with Him could provide an excellent source to answer her questions that came up. Third, she made His friends her friends. She surrounded herself with people who already had relationships with God so they could share common experiences in their spiritual growth. And fourth, she removed everything in her life that would be a hindrance to the relationship. That was the most difficult task, but as her relationship grew, the more He helped her identify those things that were standing in the way.

_____

Father, help me become more and more acquainted with You each day.

> *And those who are Christ's have crucified the flesh*
> *with its passions and desires.*   —GAL. 5:24

When I first saw Mark, he was the victim of multiple addictions. Perfectionism, success, money, and body-building had all been part of his life. He began to recognize the toll they were taking on his life—they had already cost him one marriage and two jobs. And yet they never gave him the sense of fulfillment he thought they would. He knew he had to give them up and turn to God before they took over his life. He had to destroy them, or they would destroy him.

To illustrate this point to himself in a way he would never forget, Mark held a funeral for himself. Not a real funeral, of course, but one that showed the old Mark was gone for good. He took sheets of paper and on each wrote one of his addictive behaviors. He then put them in a box, went to the backyard, dug a hole, buried his box, and put a marker on it titled "The Old Mark." Then he asked God to fill up the empty place in his life from those addictions and begin controlling his life. Now, even to this day every time one of those old behaviors rears its head, Mark looks at that marker in the backyard and remembers that the old Mark is dead and buried.

Help me see, O Lord, that my relationship with You can mean the death of my own compulsive behaviors.

*But You, O LORD, are a God full of compassion,
and gracious,
Longsuffering and abundant in mercy and
truth.*
—PS. 86:15

It is amazing how much your concept of God is influenced by your relationship with your parents and specifically your father. For those individuals like Billy who grew up in dysfunctional homes, their God concept can often be very negative and fearful. Because of the physical abuse he suffered, he saw God as a disciplinarian who stands in heaven with a club in His hand, waiting for him to step out of line just once and then, bam! This caused Billy to begin avoiding a relationship with God, for fear that no matter what he did in life it wouldn't be done right, and it was better not to have a relationship than have another one that would be painful.

While discipline and judgment are certainly part of God, they are only a small portion of who He is. When Billy began to understand the other aspects of God, he could open himself to trust Him. He learned that even though he made mistakes, God is merciful and able to forgive him. Most importantly, he began to experience the grace of God that can accept human weaknesses and still place great value and worth on his life. Billy found that a healthy and meaningful relationship with God is one based on a complete picture of God as found in His Word.

Lord, help me begin to understand You as You truly are.

> *Or let him take hold of My strength,*
> *That he may make peace with Me;*
> *And he shall make peace with Me.*
> —ISA. 27:5

So often those who turn to addictive agents to ease their pain are searching for that one commodity they feel will make the difference—peace. Keith's life seemed to have been in turmoil for as long as he could remember. That is why his need to play his guitar became so strong. The music brought him a brief relief from the misery he was feeling inside. It gave him the illusion of peace, even if it was only momentary. But that feeling became so powerful and so desirable that soon he was neglecting even his own physical needs just to buy that peaceful feeling.

Only God can provide the kind of peace that is eternal. Keith was using his music as his god, but because it never helped him face his past and confront his pain, it never really did what he wanted it to. God's peace is not based on a momentary numbing of the pain. His true peace gives you the ability to face the pain, knowing that it can be forgiven, healed, and put behind you forever. As an act of commitment, Keith gave his guitar up to God. That simple act finally gave him the peace for which he had always longed.

Father, allow Your peace to still the turmoil in my heart today.

Yet they did not obey or incline their ear, but walked in the counsels and in the imagination of their evil heart, and went backward and not forward.
—JER. 7:24

One of the strangest experiences I have ever had took place during one winter. I was working in Chicago, and I had a six-block walk from the subway to my job. Around New Year's, a storm blew in, bringing lots of ice and wind. As I headed for work, I turned a corner, and as that wind hit me full force in the face, my feet started sliding on the icy sidewalk. I had the sensation of actually losing ground as I was moving forward. My feet were moving in the right direction, but my body could not compete against the force of that wind. It took me several minutes before I was able to negotiate my way around that particular corner and get on to work.

It reminded me of Ben, a patient who was fighting his drive to be monetarily successful. Although he was trying to make progress, it seemed that the harder he tried to move forward, the more his addiction to money pulled him back. The more he tried to accomplish, the less he felt fulfilled. He finally had to admit he couldn't do it on his own and gave control to God. When he finally made the decision to do this, he found that he was no longer walking into the wind, but that it was at his back, moving him forward.

Help me rely on Your power, Lord, to get me moving forward in my life.

> Delight yourself also in the LORD,
> And He shall give you the desires of your heart.
> —PS. 37:4

Lauren started out to become a great actress so that she could somehow transcend her poverty-stricken beginning. By playing the different characters, she could escape the mundane existence she felt doomed to live. So she committed her whole being to acting, believing that if she were great enough she could achieve some level of immortality.

But somewhere Lauren's life had gotten out of control. The more she sought greatness, the harder she drove herself. And the more she drove herself, the more elusive greatness seemed to be. Her need to prove herself consumed all her energy, and even when she had nothing left to give, she gave it. Recently, the desire of her heart was simply the strength to get out of bed and face another day.

Lauren needed to discover that a relationship with God would give her all those desires that acting—her false god—could not give her. Acceptance, freedom, immortality were all hers to be had, just for the asking. Now the choice was up to Lauren—to ask or not to ask.

Father, help me always choose You to give me the desires of my heart.

*But as many as received Him, to them He gave
the right to become children of God, even to those
who believe in His name.*   —JOHN 1:12

In understanding the possibility of having a relationship with God, it is important to understand that relationship allows you to be a child of God. What exactly does that mean? For Patricia, being a child was something she had never really experienced. From the time she could remember, she had responsibilities for taking care of the other children, cleaning the house, and trying to make sure her parents didn't forget or abuse the other kids. Now she was told that God wanted to be her Father. What did that mean? How would being God's child be different from being her parents' child?

First of all, it allowed her to have a relationship with Someone who has unconditional love for her, who gave up His life for her, and who wants nothing more than to have her as His child. It also provided her with the forgiveness she needed to deal with the mistakes and failures of her past. He provided her with access to Him any time she had a need or was struggling with an issue in her life. He would understand when she hurt and would be there to put His arms around her. And perhaps most important, He promised her the victory over the negative messages from her past. When Patricia saw all that, she knew this was a Father she could trust.

Help me learn to live as Your child today, Father.

> *For if they fall, one will lift up his companion.*
> *But woe to him who is alone when he falls,*
> *For he has no one to help him up.*
> —ECCL. 4:10

In beginning to face addictive behaviors, it is so vitally important to develop support networks. Ellie, for so long, had been under the impression that she had to fight the battle alone, that she could count on no one but herself. Everyone else was not to be trusted and would take advantage of her. In fact, her addiction to her artwork isolated her and led her further and further away from people.

In recovery, it is essential to develop relationships. Not only do they help in battling addictive behaviors, but they provide the human contact so desperately needed. When Ellie finally made those contacts, it was reassuring but also challenging to be able to find someone who had dealt with the same issues that she had. She found hope that she too could recover someday. It also helped her see that she was not alone in her struggles. If you are battling addictions in your life today, become involved with the support of those around you. Find a friend or a group that will listen to you and begin sharing your experiences with them. Let them minister to you. It will go a long way to help you in the healing process.

_____

Father, help me understand that when I least desire people in my life is the time when I need them the most.

7. FALLOUT

THE GREAT PARADOX – *August 29*

He who finds his life will lose it, and he who loses his life for My sake will find it.

—MATT. 10:39

Jack was bankrupt. To look at him, you would never guess it. He owned his own chain of car washes, had a home on the lake, drove around in a European sports car. All the trappings of success were visible. Yet Jack was losing it all because of his need to have more. For in order to multiply his worth, he had gambled all of his financial worth on a get-rich-quick scheme that had failed. That one last stab at invincibility had failed, and it was going to cost him everything.

Jack was also emotionally and spiritually bankrupt. The family he had worked so desperately to provide this for left long ago, and through his back-stabbing deals he had alienated most of his friends. The control and order he had tried to place on his life seemed further away now than ever.

Jack had to learn the great paradox of life. To try and control life on one's own guarantees certain failure. But to finally give up control to God, releasing the reins of his life and admitting his inability to do it on his own, Jack could finally have the direction and stability with life he had always sought.

Help me find my control, Father, by giving that control to You.

> *For what advantage is it to a man if he gains the*
> *whole world, and is himself destroyed or lost?*
> —LUKE 9:25

In today's competitive world, the importance of having an "advantage" over your opponent is emphasized. Brett bought into that idea and believed that in order to succeed, he had to do something more or better or perfectly to have that edge that was going to push him to the top. The more intensely he pursued that goal, the more consumed he became, the better chance he had of winning. For after all, winning is everything. The man who sits on top is the man to be envied. And whatever he has to pay to get there is worth it. Or is it?

It is often interesting to see what is found in the wake of those so-called "successful" people and what that success is measured by. When Brett finally stopped his push to the top to see what it had cost him, he was amazed at the price. His success was obtained at the cost of a broken marriage and forgotten family. His physical health had suffered, and he had lost most of his friendships. And most importantly, Brett's success was obtained at the cost of being too busy for God, not having time to learn and experience the real meaning of life.

Lord, help me see the ways that my advantage is costing me.

For which of you, intending to build a tower, does not sit down first and count the cost, whether he has enough to finish it.
—LUKE 14:28

Recently, we added a room on to our house. We decided we needed more space, so we sat down with a contractor and told him about our plans. He then went over everything it would take to make the room to our specifications and presented us with an estimated cost. We looked at our budget, calculated all the facts and figures, and tried to figure out the impact this would have on our current finances.

I shared this with Rebecca, and she saw the parallel in her life. It seems she didn't count the cost of excessive exercising. She failed to realize what other areas of her life it was affecting, like her studies. Sometimes she was afraid to count the cost because if she really saw how much exercising was eating up study time and thus lowering her grades, she would be forced to have to consider giving it up. But if she didn't take the time to stop and recognize the loss of time and energy, she would ultimately lose what she was trying to achieve for herself, namely her health. The sooner she was able to count the cost, the sooner she would be able to see that the price was too high.

Give me the courage, Lord, to count the cost of the addictive behaviors in my life.

> *Awake to righteousness, and do not sin; for some do not have the knowledge of God. I speak this to your shame.*
> —1 COR. 15:34

Paul shared an interesting story with me about how finally he had begun to face the fallout in his life. He had been trying to figure out a solution to a tax problem in his business, and he had been wrestling with it for days. Finally, he fell exhausted into bed, hoping to catch a few hours of sleep before tackling it again. As he dozed off, he began to dream and suddenly the perfect answer came to him. His excitement woke him up. He dashed to his desk and began to write it down. But the more he wrote, the more his rational, logical mind started calculating the cost and he soon saw that his "perfect solution" was utterly ridiculous and totally impractical. He felt more discouraged than ever by being so fooled. That was when the light dawned.

"I realized that was exactly what my compulsion with success was doing to me. It was fooling me into thinking I could provide the answers for my life, but when I finally counted the cost and compared it to the answers for life that God showed me in His Word, it looked ridiculous. Now, every time I feel the need to use work to meet those needs, all I do is shout to myself, 'Wake up!' and turn to God again."

Help me today, Father, wake up to Your truth in my life.

Whose minds the god of this age has blinded, who do not believe, lest the light of the gospel of the glory of Christ, who is the image of God, should shine on them.
—2 COR. 4:4

While on the surface many addictive behaviors may seem relatively harmless, there is a deceitful underside to them that can be truly devastating. The problem involves the way that your addictions blind you to the cost that they are really taking on your life. Because he had such emotional deficits, Kurt's main focus in life was to feel good about himself. When he found that buying a new item of clothing gave him a feeling of satisfaction, he began to buy more clothes more often. However, no amount of clothing seemed to be quite enough to stop that longing in his heart.

As he consumed himself with getting his emotional needs met, he failed to see the toll these behaviors were taking in other ways. When he took the time to isolate this addiction and focus on the different areas of fallout, he specifically saw that he had been blinded to the financial burden it was placing upon him. When he compared what he was spending to what he was making, God opened his eyes to see that unless he stopped his spending, he wouldn't be able to provide for more basic needs. His blinded eyes were finally opened.

Lord, shine a light of Your truth on my blinded emotional eyes today.

But you are not willing to come to Me that you may
have life.
                           —JOHN 5:40

I remember in college, going through a particularly difficult semester in terms of my work load. I was taking eighteen hours, fifteen of which were in my new major of psychology in which I had never before taken a course. I was also working about twenty hours a week in a nearby town. As I felt myself becoming stretched thinner, I attempted to change my schedule, rearrange my work hours, and try different strategies on my homework. Yet it seemed like the more I studied, the more tired I got, and the more often I missed class. But I was determined to find a way to do this on my own.

Then one day while having my quiet time with God, I realized that I had neglected the most important factor of all—turning to God for His direction. After asking for God's help, I went to my teacher and told him that I was about to flunk out of several of his classes and asked for his help. I also went to my boss and informed him of the fact that I was going to have to take some time to get caught up on my studies.

With God's help in setting those boundaries, I was able to come through with fairly decent grades and not lose too much of my income from my work as well. I learned who to turn to first.

Help me turn to You in the first place, O God.

He who speaks truth declares righteousness,
But a false witness, deceit. —PROV. 12:17

A couple sat in silence across from me in my office. May, whom I had seen several times, sat with her head down and her hands folded, dejection written all over her face. Beside her, in stony silence, sat her husband, Harold. I had asked May to bring him, hoping to help him see how he had contributed to some of the dysfunction in the family. He finally spoke with a steely voice. "I know what my wife has told you about me, and you probably believe all that bunk. My kids tell me the same thing, and so do my coworkers. They are all ganging up on me, but they are not going to make me take the rap. I'm OK, and I don't care what anybody says." I asked, "Could there be a possibility that some small part of what they say is true?" His frosty glare told me all I needed to know regarding his response.

Until Harold is able to come to grips with the truth—what his behaviors are costing him—he will continue to destroy those things that are dearest to him. The willingness to recognize the truth about addictive behaviors is a difficult task for anyone. But the sooner the truth is known, the less damage and devastation will be done. Have the courage today to be willing to face the truth about the fallout in your life.

Lord, help me face the truth of my fallout today.

> *The way of life winds upward for the wise,*
> *That he may turn away from hell below.*
> —PROV. 15:24

The journey through life is often compared to a road. As with any journey, the direction that you decide to take usually determines on what road you will travel. For Lance, that road started with a commitment to himself to make sure he would never be unappreciated like he was in childhood. His road led through college, law school, local politics, and eventually the state capital where he was one of the governor's top assistants. Yet going down that road of self-fulfillment had cost him quite a bit, and the price he paid for his public popularity was to be despised and rejected by those closest to him. The road had not brought him fulfillment, and he seemed more alone and confused than ever.

Are you at that place in your life? The good news is that no matter how far down that dark and dismal road you have gone, that distance down the road to happiness and fulfillment always remains the same. It is never further away than a commitment to God. It simply involves a decision to let God be in control. When Lance looked at the road of his life, where it had led and what the fallout had cost, there was no question about making that decision.

Help me, Father, to choose the road of Your direction.

Surely every man walks about like a shadow;
Surely they busy themselves in vain;
He heaps up riches,
And does not know who will gather them.
—PS. 39:6

One of the things that compulsive people spend their time doing is building a legacy for the future. Whether it is money, power, prestige, or philanthropy, the goal is to work desperately hard to make sure the world has something by which to remember them. Martin was busy trying to build on the empire that his father had left him. The hours were ruining his health, and his wife had become a stranger. Then his father died. Martin was faced with the question: What happens to it now? When death finally came, there was not one thing in this world that went with his father into eternity. All the effort, all the drive stopped at that moment, and whatever he accumulated was simply left behind for someone else to use as they wished.

While Martin grieved the loss of his father, he also began grieving the losses of his own life. He allowed himself to see not only what it had already cost him, but what it would cost him in the future if he did not change his values. That realization helped him to begin putting his energies toward the things that matter—his relationship with God, with his family, and with his friends. That was a legacy Martin could happily pass on.

_____

Father, help me put my energies and efforts into things that will last beyond the scope of my life here on earth.

> *The sleep of a laboring man is sweet,*
> *Whether he eats little or much;*
> *But the abundance of the rich will not*
>   *permit him to sleep.*
> —ECCL. 5:12

One area of fallout that is often overlooked is the anxiousness created by compulsive behaviors. Not only was Stacey worried about accumulating more material possessions, she was consumed with making sure that she protected what she already had. Because the feeling of loss and abandonment from childhood was so painful to Stacey, she felt a desperate need to cling to what she had struggled so hard to gain for herself. This need for absolute control in her life began affecting other relationships as well. She began to distrust people and felt that somehow they were out to take away what she worked so hard to attain. The more paranoid Stacey became, the higher the wall was built, and soon she began to shut out everyone and everything in order to protect herself from further loss.

By recognizing that she was allowing material possessions to meet her needs instead of God, Stacey saw that these in effect were "false gods." She saw that if she allowed God to control her life, it would be His responsibility to care for and protect what is His. Then she could be free to start working on the other relationships in her life.

Help me trust You for all of my needs.

Why do you spend money for what is not bread,
And your wages for what does not satisfy?
Listen diligently to Me, and eat what is good,
And let your soul delight itself in abundance.
—ISA. 55:2

One area of fallout that may affect an individual is the financial burden a compulsion may begin to build. Lonnie started out collecting figurines because she thought they were pretty. Soon it became kind of an adventure for her, browsing through thrift stores and antique shops, anticipating the thrill of discovering a long lost treasure. When she brought her purchase home, she would feel excited for awhile, but the high would wear off soon enough and it would become one more piece of junk in her house. This drove her out more often and increased the amount of purchases. Her bills and basic needs began to be pushed aside, just to feed her compulsion.

In doing her recovery inventory, Lonnie discovered her biggest area of fallout was financial. When she calculated what she had spent over the last year on her collection, she saw that the same amount of money could not only pay her bills and buy her food but allow her to do things for herself that really would help her meet her emotional needs. She could go on a relaxing vacation or out to dinner with friends. Best of all, she would know that she was getting the best investment out of her money.

Help me to invest my life wisely.

For the heart of this people has grown dull.
Their ears are hard of hearing,
And their eyes they have closed,
Lest they should see with their eyes and hear
*   with their ears,*
Lest they should understand with their heart
*   and turn,*
So that I should heal them.   —ACTS 28:27

Denial can lead to further addictions. Driven by the need to be seen as the perfect father who provided everything for his children, Lou spent long hours at work to earn the money to give them whatever they wanted. The sad truth was that what they really wanted was him—being available to play catch or just sit and talk. But whenever Lou began to feel guilty about not spending that quality time with them, he would immerse himself further in work to buy something bigger and better for them.

The breakdown of his denial came one afternoon when his three children marched into his study and asked if they could make a deal. They asked if they could turn in all their games, gadgets, trinkets, and toys for one big present that would make them all happy. Intrigued, Lou responded, "Sure, what is it? You name it, and I'll give it to you." When his oldest daughter replied, "One hour a day of your time," he sat stunned. Lou finally saw the fallout of his addiction, and realized he was not providing the best gift a father could give his children—himself.

Help me see what my addictive behaviors are not allowing me to face.

There is a way that seems right to a man,
But its end is the way of death.
—PROV. 16:25

For patients who have a difficult time facing the fall-out of their compulsive behaviors, I often use the strategy of taking them down the road to see what the future may hold if the behaviors continue. Lydia was not really concerned too much about her need to call her mother long-distance every day to talk to her. Since she talked one hour a day at the cost of about ten dollars a call, we figured if she did this for twenty-five years, the cost would be one hundred thousand dollars for just under ten thousand hours. Lydia was staggered.

We then figured how much she would save by limiting herself to just one call a week. Then I asked her to list all the positive things she could do with that money and time, especially focusing on the other relationships she could use that time to build. She began to see that the compulsive phone calls were going to cost her much more than she was willing to pay and she could use the time and money much more productively.

Right now the price tag on your addiction may not seem so high, but take time to look down the road and ask yourself, "If I don't stop, what will it cost me?"

Father, help me see where my compulsions could lead me.

> *Who satisfies your mouth with good things,*
> *So that your youth is renewed like the eagle's.*
> —PS. 103:5

In considering the fallout in your life, make sure you are giving those people around you the things they need rather than the things you *think* they need. When this situation happens, it can be devastating.

Bill and Linda sat in my office, trying to come to terms with how they were using each other to meet their own needs. In effect, they were addicted to each other. Every time Bill felt down or his self-esteem needed a boost, he wanted to have sex with his wife. After all, she had been neglected by her first husband, so he felt he had to be a "real man" to her to make her feel better. Meanwhile, Linda kept trying to mother Bill since his mother had deserted the family when Bill was a child. And since Linda could not have children, that met the need for her. But they both were frustrated since the other person did not seem to appreciate their "gift."

When they finally identified their needs to each other, they saw they were usually trying to meet their own needs. And the fallout had really been their relationship. It is important to allow God to meet your needs so you can be more attuned to what others *really* need from you.

Lord, meet my needs today so I can be more useful to You.

*Beloved, do not think it strange concerning the
fiery trial which is to try you, as though some
strange thing happened to you.*

—1 PETER 4:12

This is no fun," Randy said. "I want to see what my
addictions are costing me, but I didn't realize it would
hurt so much. Does this really help, or am I just creating more pain that I will have to deal with later?" The
hurt seems to be so unbearable at times that it does not
seem to be worth the effort.

What I share with people like Randy is that there are
two kinds of pain—pain toward sickness and pain
toward healing. The example I use is having your ap-
pendix taken out. Initially, you go to the hospital because you are in extreme pain, pain that could kill you
if not taken care of. Then the doctor says you need
surgery. So you go under the anesthetic, hoping the
problem will be taken care of. But when you wake up,
you are still in pain—sometimes, more pain than before the surgery. But that is a different pain. It is the
pain of healing. You may be hurting desperately, but
as each day goes by and the wound begins to heal,
you feel better. Then you see it was worth the pain of
surgery.

Are you going through pain as you identify fallout? If
so, remind yourself it is *healing* pain, not destructive
pain, and the sooner the surgery is over, the sooner the
pain will be too.

_____

Help me, Lord, endure the pain of getting well.

> *But they refused to heed, shrugged their shoulders,*
> *and stopped their ears so that they could not hear.*
> —ZECH. 7:11

Fred was a proud man. In fact, he was addicted to his pride. He felt that whatever situation came along, he could handle it. And he always knew that he was right. When his wife tried to get him to see what his pride was costing the family, he refused to consider it. After all, it had served him well up to this point, so why should he change now?

Eventually, after much pleading, his wife got him to come to counseling. When he strutted confidently into the counselor's office, ready to stand his ground, he was not prepared for what faced him. Around the room sat his wife, his children, his boss, his pastor—even his best friend. For the next hour they spoke a litany of fallout that his pride was costing him. His children did not respect him, his friends were starting to avoid him, he possibly could lose his job. Even the church was ready to remove him from leadership. Faced with such overwhelming evidence, Fred saw that he had to begin facing his pride and what it was costing him.

Don't let pride stand in the way of your recovery. Be courageous enough to begin looking for yourself at what your addictions are costing you.

Lord, with Your intervention, help me see the fallout in my life.

A prudent man foresees evil and hides himself,
But the simple pass on and are punished.
—PROV. 22:3

In looking at fallout from addictions, it is often easy to focus on the major areas of cost and forget about the small, daily price paid for the behaviors. In fact, what you consider to be minimal and unimportant may in fact be very significant. That is why, in making your inventory, you have to isolate such addiction in order to consider fully what it may be costing you.

As Chad went through and saw each addiction and the fallout it brought, he was able to begin releasing those behaviors to God. The one thing he still had trouble doing was finding time to have a quiet time each morning with God. So he was asked to do an exercise where he broke his day down into ten-minute increments and write what he was doing during that time.

He came in next time with a sheepish grin on his face. "I found it," he said. As he looked through his day, he saw that whenever he had a few minutes, he browsed through his most recent men's clothing catalog, since dressing perfectly was part of his need for approval. In adding it up, he saw that he usually spent forty-five minutes a day on that useless exercise. "Now I see where the time for God can come," Chad said. "By giving up my other god—my wardrobe."

Lord, help me see the danger in all of my addictions, great or small.

*For by grace you have been saved through faith,
and that not of yourselves; it is the gift of God,
not of works, lest anyone should boast.*
—EPH. 2:8–9

When you take the time to calculate the losses that addictive behaviors have cost you, be careful not to use those issues as a way to create further low self-esteem. An individual who is susceptible to addictions may become addicted to finding the fallout, and use it as a club to continue abusing themselves. Ruth was a victim of sexual and physical abuse in her childhood. She had been involved in one-night-stand relationships with men for as long as she could remember. Now she had started recovery, but when she got to the fallout point on the addiction cycle, she got stuck. All she could focus on was what her sexual addiction had cost her, and she spent hours reminding herself.

While everyone suffers losses due to their addictions, it is also important to remember how much God, in His grace, protects you from further damage. To help Ruth see this, she was given the assignment of writing each day, "But for the grace of God . . . ," and filling it in with something that had *not* happened to her. Eventually, she was able to come up with items like "I never lost my job," "My life was never threatened." She came to see that while she had suffered from her addictions, except for God's grace it could have been much worse.

Lord, thank You for what Your grace has kept me from suffering.

*For you, brethren, have been called to liberty; only
do not use liberty as an opportunity for the flesh,
but through love serve one another.*

—GAL. 5:13

Freedom is something that everyone longs for. People
march for it, fight for it, sometimes even die for it.
There is always a cost involved to obtain freedom.
Sometimes addictive behaviors allow you to think you
can avoid paying the price for freedom. But avoiding
those realities can cost much more than what you
would have paid for true freedom in the first place.

Donna thought she was gaining freedom through
her excursions to the mall. When she walked out the
door and got into the car, it really was an exhilarating
feeling for her. She was free from the housework, free
from the bills, free from the creditors' phone calls or
threatening letters. But what Donna needed to see was
that this was not true freedom but simply escape which
created more bondage. When she got home, all those
things still existed, and the more she put them off, the
less free she was. Donna had to learn that the "freedom" from her responsibilities was costing more than
actually facing them. When she finally began paying
off each debt and accomplishing each chore, she found
she really was free.

*Help me see, Lord, that the price of freedom is not nearly as much as
the cost of avoiding it.*

> *Though his hatred is covered by deceit,*
> *His wickedness will be revealed before*
> *the whole congregation.*
> —PROV. 26:26

Looking at the various ways that fallout has been created in your life, one area that is most costly is in personal relationships. Even the most seemingly innocent of behaviors can have a dark underside if used to get back at another person. This passive-aggressive anger is all the more deadly because it can go unnoticed since it is covered by actions that are not "bad" in and of themselves.

On the surface, Luke seemed like such a caring husband, always bringing home little candy treats for his wife or taking her out to dinner. These appeared to be loving acts, except for the fact that he knew his wife had a weight problem. She was outgoing but was self-conscious about her size. Luke, on the other hand, had few friends because he was so controlling in his relationships. When he assessed his relational fallout, he realized he was trying to keep his wife heavy in order to punish her for having so many friends. He felt if he could limit them, he could have more control of her time. What he actually was doing was creating more unhappiness in her, which only made her more miserable. By admitting his insecurities, he removed the need to passively hurt his wife, which allowed them to improve their relationship.

Help me see how I am taking out my anger passively on others, Lord.

That the LORD your God may show us the way in which we should walk and the thing we should do.
—JER. 42:3

One of the most intriguing experiences I have had in my life was visiting the catacombs in Rome. From a practical view, the thing that sticks out most in my mind is remembering how necessary it was to stay as close to the guide as possible at all times. He would lead us down a particular tunnel, and then almost before we would know it, it would disappear from our eyes, taking a sharp left or right turn. And then about the time we would gain our bearings again, it would turn again. The maze of passageways was almost beyond belief. I truly believe that if that guide had disappeared, we would still be wandering around the labyrinth today.

In the emotional maze of your past, you also need guidance to help you identify fallout. The source of help can come from three places. First, you must allow God to show you through prayer and His Word the areas that need changing. Those closest to you—family, friends, coworkers—can also be a source of direction for they have observed your life firsthand, and understand your losses. The third place to go for help is a support group, for others who have been through that maze before can help you through it. For with guidance, you can break free of the maze of your fallout.

Lord, please guide me out of the maze of my past.

> *To give light to those who sit in darkness*
> *and the shadow of death,*
> *To guide our feet into the way of peace.*
> —LUKE 1:79

One negative consequence of fallout is the loss of your perspective on reality. You can become so narrowly focused on those few behaviors that seem to give satisfaction in life that you do not recognize how far from the truth those negative behaviors have brought you. Take the time to look around and see where that path brought you. Often, it is a cold, dark, lonely place, and when you finally take the time to see what your addictions have cost you, it can create an overwhelming sense of grief. In that emotional darkness, you can become very frightened. Often that fear will lead you to indulge more into addictive behaviors to block out the grief so that you will not have to face it.

When you finally find yourself at that dark and lonely place, you need to recognize that there is a source of light that can shine into the blackness of your pain and help you to begin to grieve those losses in a healthy way. Not only does that source give His light to help you see what you've lost, but He also gives you the strength to go through the process of grieving those losses so that you can finally give them up. Then you can balance those losses by seeing all God's grace can provide for you, such as forgiveness and direction. You don't have to sit alone in darkness anymore.

Help me begin my journey into Your light today, O Lord.

*Keep yourselves in the love of God, looking for the
mercy of our Lord Jesus Christ unto eternal life.*
—JUDE 21

When a person begins adding up the cost of the fallout that has been created by his addictive behaviors,
there is almost always an overwhelming sense of loss.
When Sondra took the time to calculate the toll her
compulsive cleaning had taken on the relationships in
her life, she began to become aware of the incredible
amount of energy that it sapped from her. She began
to see what she had given up to gain the little comfort
she could from her perfectly clean house. This became
painful when she tried to figure out how to begin to
pay back all that lost time. When she realized how
much hurt and damage those behaviors created in her
family, she began to recognize there was really nothing she could do in human terms to make up the difference.

There is in fact only one thing that can ever settle
the account—God's mercy. Sondra had to ask God's forgiveness for the price she had paid for her perfectionistic cleanliness. But she also had to realize that there
were many things she still had to be thankful for—her
home, her husband, her health. In fact, each time one
of those losses came back to haunt and defeat her, she
would respond by saying out loud, "But for God's
mercy I could have lost . . ." and named something He
had provided for her. She was able to learn to accept
what she had lost by emphasizing what she had not.

Lord, thank You for Your incredible mercy that You have shown me.

> *Keep your heart with all diligence,*
> *For out of it spring the issues of life.*
> —PROV. 4:23

Sometimes you learn more about an individual from what he ends up *not* having in his life rather than what he has. When Howard Hughes finally died, there was virtually no one around for he had kept himself in isolation for so long. He had no friends and it was thought that his last will was given to an individual he had only known for a few hours. At one time he may have been identified as the richest man in America, but at the time of his death, he was remembered more for being a paranoid, lonely, isolated man.

When you look back at your life, are you able to identify more of what you *have* or what you *don't* have? Can you look back on your life and see the things that were very dear to you that have now disappeared because of your addictions? You must recognize that sooner or later, if your heart is set on a course of destruction, you will end up losing everything that is important to you. It will be easier to list the things you don't have rather than the things that you now have. Take the time today to finish this statement: "If I don't stop my _____ behavior, I could lose _____." Then allow God to change that behavior, so you won't have to deal with that loss.

Help my heart focus on what I am losing by not trusting You.

He who loves silver will not be satisfied with silver;
Nor he who loves abundance, with increase.
This also is vanity.   —ECCL. 5:10

Darla had always been concerned with her figure, and she always had been an advocate of good exercise. But lately, it seemed that she was having to exercise more in order to feel good, and that feeling was becoming more short-lived. She began to crave that exercise time, even at the sacrifice of time for her family. Then she began to take longer lunch hours and leave work early, just to get that exercise "high." The strange thing was that the more she exercised, the less she really enjoyed it.

When the enjoyment becomes less important than the pursuit, you will begin to experience the fallout. Your focus becomes singular, and the enjoyment in your day-to-day living becomes replaced by the need to continually feed your quest. And once that quest is started, it becomes a never-ending journey into compulsion, unless you reach a decision to get off the cycle before the damage becomes too great. Darla had to not only face the fallout of her exercising but look to see what emotional need she was trying to satisfy so she could begin facing those needs directly.

Help me see what needs I am trying to satisfy by my compulsions.

8. VIOLATION OF VALUES

September 23 – THE MESSAGE OF THE MIRROR

> *For if anyone is a hearer of the word and not a doer, he is like a man observing his natural face in a mirror; for he observes himself, goes away, and immediately forgets what kind of man he was.*
> —JAMES 1:23–24

Have you ever known a person who can't pass a mirror without looking? My wife has a friend like that. If Gayle happens to be over at our house, she will not pass by a mirror without stopping to take a look at herself. She is compulsive about her appearance. The interesting thing about Gayle is that these views into the mirror never seem to have any lasting effect on her. She may make a few sweeps at her hair or straighten her collar, but somehow she always manages to look a little unkempt. It is as if when she walks away from the mirror, she forgets about anything it may point out to her.

That is also how Gayle uses God's Word in her life. She may read that focusing on her appearance is not healthy for her to do and she may even recognize it intellectually. But it seems that those acknowledgments never get past her mind and into her heart, and those changes are never made. She momentarily recognizes what needs to be done but never seems to take the time to make the change. Only by honestly confronting those behaviors can they ever start matching up to her beliefs.

Help me, Lord, work on making my behaviors match my beliefs.

*Woe to you, scribes and Pharisees, hypocrites! For
you are like whitewashed tombs which indeed
appear beautiful outwardly, but inside are full
of dead men's bones and all uncleanness.*
—MATT. 23:27

In the town where we used to live, there was a favorite
spot for wedding parties to have pictures taken. There
was a little creek flowing into a pond, and all around
the pond were beautiful weeping willow trees and tall
pines. The lawn was manicured like a golf green and it
always seemed to be so peaceful and tranquil there.
However, this pastoral spot was also a cemetery. If the
photographer turned too far to the right or left from the
shot he was taking, the pictures would be ruined because of the head-markers and gravestones.

That was how Crissy treated her life. She worked so
hard to make the outside attractive and beautiful,
never allowing others to see what was really on the
inside. It was her way to avoid dealing with the real
issues of pain and anger she felt inside. What Jesus is
saying in this verse is that the Pharisees' lives were a
sham, just a beautified cemetery. The point He was
making was that a person should quit focusing on the
outside and begin looking at what's going on inside.
Only by identifying the violated values behind the ob-
sessions with beauty could Crissy ever be free of them.

Help me work on the inside as well as the outside of my life.

> *Therefore, when you do a charitable deed, do not*
> *sound a trumpet before you as the hypocrites do*
> *in the synagogues and in the streets, that they may*
> *have glory from men. Assuredly, I say to you, they*
> *have their reward.*
> —MATT. 6:2

In honestly looking at the behaviors in your life, one thing you have to question is your motivation behind doing something. Sometimes it is easy to deceive yourself into thinking that you are doing something for the right reason simply because you are doing a good deed. You tell yourself, *After all, isn't it important that this particular thing be done? And if no one else is going to do it, why shouldn't I step in and be the one to take care of the situation? How can doing something good be bad?*

Because of the low self-esteem brought on from the past, Warren felt he always had to be the one to volunteer for any project, to make sure he was needed. When good deeds are done with the motivation of making yourself feel better about yourself, they can turn out to be very selfish acts. Check to see if you have some personal, self-satisfying motive behind doing some of the things that you do. If you simply cannot say no, that is a good indication that it is not the deed that is important but rather the reason you are doing it.

Warren had to ask himself if he was doing this for others or for Warren.

Lord, honestly search the motives behind the actions I am doing in Your name.

There is a generation that is pure in its own eyes,
Yet is not washed from its filthiness.

—PROV. 30:12

If you were to go to any high school in the country, there is one common element that you will find—social groups. Some of these groups are pretty standard, like the "jocks" or the "brains." One group you are fairly sure to find is the group I call the "Mutual Admiration Society." This group is made up of the more socially elite kids, who usually have everything they ever wanted. The sole purpose of this group is to continually reinforce to each other how wonderful they all are and how great it is that they are all together. Because they are blinded to anything other than the need to maintain the group, they ignore the characteristics of their lives that will eventually cause their destruction— backbiting, envy, jealousy.

The philosophy of that group had pervaded Jenny's life. She was so interested in maintaining a positive front and reinforcing her image to her friends that she failed to look at herself and see that the attitudes she was practicing were the very attitudes she spoke against. What Jenny had to do was step back and pretend she was evaluating her life from a third-person perspective, like God does. By taking His view she could see the areas that needed to be changed and could more readily turn to Him for His help.

Lord, make me aware of who I truly am and what I truly need to be in Your eyes.

> *Let us search out and examine our ways,*
> *And turn back to the LORD.*
>
> —LAM. 3:40

In dealing with the violation of your values, a surface examination is usually not enough to identify the problem. You need to be willing to take a deeper look because you have become so expert at fooling yourself. Because of the ability you have developed to overlook a particular area of your life, you probably need someone else's help in identifying that area.

My wife will ask me to go and find a brush in the bathroom. Because I have looked at that room so many times and have more or less blinded myself to everything in there, I have a difficult time seeing the brush. I will tell my wife that I absolutely cannot find it, and she will come in and point it out to me even when I had been staring at it all the time.

Sometimes you have chosen to overlook certain behaviors for so long that you will be unable to see how negative they are. Try seeking the aid of a trusted friend, someone who can help you more clearly see the truth even when you can't. By allowing God to use that person in your life, you can begin working on those issues.

Lord, begin to search my heart and let me know the things I need to change.

They profess to know God, but in works they deny Him, being abominable, disobedient, and disqualified for every good work.

—TITUS 1:16

If you want to determine what people truly believe, do you listen to what they say or watch what they do? Words are a powerful tool. Kip was not very old before he learned that he could make his words say anything that someone else wanted to hear, regardless of what he believed. In fact, he became an expert at saying the right thing because he liked the response he got when his friends heard what they wanted. He took this practice into adulthood, recognizing that the more people heard what they liked, the more approval he received.

But the way to truly measure how individuals believe is to watch what they do rather than just listen to their words. Kip had told his bosses for years that he was appalled by insider trading even though the practice had won him a higher position in a New York stock company. But the day he was caught on the phone giving privileged information to a client, his world came crashing down. Kip had to finally realize that his true character was reflected by his actions and he needed to do a moral inventory so he could begin identifying just what he actually did believe.

Help me work on making my actions match my words.

> *An angry man stirs up strife,*
> *And a furious man abounds in transgression.*
> —PROV. 29:22

One of the ways that a violation manifests itself in a person's life is in the area of anger. On the surface, Naomi seemed to be very content with her life. If you were to question her she would deny that she had anger and claim that she had virtually eliminated it from her life.

But, in looking a little deeper, the more subtle evidences of anger could be seen. There was a long-standing grudge toward her mother that had never been resolved where just the mention of her name caused Naomi to boil inside. She was continually late, unwilling to do even the smallest favor, made excessive demands, and always had an excuse for her failure. These kinds of behaviors were not as obvious as yelling or screaming, but they had more long-term effects because Naomi was unaware of how damaging they really were.

To begin acknowledging the anger in her life, Naomi asked God to help her identify everything she was angry about. Then she identified who had made her angry, what caused that anger, and what effect it had on her life. By making this "grudge list," she was able to bring it to the surface so it would no longer need to come out in subtle ways.

Lord, help me see the subtle ways that I am expressing unresolved anger in my life.

For the wrath of man does not produce the
righteousness of God.
　　　　　　　　　　　　—JAMES 1:20

One of the ways to fool yourself about the negative behavior in your life is to convince yourself that you have a *right* to be angry. If you were to be asked, you certainly would agree that self-centered anger is wrong. However, when it applies to you, your anger has a reason to be justified. Jack always had a *reason* for his anger. Maybe he was angry at some unethical principle he saw at work. Maybe he was expressing outrage at the treatment of a minority group in the community. Perhaps his wife didn't handle a problem with the children well, and he felt his anger was justified for the kids' sake. Whatever the situation, the reason for Jack's anger was always the other person's fault, not his.

What Jack failed to see was that his angry responses had nothing to do with the other person but with how he felt about himself. Rather than try to right all the wrongs he saw through his anger, Jack needed to focus on the origin of the anger in his life and what he could do to resolve it. Only when he began to let go of that anger could he act in a responsible manner that would help right some of the wrongs that he saw in his everyday world.

Help me see, Lord, that often the source of anger starts with me.

> *I acknowledged my sin to You,*
> *And my iniquity I have not hidden.*
> *I said, "I will confess my transgressions*
>   *to the Lord,"*
> *And You forgave the iniquity of my sin.*
> —PS. 32:5

One of the difficult tasks in life is confronting the continued desire to run away from problems. Because he needed to be so protective of his emotions in the past, Carl was overwhelmed at the thought of doing an inventory of violated values. He had spent his adulthood building a life-style that would allow him to ignore his past, or so he thought. By creating the illusion of the successful businessman, committed to the good of the company, he felt he could keep enough distance from the selfishness inside that he would never have to deal with it.

In making his moral inventory, Carl had to finally come to the point where he had to list the things he was afraid of—identify his fears. Once he identified those fears, he began to realize the motivation behind his need to run so hard to prove himself. As he named those fears to God, he realized that God was more powerful than all of those fears put together. And since Carl no longer had anything to hide, he also had nothing to fear.

Help me, Lord, no longer hide myself from You.

For I will declare my iniquity;
I will be in anguish over my sin.
—PS. 38:18

One of the things any person traveling overseas must do upon reentering the United States is to declare to the customs agent what he has purchased on his trip. Sometimes, if one hasn't kept track of how much he has been spending along the way, trying to remember everything can be a time-consuming task. This is just a way of assessing how much a person has spent on overseas goods so that the proper duty can be paid upon reentering the country. And the more one buys, the more one pays.

In a sense, that is the same thing you need to do in dealing with your addictions. Make an honest assessment of what behaviors in your life do not match up to your values so you can become aware of how they are affecting you. Once you see how much they have cost you, you will want to give them up. The difference between the customs agent and God, however, is that the price has already been paid for those behaviors. It is simply up to you to declare it then hand it over to Him.

Lord, give me the strength and courage to identify the things in my life that need Your forgiveness.

But You are God,
Ready to pardon,
Gracious and merciful,
Slow to anger,
Abundant in kindness,
And did not forsake them.
—NEH. 9:17

Clark tried to be all that his parents told him he couldn't be, running from their mockery of his size by being a super athlete, a Saturday afternoon hero to millions of young boys. The more popular he became, the more unwilling he was to look at what his life had become. He proclaimed physical fitness, but he had become addicted to steroids. He was so involved in his success that he was not aware of his bondage, and what he expressed publicly did not match up to how he was living.

God provided everything Clark was looking for. He provided forgiveness for all the values he had violated. He provided grace and mercy to heal the mocking voices of the past. When, because of his weaknesses, Clark didn't live up to the standards God had for him, He was slow to anger. And when the lights went down and the cheers died away, Clark was still special enough to God to be there no matter how he was feeling. He was always there, waiting to meet every need Clark ever had.

Lord, help me see that everything my addictive behaviors cannot provide, You have already given me.

Peace I leave with you, My peace I give to you; not as the world gives do I give to you. Let not your heart be troubled, neither let it be afraid.
—JOHN 14:27

Do you live in fear?" When I asked Grant this question, he responded that he did not. He considered the security of his home, his family, his job, and generally felt he was not overwrought with fear. I reminded him that often people have emotional fears, fears that involve abandonment, lack of self-esteem, the realization that perhaps they will not live up to others' expectations. Those kinds of fears can be subtle.

When he looked closer, Grant found there were fears. He was afraid of not appearing socially acceptable, so he went ahead and joined the country club, even though he couldn't afford it. He was so afraid of not being successful that he began to violate the ethics at work that he had so strongly defended. In his Christian life, he was so afraid of not appearing perfect, that he ended up putting demands on himself and his family that he would have called inexcusable if he had seen them evidenced in another family.

Grant recognized that God's peace could calm every one of his fears. God does not want you to live in fear but rather in the peace that only He can give. When Grant relinquished control of his life to God, he recognized that he had nothing to fear.

Help me have Your peace in my life today.

As soon as Jesus heard the word that was spoken,
He said to the ruler of the synagogue, "Do not be
afraid; only believe."
—MARK 5:36

For Clara, changing the faulty belief system that developed from her dysfunctional past was one of the most difficult parts of her recovery. Even though that belief system was creating an addiction to dieting that was controlling her life, even though those beliefs were costing her everything, even though they were creating an almost unbearable weight of guilt, it somehow seemed easier to live under the burden of the familiar rather than risk the unknown. After all, the old saying goes "my belief may not be right, but it's mine," and for Clara it was all she had. Even when it was violating her own values, it was easier than to risk possible failure.

Jesus' words seem so simple here, but there is a profound truth behind them. Only by believing in Him can the sources of our pain ever be addressed, but for those who have never trusted *anyone,* that can be an overwhelming task. Clara began to realize that in spite of what her fad diets were costing her, they still weren't providing her with what she wanted. She began to accept the unconditional love that God had for her, and by finding her value in Him, she saw that she not only did not have to be afraid of herself anymore, she did not have to be afraid of God either.

Lord, calm my fears as I put my trust in You.

There is no fear in love; but perfect love casts out fear, because fear involves torment. But he who fears has not been made perfect in love.

—1 JOHN 4:18

There was a song a while back that said "What the world needs now is love, sweet love." Ellen attempted to make that song the story of her life. She had felt so unloved in her childhood, she was determined not to ever be without love again, so she began a long series of destructive relationships. What she could not see was that it was not love that was motivating these relationships, but rather her fear—fear of rejection, being alone, abandonment—all the things she was never going to feel again. Those fears led her to do things she knew were wrong by simply trying to get her needs met. And when finally driven by her guilt to escape the current relationship, she ended up feeling alone, abandoned, rejected again. This was not perfect love.

Perfect love is the kind of love that Jesus demonstrated while He was here on earth. That love wasn't based on fear or expectation. God never forces or demands you to love Him to get His own needs met; rather, He simply loves you and allows you to make the decision to love Him back. When Ellen was able to experience that kind of unconditional love and recognize through His promises that He would never abandon her, then she was on the road to developing that perfect love in her life.

Lord, help me seek after Your perfect love for my life.

> *But if you have bitter envy and self-seeking in your*
> *hearts, do not boast and lie against the truth.*
> —JAMES 3:14

One of the things that often becomes difficult for people to see is how selfishness motivates their behavior. This is especially true in the area of values, for people always like to think they have the purest of motives behind all their actions. However, in any behavior you are engaged in, no matter how obsessed you are with it, you can always convince yourself of some positive motive and therefore justify yourself to those around you.

You must realize that your motives are not often as pure as you would like them to be. Many of the community service projects Jason was involved in were simply a means of having his own need for approval met. In the very act of trying to prove to the world how unselfish he was, he was being selfish. In order to help himself see this, each time he provided some "good" service for the community, he began to ask himself how it made him feel and identify what specific need it was meeting in his own life. Checking his motive was what finally allowed him to stop his compulsive helping.

_____

Father, help me see how my selfishness is motivating me to do things.

THE SOURCE OF SELFISHNESS – *October 8*

*Let nothing be done through selfish ambition or
conceit, but in lowliness of mind let each esteem
others better than himself.*　　　　—PHIL. 2:3

Margie was the least selfish person in the world. Or
so she thought. She worked long hours and sacrificed
many personal pleasures so her children could have
the best of everything—clothes, cars, a beautiful home.
If anyone needed a helping hand or a listening ear,
Margie was always right there. If a coworker had to go
to the dentist or needed to run an errand, all they had
to do was ask Margie—she would pick up the slack.

But Margie couldn't enjoy any of those things she
was involved in. When she came into counseling she
was tired, depressed, lonely. She felt totally unappreciated for all her hard work. "So how can I possibly be
selfish?" she asked.

The reason Margie was selfish was that she was not
doing all those things for all those people—she was doing them for Margie. In looking back, Margie began to
see that by never getting the approval she needed as a
child, she was driven to get it as an adult, except that
she could never get enough to offset that deficit. Only
by accepting God's approval for her life and identifying
what unmet needs her compulsive giving was attempting to fulfill, could she finally start enjoying what she
gave to others.

_____

*Help me, O Lord, to begin to see where my "selflessness" is really
"selfishness."*

A scoffer does not love one who reproves him,
Nor will he go to the wise.   —PROV. 15:12

Erica wanted perfection. She had spent her total energies and income creating a perfect world inside her apartment. To escape the shame of her childhood poverty, she had surrounded herself with the most expensive, exclusive possessions money could buy. Yet because she couldn't afford to eat and had to work longer hours to get more money, her health was in serious danger, but Erica chose not to see that. The price of her perfection was denial.

No one is immune to denial. Everyone has those behaviors or relationships that he has been involved with for so long that he doesn't have a true perspective on them. Allow yourself to be open to the wisdom of those around you, so you can see the areas where you are not only behaving in destructive ways but violating the very things you say you stand for. Erica's wall of denial finally began to come down when she was confronted by members of a support group she had been attending. Through their loving but firm confrontation, she was able to finally face the unmet needs she had been denying all along.

Lord, help me listen to those around me who want to help me.

Hypocrite! First remove the plank from your own eye, and then you will see clearly to remove the speck out of your brother's eye. —MATT. 7:5

I used to wear contact lenses, and one of the most aggravating things was to get a speck of dirt in my eye. My eye would water, my vision would become blurred, and the pain would cause me to be unable to focus clearly. No matter how I squinted or strained, until I got that piece of dust out of my eye, I was unable to see anything. In fact, once I got the speck out of my eye, it took a little time for my vision to clear enough to where my observation powers returned to normal.

Chad had blurred vision too, only it was with his emotional eyes. Because of the "plank" of self-centeredness in his life, not only was he unable to see the weaknesses in his own life, but he spent most of the time pointing out others' weaknesses to make himself look good. But it didn't make him feel any better because that self-centeredness was causing his pain. In order to finally be free from it, each time he found himself criticizing someone, he would stop and ask himself, "What am I trying to avoid facing in my life?" By answering that question, he could begin to remove that "plank" from his eye, and get a clearer perspective on his life.

Lord, make me aware of the behaviors in my life that are blocking my vision.

Even so you also outwardly appear righteous to men, but inside you are full of hypocrisy and lawlessness.
—MATT. 23:28

As I discuss the violation of values with people in counseling, I often share the opening of a story I once read. The setting was a southern Georgia town on a hot, sultry day after a long summer without rain. Several boys decided to go swimming in the local pond. As they approached the pond, everything on the surface was perfectly tranquil. But as the first boy swung out over the pond and hit the water, the whole pond began churning. As his horrified friends looked on, he struggled to get his head above water. He was only able to get out one word before he sank back to the bottom— "Snakes!" The pond was full of water moccasins.

While that is a startling story, it brings home a point. Perhaps on the outside you appear to be in perfect control—everything is tranquil. But underneath, you are churning with anger and resentment, and your need to be in control is your way of proving you do not have to face those issues. Let one unforeseen circumstance break the surface of that calm, and suddenly your whole life is churning with anger—violating every principle you propose to stand for. If that is your life, you need to stop pretending to be in control and begin identifying the sources of your anger that lie under that calm surface.

Help me look under the surface of my life.

Behold, God is my salvation,
I will trust and not be afraid;
"For YAH, the LORD, is my strength and my song;
He also has become my salvation."

—ISA. 12:2

One of the biggest motivators that lies behind the violation of values is fear. Often it is the basis behind anger, resentment, and even self-centeredness. On the outside there may be a tough exterior, but underneath lies a huge pool of fear. Natalie thought that she was involved in her charities and causes because she wanted to make a difference in the world. She viewed these avocations as a way for her to give of herself. But when she looked at what was behind her involvement, she saw that she became fearful each time one of these causes ended. She identified her fear of not being recognized or mattering to anyone as driving her to continue her addiction to causes.

When she became aware of this, she realized she needed to allow God to remove that fear. In fact, she saw it as a pool of fear, and each time she became afraid, she asked God to "drain" just a little more fear off the pool. She knew once that fear base was removed, the power it held in her life would be too.

Take away the base of fear that is driving my addictions, O Lord.

> *And He said to them, "You are those who justify*
> *yourselves before men, but God knows your hearts.*
> *For what is highly esteemed among men is an*
> *abomination in the sight of God."*
> —LUKE 16:15

So often in today's world, there is such a need to justify and prove one's worth to others. Larry soon found it was no longer enough to evaluate his strengths and weaknesses and base his potential on his character. He found that quantity had replaced quality as the ultimate criteria, and what he did was much more important than who he was. Given that kind of philosophy, it became less and less difficult to violate the values he held in order to achieve success in the marketplace. If success at any price was the battle cry, then the casualties of war were the principles of honesty and integrity that Larry had to violate in order to achieve his goals.

But God knows your heart. You can do all the justifying before others you want, but your beliefs cannot be something that you can sacrifice at the expense of gaining approval. Larry had to once again recognize that he answered to God for his life, and in His eyes, quality will always outweigh quantity, no matter what the situation. By placing his life back under God's control, he saw he no longer had any reason to try and live up to others' standards.

Lord, give me the courage not to sacrifice my beliefs simply to justify myself before others.

And whoever exalts himself will be abased, and he who humbles himself will be exalted.

—MATT. 23:12

Every year, Mark won all the top sales awards his company gave out. At the banquet each year when his name was announced, and he came to the podium to accept the award, you could almost anticipate what he would say. Usually he claimed that he never expected to win this award, and what an honor it was to be chosen, and then he would proceed with a litany of thank-yous to all the people who helped him along the way. His belief was that if he could make himself look more humble and unassuming, then he would be more deserving of the award, and his receipt of it would be more accepted in that community.

This grand show of self-humility was a ploy. In actuality, Mark was attempting to use this humility to gain others' approval so he could continue to build his ego where he needed it most. Mark needed to recognize that true humility establishes worth from God's perspective; it is not the kind of humility where he had to minimize himself in order to get people to like him. Rather, it is the humility that says, "I can love myself because God loves me."

Lord, help each of us recognize what true humility is.

For as the churning of milk produces butter,
And as wringing the nose produces blood,
So the forcing of wrath produces strife.
—PROV. 30:33

There are certain events in life that produce natural consequences. If milk is churned long enough, it will eventually turn to butter. If a person gets pummeled in the nose long enough, he will develop a nosebleed.

If you continue letting your anger out in unhealthy ways, sooner or later it will create problems in your life. If you have not gained control of your temper, it will cause trouble. Those individuals who are attempting to deal with their tempers must recognize how much unresolved anger contributes in developing and continuing some of their compulsive behaviors.

Jolene had such a need to always appear in control, she would deny her angry feelings until they would explode. Because of the unpredictability of those outbursts, her family began avoiding her and her boss was about to fire her. Jolene needed to see that her anger was fueled by her fear—fear of not being in control at all times. Once she identified that fear, through accepting God's forgiveness and worth, she saw she didn't have to be "perfect" anymore. Then the natural consequences of her anger could be controlled.

Lord, help me deal with the anger as it manifests itself in my life.

*For they bind heavy burdens, hard to bear, and lay
them on men's shoulders; but they themselves will
not move them with one of their fingers.*
—MATT. 23:4

People who are violating their own values often expect things from others that they would never do themselves. Dave gave a litany of all the things that his wife, Cindy, wasn't able to fulfill in their marriage relationship. When he was finished, I asked Dave if he thought his expectations were too high. He replied that he felt that they were not. I then questioned him as to how many of those expectations he would be willing to fulfill himself. After thinking a moment, he replied, "Not very many I suppose, but then those things are not my job."

Dave was missing the point. He was unwilling to recognize that he was violating his own value system by expecting more from her than he was willing to give himself. He was out to get his needs met at any cost, and if that contradicted his belief of what a true marriage involved, it was worth the price.

Dave had to recognize that he could not expect Cindy to do what he would not be willing to do himself. By asking himself "Would I do this?" he brought his expectations more in line with his beliefs.

Lord, help me see that what I expect of others I need to expect of myself as well.

In the day when God will judge the secrets of men
by Jesus Christ, according to my gospel.
—ROM. 2:16

Whatever personal values you are secretly violating by your addictive behaviors, you must recognize that God is aware of those behaviors and the motivations behind them. Ken got by with his addiction to pornography because he became an expert at denial, both to himself and to the people around him. He believed that because he kept to himself, and did not share his feelings or emotions with anyone, then no one could judge him on his behaviors. The more secretive he became, the more he was able to deny the reality of the situation, and the more attached he became to his hidden addiction.

Whatever secrets he had from his family and friends, and however he tried to fool himself, Ken had to recognize that God was not fooled. God was aware of how much Ken's life matched up to what he said he believed. God knows your actions as well as your thoughts, and if you give Him control of your life, He controls both. When Ken saw he could not fool God, he realized he could no longer fool himself. Once he acknowledged these behaviors, placed them under God's control, realizing if God knew about them anyway, then He could take care of them.

Help me realize, Father, that whatever secrets I am trying to keep,
You know them anyway.

9. GUILT

LOAD LIMIT – *October 18*

For my iniquities have gone over my head;
Like a heavy burden they are too heavy for me.
—PS. 38:4

How often have you seen a "load limit" sign on an elevator, on a highway, or on the side of a truck? The purpose of the load limit sign is to identify the maximum amount of weight that can be carried by that particular object. Any weight beyond that amount tends to put too much strain on the object and damage results. The longer those signs are ignored and those limits are exceeded, the more severe the damage will be. Finally, there comes a point where the burden is just too great, and the object begins to fall apart under the weight of the load it is carrying.

While there are no particular specifications for load limits in your own life, the burden that you carry around as a result of your painful past often exceeds the limits that your life was intended to bear. The impact may be subtle at first, but the weight of the burden begins to show wear. Eventually, there is a point where the burden becomes too heavy to bear, and you begin to crumble under the weight.

Are you exceeding the load limit of guilt? It is time to become fearlessly honest with yourself by admitting your guilt to yourself so you can begin observing the load limit signs in your life.

Help me, Lord, observe the load limits in my life.

Let us draw near with a true heart in full assurance of faith, having our hearts sprinkled from an evil conscience and our bodies washed with pure water.
—HEB. 10:22

In attempting to deal with addictive behaviors, the question to ask yourself is where those behaviors are leading you. Because of the great amount of guilt that he had, perfectionism led Clint away from the truth and into a pattern of trying to atone for his past mistakes. Because of the guilt he felt about all of his failures and inadequacies, he strove harder and harder to make up the difference, rather than allow God to take care of the guilt in his life. That led him further down the path of self-fulfillment which only led him further into his perfectionism.

Clint needed to allow the guilt in his life to draw him in a different direction. If he chose, it could lead to the Person who could truly begin to forgive his guilt, the One who has already paid for it—God Himself. Clint was able to see that he could never make up the difference for the faults in his life. The price that Jesus paid for him had already taken care of that. Understanding and accepting His forgiveness through studying God's Word gave him the assurance of eventually being able to lead a healthy, whole life.

Lord, allow my guilt to draw me toward You.

Wash me thoroughly from my iniquity,
And cleanse me from my sin.
—PS. 51:2

After working at some particular task that has gotten you all dirty and sweaty, there is nothing more refreshing than stepping into a hot shower to clean off. That water splashing down on you, rinsing away all that grime, is a great feeling, and no matter how tired you are from the efforts of the day, it has the power to revive you again. Stepping out of that shower, clean and refreshed, is exhilarating. You feel like a new person!

Laura thought, "Wouldn't it be great to feel washed clean on the inside like that?" For so many years, her compulsive work habits had allowed her to deny her guilt feelings. Emotionally, she had been covering them up, trying to fool herself. But she finally had to recognize that God wasn't fooled. He is not in the business of covering up. What He wants to do is help you be free of that guilt once and for all, just like that dirt going down the drain in the shower. He wants to take your life and scrub it clean. When she finally got the courage to admit her guilt to God and literally hand it over to Him for forgiveness once and for all, she felt as clean on the inside as a refreshing shower would make her feel.

_____

Father, allow Your love to wash me clean from all the iniquities I have.

> *For whoever shall keep the whole law, and yet stumble in one point, he is guilty of all.*
>
> —JAMES 2:10

Jake tried to fool himself into believing that because his compulsions were often in those areas classified as "good behaviors" such as church involvement, they really couldn't be that destructive. He tended to minimize the negative effects of these behaviors by blaming his family for not understanding how much time his church activities took. After all, he justified the cost by pointing to the results as being worth the price. "If something turns out good, how can it be bad for me?"

No matter how you try to sugarcoat it or deny the negative effects in your life, it is still wrong. Jake needed to realize the domino effect of the guilt—because he felt like he was losing his family, it made him feel more guilty which made him need to prove his worth all the more by being the best Sunday school teacher or the most faithful choir member. What Jake needed to admit before God was that he was guilty and incapable of doing it on his own. By admitting it to God, then allowing God to help him make amends to his family, he would no longer need to do his "good deeds" for the wrong reason.

Father, help me recognize what "good" things I am doing for not-so-good reasons.

For he who lacks these things is shortsighted, even to blindness, and has forgotten that he was purged from his old sins.
—2 PETER 1:9

One of the things everyone suffers from at some time or another is forgetfulness. The way I normally experience this is forgetting where I put the car keys. Usually this causes a minor inconvenience, but if I am in a hurry, it can turn into a major problem. I might also forget things that affect other people's lives, such as appointments or special events. This can lead to disappointment and hurt feelings and may hurt a relationship. No matter what it is I forget, though, it usually ends up costing me something. It may be time, it may be energy, it may even be relationships, but there is usually a price tag because of my forgetfulness.

One place my forgetfulness really does cost me is in my emotional life. As daily pressures build up and more demands are placed upon me, once again I feel the need to prove my worth to the world. The guilt of all my old failures and weaknesses surfaces. What I have forgotten is that God has forgiven me and that I don't have to allow that guilt to control me any longer. When those doubts and fears arise, claim God's power and remember that if you have trusted Christ, you don't have to feel guilty any longer.

Help me always remember that I am forgiven in You.

If we confess our sins, He is faithful and just to
forgive us our sins and to cleanse us from all
unrighteousness.
—1 JOHN 1:9

It is said that confession is good for the soul. While that may be true, confession serves a much greater purpose. If confession were simply good for you, like taking your vitamins, it would be something you could arbitrarily choose to do as you felt the need arise. It would be a ritualistic exercise that would simply be used for selfish whims to make you feel better when you were down.

However, Priscilla soon saw that confession had become another compulsion. It was through her study of God's Word that she began to understand true confession. True confession involved an understanding of who she was in God's eyes and that by herself she had no possible way to get rid of the guilt she felt. She also had to understand that God provided for guilt by providing His Son as the ultimate sacrifice, and that would take care of all the guilt she had, not just the guilt feelings. Guilt was avoidable to her for the asking, by simply accepting it as a gift. Priscilla began to recognize that confession was not just good for the soul, it was vital for her existence.

Lord, help me understand the need for confession.

I will return again to My place
Till they acknowledge their offense.
Then they will seek My face;
In their affliction they will diligently seek Me.
—HOS. 5:15

Why does it seem that as long as things are going well, people seem to forget the importance of acknowledging God's place in their lives? The better things were for Colleen, the less she seemed to need God and the more she tried to handle things on her own. Even when she began to recognize her old ways creeping back into her life, she tried to minimize it and would simply chalk it up to her human weakness. It was only when her addictions began to control her again, when her pain seemed to be getting out of control, when her guilt felt overwhelming, that she finally would turn back to God and remember what He had done for her.

Colleen needed to remember that God is available on a day-to-day basis. His forgiveness has not been designed just for those times of desperation, but to be used and appropriated as the need arises. The same forgiveness that can take away the mounds of guilt that have built up over the years can also have the power to forgive your sins on a daily basis. In fact, Colleen found that when she confessed her guilt and applied God's forgiveness at the moment it was needed, she never reached those points of desperation in her life.

Lord, help me not just wait for desperate times to allow Your forgiveness to work in my life.

> *The pains of death encompassed me,*
> *And the pangs of Sheol laid hold of me;*
> *I found trouble and sorrow.*
>
> —PS. 116:3

When Patrick finally came to that place in the cycle of addiction where his guilt seemed to overwhelm him, it was very frightening for him. At the point where he needed to be the strongest, it seemed that he was the least capable of fighting the battle. He began to look back over his life and recognize how much time and energy he had wasted, the incredible cost of his drive for success, and how little it had provided. It was then that the guilt started eating away at him and he felt defeated by his inability to relinquish the past.

Do you feel that you are at the very depths of despair in your life, that all your frantic efforts to gain your worth and improve yourself have been fruitless? Do you see a trail of ruined relationships and wasted time in your wake? Turn to the God who can forgive and forget that past. Once Patrick saw how God's power could change that old life into something new, he practiced the principle of endorsing himself. He gave himself permission to focus on the positive changes in his life such as his new ability to say no when he was tired. He reminded himself constantly of those changes. That new outlook changed his despair into great joy.

_____

Meet me today in my hour of need, O Lord.

*For godly sorrow produces repentance to salvation,
not to be regretted; but the sorrow of the world
produces death.*   —2 COR. 7:10

In discussing the nature of true repentance from guilt
with my patients, I often remind them of a scene in the
movie *Gone with the Wind*. After Scarlet O'Hara's second husband whom she really didn't love dies defend-
ing her honor, she gets drunk, hoping to remove the
pain of the guilt. When Rhett Butler comes to call, she
has to face him. She breaks down and begins pouring
out all of her false guilt and making rash promises
about changing. Mr. Butler laughs in her face, at which
she becomes irate. She questions why he doesn't believe her. His response is a classic. He says to her,
"Scarlet, you are not upset because you feel sorry; you
are upset because you got caught."

Like many individuals, Scarlet never learned to separate true guilt from false guilt. Guilt can be used as a
positive tool to help a person repent from selfish ways
instead of overreacting and setting up standards that
are too high. A person who truly feels repentant, will
admit her mistakes, ask God to forgive her, and with
His help slowly begin making those changes that will
lead her to a healthier life-style.

Lord, help me have true sorrow over the guilt in my life.

Behold, the former things have come to pass,
And new things I declare;
Before they spring forth I tell you of them.
—ISA. 42:9

It was amazing for Troy to understand that God not only wanted to remove the guilt from his life, He also wanted to replace it with a new life-style. God's ability to remove the guilt was enough for Troy. But Troy learned through His Word exactly what he could expect when he turned his life over to Him. He promised unconditional love and worth that allowed Troy to give himself permission to take care of himself and not overwork himself. God took away those negative messages and replaced them with the hope and assurance needed for making competent decisions such as how much time he could spend at the office. He learned that no matter where he was, God would always be with him, to help him reinforce his new boundaries of not working past six o'clock. In God's plan, getting rid of the guilt is just the first step—there is a whole new life-style to embrace.

_____

Lord, help me recognize that removing the guilt is only the beginning of what You have for me.

Then I will give them one heart, and I will put a new spirit within them, and take the stony heart out of their flesh, and give them a heart of flesh.
—EZEK. 11:19

I recall as a young child what a major news event it was when Dr. Christiaan Barnard performed the first heart transplant. It seemed almost inconceivable that a doctor could take a living heart from one body, place it in another individual, and that person would go on functioning for many years. This was moving a vital organ from one person to another and expecting it to function just like it did the first time. That person had been given a second chance on life for they would surely have died without the new heart. Since that first operation, hundreds of people have been given the opportunity to live longer healthier lives because of this miraculous procedure.

Yet, that is exactly the kind of operation that God has been performing throughout history. When Aaron finally realized that all of his driven efforts to be a perfect father and husband were not making him feel any better, he had to admit he could not do it on his own. By depending on God's gift of salvation to pay for all his guilt and turning that guilt over to God, He placed within Aaron a new heart. That new heart allowed Aaron to finally forgive himself, and he eventually learned how to love and forgive others.

Transplant your guilty heart with God's heart of love today.

"For though you wash yourself with lye,
and use much soap,
Yet your iniquity is marked before Me,"
says the Lord GOD.
—JER. 2:22

What kind of "soap" are you using to rid yourself of guilt today? Stew used an exercise of listing the "brands of soap" with which he was trying to clean up his life. One "brand" was his need to be involved in several community organizations in order to clean up his unworthiness. Another "brand" was his perfectionism which he used to wash away his past failures and weaknesses. A third "brand" was his drive for success in his business to remove all the negative messages about not amounting to much. When Stew identified all these, I asked him how they were doing in their job of cleaning him up. He responded that not only were they not making him feel clean, but the more he "scrubbed" with them, the more he saw how "unclean" he was.

What Stew needed to do was change his brand of soap. God has provided the cleansing agent through Christ's death on the cross, and it is strong enough to wash away anything your life would produce. When Stew chose to allow God to wash his life, he saw that the other brands were of no further use to him, so he could pitch them forever.

―――――

Father, please help me allow Your love and forgiveness to cleanse my guilt today.

*Therefore, if anyone is in Christ, he is a new
creation; old things have passed away; behold,
all things have become new.*   —2 COR. 5:17

Teresa sat crying in my office. "It is so hopeless," she said. "It seems like everything I've touched in my life has fallen apart. I have made a mess of everything, and there is nothing I can do to change it." After several moments of silence, she lifted her head and quietly said, "If only I could start all over again, if only I had another chance to do it right."

Looking back at the past, many people feel the same way. They see all of their failures, all of their mistakes, and feel the weight of the guilt of things they have done, and wish there was some way they could just stop it all and start over again.

That alternative *is* possible, even for Teresa. Of course, her first step was to confess her failures to God and allow Him to do for her what she couldn't do for herself—forgive her past. Once she accepted that, she could make amends to all the individuals she had hurt through her destructive relationships. She contacted all those individuals, admitted she had caused them pain, let them know how sorry she was, and put the relationship back in its proper perspective. In this way, she really was starting all over again.

Lord, come into my life and make me the new creature that You want me to be.

And have put on the new man who is renewed in knowledge according to the image of Him who created him.

—COL. 3:10

In dealing with the guilt in his life, one of the important things Bud began working on was changing the negative messages he believed about himself. Because these messages were so ingrained, and he had been repeating them to himself for so long, they were very difficult to remove. The more he repeated them, the more he believed them, and because he was only viewing himself from his skewed perspective, the more their supposed "truth" made him feel guilty. This cycle fed on itself, and drove him deeper and deeper into his drive for proving himself.

Bud needed to break out of this cycle with a brand new perspective of himself. The only way he could gain this new perspective was to get a different viewpoint. He found three sources for that new view. First, he began to study God's Word each day to learn the worth and value that God found in him. Second, he developed a close relationship with a friend who listened to and nurtured him without judgment. Third, he joined a support group that helped him see he was not unique in his weaknesses or his struggle. Bud soon saw that he wasn't the person his faulty perception had told him he was.

Father, help me use the knowledge You have given me in Your Word to begin dealing with the guilt in my life.

*Be kind to one another, tenderhearted, forgiving
one another, just as God in Christ also forgave you.*
—EPH. 4:32

One thing that guilt often does is cause you to act in
negative ways toward the people around you. Elaine
grew up with no support from anyone in her family, so
whatever she got in life was something she had earned
on her own. Whenever she had to deal with other people, she made sure to gain whatever advantage she
could over them, even if it meant making herself feel
better at their expense. Often that caused guilty feelings, but that guilt only fed her low self-esteem and
caused her to excuse her one-upmanship because of
their stupidity, as if to justify her own negative behaviors.

Elaine had to become aware of how that guilt in her
life was spilling over to other people and how negative
her treatment was of them. She started to allow God's
forgiveness to become evident in her life, so that forgiveness could spill over into the lives of other people.
Elaine recognized that she was taking out her tensions
on others in her life. She saw that if she truly had accepted the flaws in her life and those in her family, she
could forgive the weaknesses in those around her as
well.

*Lord, help the forgiveness I feel in my life through You touch those
people around me.*

Therefore, as the elect of God, holy and beloved, put on tender mercies, kindness, humbleness of mind, meekness, longsuffering. —COL. 3:12

I don't understand it," Byron said. "I've been coming to counseling for over a year now, and I've come such a long way. I've looked at my past, identified negative messages and emotional pain, made great strides in breaking my addictions. I've even sorted out the true and false guilt I've been carrying around. I turned over control of my life to God several months ago, and it did make a difference. But it seems that all those qualities I want just aren't happening. Now I'm feeling guilty again. What am I doing wrong?"

While all these characteristics are available, Byron had to understand that they do not flow naturally from our lives. Notice that this verse says to "put on" these qualities. The idea is that in order to demonstrate these qualities, there has to be a continual active choice on the part of the individual to behave this way. What helped Byron in making this choice was to understand that when God forgave him and removed his guilt and replaced it with His love and worth, then he could begin to choose to demonstrate these qualities without the feeling that he was doing it somehow to look good. It was up to Byron to make that choice daily so those qualities could continue to be seen in his life.

Father, help me daily choose to demonstrate Your love in my life.

For God will bring every work into judgment,
Including every secret thing,
Whether it is good or whether it is evil.
—ECCL. 12:14

There's a saying in recovery that states, "You are only as sick as your secrets." Unless you are continually willing to be honest before God, your guilt has the capability of placing you right back on the cycle of addiction.

Sabrina had been progressing through her recovery slowly but consistently. She had seen many positive changes in her life. She was really getting a handle on her need to "buy" herself the love that her father never gave her. Then she started becoming more guarded in her sessions and missed several in a row. When she finally returned, she made a confession—she had begun a relationship with a married man and by not dealing with it right away, the guilt brought back all the old feelings of unworthiness, shame, and compensations which only made her feel more guilty.

Sabrina needed to recognize that disposing of guilt is an ongoing process. She needed to address the true guilt of the illicit relationship by breaking it off and the false guilt of being unlovable by handing it back to her father. By continually assessing the guilt in her life, she never needed to be victimized by it again.

Lord, help me willingly deal with the guilt in my life.

> *"Only acknowledge your iniquity,*
> *That you have transgressed against the LORD your*
>   *God,*
> *And have scattered your charms*
> *To alien deities under every green tree,*
> *And you have not obeyed My voice," says the LORD.*
> —JER. 3:13

Mitch was tired of hiding his guilt. All the effort and energy spent on his drive toward success over the years had worn him out, and he saw the destruction it had produced in his life. His wife had left him, he had no contact with his children, but still he kept trying to pretend that everything was OK by losing himself in his work. Then the day came when his boss informed him that he was being let go—he wasn't functioning up to his potential. Not only was Mitch emotionally devastated, but the very thing in life he had used as a cover for his guilt was now the cause of it.

In order to begin facing his addiction to work, Mitch finally had to take the step of acknowledging his guilt. He first admitted it to God, recognizing that while he wasn't unique in his guilt, he still needed God's forgiveness to take it away. He then admitted it to himself by writing out all the ways he had wronged himself, his family, and God. By developing this personal honesty, he gained the courage to take the third step and acknowledge his wrongs to a friend. By admitting his guilt, there finally came that sense of relief for which he had been searching.

————————

Help me acknowledge my guilt to You today, O God.

You are already clean because of the word which I have spoken to you.
                                        —JOHN 15:3

Have you ever decided to help somebody out by doing some special task for them, working hard to make sure it is done as thoroughly and efficiently as possible, only to have them respond "Well, thank you very much, but this particular assignment has already been done"? There is hardly a more frustrating feeling in the world. You feel all your time and energy has been wasted, that all your good intentions are for nothing, and, in fact, you may feel silly for even making the attempt.

Julie was trying to get rid of the guilt in her life by being the perfect mother with the goal that if she could somehow make her children's lives better than hers, she would finally be free of the guilt she felt from divorcing their father. Removal of guilt through perfectionistic behaviors was really a waste of time. Not only could Julie never achieve it, but it has already been accomplished anyway so there was no point in her trying to do it again. Rather, she needed to accept God's forgiveness of guilt in her life and use her time and energies productively by making amends to her ex-husband and children.

Lord, help me not to waste any more energy trying to do something that You have already done for me.

And do not be conformed to this world, but be transformed by the renewing of your mind, that you may prove what is that good and acceptable and perfect will of God.
—ROM. 12:2

In dealing with guilt feelings, you must allow God to begin changing the negative messages you often believe. As Casey initially committed his life to God, God began to change Casey's distorted earthly thoughts to messages that reflected His love. But, as Casey began to face new situations on a day-to-day basis, guilt once again entered his life and drove him to negative behavior patterns. Because guilt always has the possibility of returning, you continually must allow God to renew your mind and scrutinize your thinking process.

The idea of allowing God to renew your mind can be compared to renewing a magazine subscription. Initially you subscribe to the magazine in order to begin receiving it. Periodically, when that subscription runs out, you renew it. While God's love never runs out, sometimes your own negative thinking can get in the way, and you must periodically ask Him to renew your mind to allow His love and grace to control you. Once Casey started making this renewal a daily practice in his life, his behaviors consistently began to reflect the new thinking that God placed in his mind.

Lord, let me allow You to continually be renewing my mind.

Repent therefore and be converted, that your sins may be blotted out, so that times of refreshing may come from the presence of the Lord.

—ACTS 3:19

Repentance is something that God calls you to do. But it is not an easy task. As Nina began to come to terms with the false guilt in her life, she was able to realize that there was nothing she could do to ever meet the unfulfilled needs of acceptance and approval she had felt. She was able slowly to turn over her needs to God and stop using superficial sexual relationships to meet those needs.

She saw that in order to finally put her sexual addiction behind her, it was not enough to say "I know God can forgive me" and continue to behave as if nothing had changed. She had to make amends. This involved two steps for Nina. First, she needed to express her regret and sorrow over her past behavior to those individuals she had hurt. But in some cases, she had to take a further step of acting on that repentance by breaking off those relationships in which she still felt vulnerable. Though it was a difficult and painful step, it allowed her the opportunity to be truly free from her guilt.

Father, help me see that true repentance is true freedom.

He will again have compassion on us,
And will subdue our iniquities.
You will cast all our sins
Into the depths of the sea.

—MIC. 7:19

Crystal believed that she had done too much to be forgiven. When she thought of a holy God having that kind of concern for an individual like her, her human response was to feel more guilty and more isolated than she had before. She knew that no matter how desperately she tried, she would never match up to God's perfect standard. How could He accept her, if she couldn't even accept herself?

That is where the compassion of God comes in. Not only does He love you with a love you will never understand, but He loves, knowing full well what your life is like. And the greatest part of His love is that He doesn't just promise to make you feel better about your life, He actually promises to remove that guilt. When Crystal began to experience God's compassion in her life, she saw that she too could have compassion for herself. She began to start each day by thanking God for His compassion and then promising to take care of herself since she was so special to Him.

Father, help me take advantage of the compassion You want to show me in my life today.

Even in laughter the heart may sorrow,
And the end of mirth may be grief.
—PROV. 14:13

Ron had a sexual addiction which had been created by some severe emotional and sexual abuses in his early life. However, whenever we began exploring specific instances that occurred in his life, he would begin giggling. Initially, I thought this was perhaps just a response to the embarrassment of discussing the particular situation. But as our counseling progressed, I became more aware that this laughter was in fact a defense mechanism to help him deal with the guilt. The laughter allowed him to carry around this false guilt for many years, and it ended up nearly destroying his life by creating a sexual addiction which he found very difficult to break.

By doing an inventory of his guilt, Ron was able to separate the false guilt he felt because of the abuse from his mother, from the true guilt he felt toward his addiction. In the process, he was able to give his false guilt back to his mother and his true guilt over to God. He was also able to finally remove that mask of laughter that he had been hiding behind all these years. What mask are you using to hide your guilt?

Father, help me recognize where I am hiding guilt in my life.

> *But in a great house there are not only vessels of gold and silver, but also of wood and clay, some for honor and some for dishonor. Therefore if anyone cleanses himself from the latter, he will be a vessel for honor, sanctified and useful for the Master, prepared for every good work.*
>
> —2 TIM. 2:20–21

Louann had a need to feel useful and that had created much of the guilt in her life. Whenever she saw a job at church that needed done, she would volunteer her services. Then she began to feel taken advantage of as more and more would be demanded of her. She would end up resenting the job or quitting altogether. She saw this as failure because she couldn't do everything, and the more failure she felt, the more guilt was created. Rather than feeling useful, she felt useless.

In order to become the useful person she desired to be, Louann had to begin setting boundaries for herself. By identifying her strengths and weaknesses and turning them all over to God, she began to see her worth in Him because He accepted her as she was. Once she began to see she no longer had to feel guilty because of her limitations nor prove her worth by her activities, she could set boundaries for her church work that not only allowed her to be useful but removed the guilt from saying no.

Lord, help me be useful today.

The LORD is righteous in all His ways,
Gracious in all His works.
The LORD is near to all who call upon Him,
To all who call upon Him in truth.
—PS. 145:17–18

When Beth began to think about the holiness and righteousness of God and look at her life in comparison with all her guilt and failures, it was intimidating. She began to develop the idea that because she was so guilty and God is so perfect, the last person He would be interested in was her. She felt that however much God might provide for her, He must be very far away, for He would not want to be anywhere near the kind of person that would have all that shame in her life. That was the way she felt her family treated her, so her guilty conscience led her further from God.

When, through long hours of counseling, Beth finally made the decision to believe that God would always be with her, she found Him near her whenever she would read His Word and meditate on its truths. She started attending church and found that she could sense His presence in the music, the preaching, and the fellowship. She joined a support group, and heard His voice minister through other people as they spoke of their own struggles. And, perhaps most importantly, she found that whenever the guilt and shame began to attack her again, He was only a prayer away.

Father, thank You for Your availability in my life.

Part 3

RECOVERY

Do you not know that those who run in a race all run, but one receives the prize? Run in such a way that you may obtain it. —1 COR. 9:24

Everyone needs something to look forward to. Whether it is a special event or a completed project, or even a ten-minute coffee break, people like to keep looking toward those positive things that they hope will happen in the future. It is the promise of those things that keeps you motivated, that keeps you working toward those goals you have set for yourself.

This is also true in the recovery process. You try to set goals for your life in order to feel a sense of achievement and have something to work toward. When you meet those goals, you congratulate yourself and begin setting new goals to further your recovery. Whatever those goals are, they help reinforce that you are on the right track and that your efforts are worth the time spent.

As you begin to set your goals for recovery, take time to look at what it is you want to accomplish. Determine from which things you need to be free forever and which behaviors you simply will need to balance. Most importantly, spend time with the Lord to see what type of person He wants you to be. Since He made you, He understands more than anyone what is best for you.

Lord, help me continue to work toward those goals that You have set before me.

Therefore we make it our aim, whether present or absent, to be well pleasing to Him.

—2 COR. 5:9

In trying so hard for so long to please everybody else around her, Josie never felt that she had ever achieved that goal. It was hard to imagine that she could actually do something that someone would find acceptable, let alone God. Yet she had learned through her counseling that it was important to accept God's approval, and this included her recovery goals.

Josie decided to set particular benchmarks along her recovery, and as she achieved each of those, she would give herself some small reward, not only to reinforce her success, but to remind her that God was also pleased with her efforts. Whenever she was able to go for one week without buying anything other than her essential needs, she could reward herself by permitting herself to purchase one item under five dollars strictly for her enjoyment. She would also document the success in her recovery notebook and thank God for helping her achieve her success.

This did not mean that Josie never failed. But she learned that God forgives and always was willing to help her get started toward her goal again.

Lord, help me see that I can please You in my life.

Free, yet not using your liberty as a cloak for vice, but as servants of God. —1 PETER 2:16

One of the exciting things Hope discovered in her recovery was that she could actually feel free. Of course, that was what she had been looking for, but she had decided long ago that it would never come. In fact, what she had done was trade in her freedom on the security of her home and family. If she could not experience that freedom she was looking for, at least she could find her identity by becoming the perfect wife and mother. Security actually became her escape, and any spontaneity she might have felt was quickly put down because that might upset her perfect control.

By giving up your control and placing it in God's hands, He offers you the balance of security and spontaneity. His love is strong enough to hold you to Him, yet flexible enough to allow you to be yourself. When Hope began to see that she could be secure and spontaneous at the same time, she gladly traded control of her life for the privilege of feeling free. By allowing herself permission to express her individuality, she found herself more secure in God's love than her control ever provided her.

Lord, help me see that I can be secure and free with Your love.

> *Then Samuel spoke to all the house of Israel,*
> *saying, "If you return to the LORD with all your*
> *hearts, then put away the foreign gods and the*
> *Ashtoreths from among you, and prepare your*
> *hearts for the LORD, and serve Him only; and He*
> *will deliver you from the hand of the Philistines."*
> —1 SAM. 7:3

During recovery, there will be outside forces against you. In this verse, Samuel gave the children of Israel the prescription for how to be delivered from their enemies. That same prescription is just as practical today.

First, you willingly choose to stop what you are doing and change the direction of your life by committing yourself to God.

Second, in order to commit yourself to God completely, you must remove all other gods from your life. Whatever addiction you have been using as a substitute for meeting the needs that God desires to meet in your life, that is the thing that you must be willing to get rid of.

Third, allow God to change your attitudes and thoughts about yourself and the relationships around you. This involves setting goals, giving yourself permission, enforcing boundaries, and developing accountability.

Fourth, you must be willing to do whatever He asks you to do in your recovery process. It may be painful, it may be costly, and you may not always immediately see the reward, but trusting Him is the basis for handling whatever circumstance develops.

Help me, Father, to apply these principles in my life today.

Commit your works to the LORD,
And your thoughts will be established.
—PROV. 16:3

One of the things I can remember as a child was going on family vacations. I can remember all the anticipation leading up to the day we would leave, then everyone piling in the car for that journey to a new and exciting place. But one of the things that I also remember about starting the journey was that just before we pulled out of the driveway, my father would always ask one of us to pray and ask for God's guidance and protection on our trip. That was always a very comforting thing for me because it helped me realize that God was in control of our journey and that whatever happened would be in His plan for us.

You need to apply that same principle to your journey into recovery. Commit your journey to the Lord, and ask for His protection and guidance along the way. This is something that needs to be done each day because each day will bring its own difficulties. When you take that time in prayer, you can rest in the knowledge that no matter what you encounter along the way, He is aware of it and has allowed it in your life. In that way you can have the reassurance that the recovery process will be a productive journey.

Lord, help me commit today's journey to You.

> *I press toward the goal for the prize of the upward
> call of God in Christ Jesus.* —PHIL. 3:14

Goals are an important part of the recovery process. Once you have become aware of the unmet needs in your life, recognized their sources in your past, committed yourself to working on the issues with God's help, then you must begin setting personal goals. These goals allow you to address specific behaviors so that as one area of your life is dealt with, you can move on to another. It also is a great reinforcement to be able to chalk off the specific goals you have set as you are able to complete the tasks.

For Warren, setting specific goals was a difficult process. He had always allowed others around him to more or less dictate his direction in life. Now he needed to commit himself to his own goals. His first goal was to set boundaries on his relationships. He set specific time limits as to how late he would stay at a friend's house and limited the number of visits each week. And as part of his goal, he set a priority of spending one-half hour each day developing his relationship with God through prayer and Bible study since that was one relationship he needed to help him with his other goals.

Lord, help me set my goals in recovery.

Let your heart therefore be loyal to the LORD our God, to walk in His statutes and keep His commandments, as at this day.

—1 KINGS 8:61

I have a friend who once lived in a university town that supported a great football team. Whenever I would go to visit him on a fall weekend, I had no doubt what would be in store. From the time I arrived in town on Friday night, the conversation started about the team's record. When we got up on Saturday morning, the pre-game show would be on the radio, so we could listen to it as we got ready. Of course, he had to wear the appropriate colors and take all the appropriate paraphernalia to show support. And no matter how the team performed that day, his focus would be on the way they could improve for next time. There was no mistaking his loyalty.

You must develop that same kind of loyalty to the moral and spiritual values of God. Al told me, "By recognizing the values that God has for me, I am able to rise above the day-to-day trials that my addictions used to make me fear." By holding to those values, Al was able to focus more on the good "plays" he had made that day, and how he could improve the ones that weren't so good. By developing those values, God not only became a way to solve those problems, but those problems became a way to get close to God.

Lord, help me today be loyal to Your values.

For the eyes of the LORD run to and fro throughout the whole earth, to show Himself strong on behalf of those whose heart is loyal to Him.
—2 CHRON. 16:9

As Sandy began to turn more and more of her life over to God, she sometimes felt that perhaps she was asking too much of Him. The negative messages she received from past relationships often led her to believe she was demanding and expecting too much and perhaps she should back off before she inevitably got hurt. Sandy had difficulty believing there was Someone who would want to help her out, who cared enough about her to listen to her needs and meet them wholly and completely even when she had failed so much.

It is perfectly acceptable for you to come to God with your needs. He is actually searching for those who are willing to come to Him and allow Him to work in their lives. The more personal that relationship is, the less chance there will be for insecurity to lead you back to your addictive behaviors. And like Sandy, you need to realize that God is the only perfect One in the relationship anyway so if He can accept your weaknesses and imperfections and still desire that relationship, then you must desire it as well.

Lord, help me respond to Your desire to be in my life today.

Create in me a clean heart, O God,
And renew a steadfast spirit within me.
—PS. 51:10

When Jessica finally got to the place of recovery, she found there were two ways God wanted to help her with the recovery process. The first thing He wanted to do was give her a new start in her life. When she committed her life to Him and confessed her sins and asked for His forgiveness, He started her out with a brand new life. This new life was no longer controlled by her dysfunctional past but was a life in which she was free to make the positive choices that would lead her toward health. This was so different from the dependence on her own successes to determine her worth, since that was so unstable and unpredictable.

Once He began this process, however, He didn't get it started and then leave her on her own. He also wants to be actively involved in the day-to-day progress of Jessica's life. He desires to continue to renew the promises that He gave to her and in new and exciting ways, demonstrate how complete His love is. God recognizes that recovery is not an event but rather a process and He promises to give you help along every step of the way. That's why Jessica set aside time each day to read His Word and pray for His guidance in her decisions.

Lord, help me accept Your power in my life wherever I am in my recovery.

> *But those who wait on the Lord*
> *Shall renew their strength;*
> *They shall mount up with wings like eagles,*
> *They shall run and not be weary,*
> *They shall walk and not faint.*
>
> —ISA. 40:31

One of the most difficult parts of the recovery process is to wait for God's timetable in your life. Often, in your drivenness you want to rush in and complete the recovery process as quickly as possible. But God has lessons for you to learn along the way, to teach you balance in life.

Notice that in this verse, God identifies three possible places where you may be in your recovery process. At times you may have a major breakthrough, and feel like you are soaring above the clouds, like eagles. There may be times in the process when there is no exceptional task to be completed but rather you are working daily through your negative beliefs, moving along at a fairly good pace. However, there are other times when it is all you can do to walk from one hour to the next because of the intensity of the struggle. Wherever you are in your recovery process, God has promised to renew your strength so you may be able to fight the difficulties and emotions you are dealing with at any time. So claim that promise today. Whether you are flying, running, or walking, God's strength is available to you.

Wherever I am in my recovery, Lord, give me the strength to go on.

You are wearied in the length of your way;
Yet you did not say, "There is no hope."
You have found the life of your hand;
Therefore you were not grieved.
—ISA. 57:10

When Don first began dealing with his addictive behaviors there was a great deal of energy and motivation to finally begin the tasks he had been putting off for so long. As is usually inevitable in recovery, there is a weariness that sets in. In fact, Don came in my office one day and said, "If I had known that it was going to be this long and this difficult, I don't know that I would have started at all. I just feel like I need a break." It is a long and difficult task and if there is no relief, discouragement sets in to the point that sometimes it begins to hinder progress.

Don had to realize that he could not become compulsive about his recovery too. The times of struggle and effort need to be balanced by times of rest and relaxation. Don took up tennis, and while he realized he was susceptible to becoming addicted, he dealt with that up front by limiting himself to three hours a week. Don found that it not only gave him a rest but allowed him to be more energized when he did work on his recovery. So if you are at the point of weariness today, do not lose hope. Just take a break.

Lord, give me Your strength in my weariness.

*When the kindness and the love of God our
Savior toward man appeared, not by works of
righteousness which we have done, but according
to His mercy He saved us, through the washing of
regeneration and renewing of the Holy Spirit.*
—TITUS 3:4–5

In the recovery process, an individual needs to be careful of falling back on negative thinking patterns. As Toni began to make progress and rely on God's power to help her deal with her workaholism, she was able to see that she was capable of making positive decisions about her life. As she made these decisions and started seeing the effects, there was a tendency once again toward feeling that these positive decisions were earning approval in her life. Because she never felt good about anything she had ever done before, that positive feedback became addictive too, and Toni began to count on her own strength to face the issues in her life.

It is God's power working in you that allows you to make healthy decisions. His forgiveness of the guilt in your life and His love in meeting your emotional needs are what provides you the worth and security for making good decisions. Each time Toni made a positive choice for her life, she began taking the time to immediately stop whatever she was doing and thank God for helping her once again. That way, she never allowed herself to forget His power.

Lord, help me never forget that it is through You I can recover from my addictive behaviors.

Therefore we do not lose heart. Even though our outward man is perishing, yet the inward man is being renewed day by day. —2 COR. 4:16

You have learned how outward appearance can be deceiving. While the outward appearance of your life may seem to be together, inside it can be falling apart as a result of your negative beliefs and unmet emotional needs. However, in the recovery process, often the reverse is true.

Because Kent stopped his speculative investing and discontinued his long-term relationships with those brokers, it seemed outwardly that he was losing everything important to him.

While Kent was giving up all those external things he had been selfishly using to meet his needs, inside he was allowing God to start meeting those needs. God was helping Kent recognize those things he could live without, which allowed Kent to continue setting boundaries. Although externally the changes may not be seen right away, inside He is working to change you so your relationships and behaviors will eventually reflect His love and power working inside your life. If God is working on your inward self, then recovery is indeed taking place.

Lord, help me not focus on what is happening outside my life but what You are doing inside to make me more like You.

> *As iron sharpens iron,*
> *So a man sharpens the countenance*
> *of his friend.*   —PROV. 27:17

In the recovery process it is important to develop accountability in your relationships. These are not the kinds of relationships you had in the past where you either totally depended on others to meet your needs or they totally depended on you to meet theirs. Those all-or-none relationships were destructive and need to be thoroughly examined and reevaluated as a part of the recovery process.

The type of relationships that God wants in your life involve those friends who can help in the recovery process. What kind of characteristics do you look for? You need an individual who will be honest with you, who will encourage you when you need it, and who will take the time to journey with you down that road to recovery. That friend must be aware of the struggles you face so he or she can help you become aware of possible negative situations you may not be able to see objectively. Those are the friends who spur each other on to the healthier lives that God encourages you to find and keep. Look for that person today and begin to allow him or her to share in your recovery.

Lord, bring those relationships into my life that would help me in my recovery.

For our light affliction, which is but for a moment, is working for us a far more exceeding and eternal weight of glory. —2 COR. 4:17

One of the problems that goes along with recovery is a very limited perspective. Because survival was her main concern, Jan was only able to recognize how a particular event affected her in the present. Whenever she began feeling pain, her only goal at that point was to relieve that pain as quickly as possible. It was that desperation that led her to her compulsive spending. And even in her recovery, it often led her to a sense of panic.

You must take your eyes off what is happening in the present and begin to trust God for what He is going to do in the future as a result of the situation happening right now. Focus more on the eternal aspect of your life and realize that the pain and suffering of your recovery is not very long when compared with eternity. Each time Jan faced a painful situation, she reminded herself that God has already secured her future so she had nothing to worry about. The more eternal her perspective became, the more she was able to deal with the afflictions that she suffered each day.

Help me, Lord, gain a more eternal perspective of my life.

*May He grant you according to
your heart's desire,
And fulfill all your purpose.*
—PS. 20:4

As you commit your life to God in the recovery process, one of the things you begin to understand about Him is how much He wants to meet the desires in your life. Susan had been confronting the negative messages from her past, and she had recognized how distorted her concept of God was. She limited herself in how much time she spent on her painting, realizing that it had become the god she had been searching for all along. But even as her God-concept changed and became healthier, often she still did not feel she had the right to ask God for the things she wanted in her life. Guilt still reared its ugly head, and she assumed that because of all that God had already done for her, she had no right to come to Him with her requests.

Unlike the limited fulfillment of Susan's painting, there is no limit on how many of your needs God can meet. In fact, in order to help her see the extent to which He could help her, Susan set as one of her goals specifically to ask for one thing each day. When she saw that need met, she wrote it down, and as that list lengthened, she discovered that no matter what the need, she could ask.

---

*Help me understand, Father, that You want to meet all the needs in
my life.*

The counsel of the LORD stands forever,
The plans of His heart to all generations.
—PS. 33:11

As you move along in recovery, you will begin to see how unchanging God's principles are. In Clarence's life, because of the instability of living with an alcoholic father whose mood was totally unpredictable, nothing was ever permanent. Clarence's own belief system continually changed to suit the purpose of avoiding pain and gaining approval and even his relationships were kept only as long as they were fulfilling a need in his life. Change became the norm, and no attitude or action was indispensable.

That is why God's Word was the only source of stability that Clarence ever found. The principles are eternal, and they are not subject to change because of the circumstances or situations that may surround them. God has been giving the same love, the same worth, and the same forgiveness to individuals as long as mankind has existed, and will continue to do so through eternity. These principles have always worked in the past, and that gave Clarence the guarantee that they would continue working for him. He derived great comfort knowing he would not wake up the next morning and find a different set of rules. God's plan for recovery always remains the same, and you can always count on Him to be all He promises to be.

Lord, thank You for the unchangeableness of Your plan.

*We then who are strong ought to bear with the
scruples of the weak, and not to please ourselves.*
—ROM. 15:1

As you become more involved in the recovery process, it is important to examine the basis for your relationships and examine them carefully. Often your
unmet emotional needs can lead you into situations
that are as unhealthy for you as they are for the other
individuals. However, you also must understand that
you cannot abandon or reject all other people in your
life. It is important to have others to share with, to help
you get up when you stumble and fall, and to encourage you when you are heading in the right direction.
God created the church for people to be available to
each other in those times they need a friend with
whom to share and pray.

In developing those healthy relationships, there are
basically three individuals who you need to find. You
need someone to look up to, to give you guidance and
encouragement and wisdom in your life; you need
someone to walk along beside you to share in your
everyday trials and tribulations; and you need someone you can reach out to and help by sharing the experiences of your own life to disciple along in his or her
growth. If you use these kinds of criteria for developing relationships, then your friendships will truly be
productive.

_____

Lord, help me choose relationships that would aid me in my recovery.

No temptation has overtaken you except such as is common to man; but God is faithful, who will not allow you to be tempted beyond what you are able, but with the temptation will also make the way of escape, that you may be able to bear it.

—1 COR. 10:13

The road to recovery is a struggle. Many times it will seem that you take three steps forward followed by two steps back. There is always the possibility of lapsing back into those behavior patterns when certain situations create painful memories.

Shawn found that each time he felt he had turned the corner in setting limits on his work, his boss would come in with some new project and Shawn's need to be over-involved would rush back in. Each time this happened, Shawn felt trapped because he knew the decision he needed to make but felt too weak to make it. In making his contract with himself for setting boundaries on work, he realized that part of that contract would involve turning to God and asking His guidance before he ever listened to or looked at the proposal. That way, if he said no, he realized that it would be God's way of allowing him a way of escape, and he could be satisfied with his decision.

God has not promised that He will make the road easy for you. What He has promised, however, is that there is nothing that will come your way that He cannot help you say "no" to.

Lord, thank You for providing those ways of escape in those times of trials.

*Bearing with one another, and forgiving one
another, if anyone has a complaint against another;
even as Christ forgave you, so you also must do.*
—COL. 3:13

Forgiveness is an integral part of the recovery process. Hope's first step of forgiveness was to see how she had been hanging on to the past and was using the verbal abuse she had been given by her father to excuse her own anger. By recognizing the anger that was the basis for her drivenness in her career, she saw how it would eventually destroy her unless she released it. The only way she could release it was to give it to God. Through His power she was able to forgive her father. The problem was, each time she saw him, he verbally abused her again, and it created anger once again.

While it is easy to forgive those people who you no longer see, it is more difficult to forgive those people with whom you still have contact. Paul's words imply a continuing relationship. The basis for being able to forgive other people is to recognize how much God forgives in your life. Hope saw that she would fail at times but God was still willing to forgive her. The more she was able to see the extent of God's forgiveness in her life, the more she could forgive her father. While forgiveness may sometimes seem very difficult, if you are ever going to have healthy relationships, you must learn how to practice forgiveness.

Help me learn how to forgive those who have hurt me, Father.

Stand fast therefore in the liberty by which Christ has made us free, and do not be entangled again with a yoke of bondage.　　　　—GAL. 5:1

One of the movies that my daughters enjoy watching is *Pinocchio*. Through various mishaps and adventures, a little wooden doll eventually earns the right to become a human boy. There is one factor of this story that continually frustrates me. It seems that whenever Pinocchio escapes from whatever mess he got himself into, he is always enticed to go back into some other form of bondage. Although he truly enjoys being free, he just does not have the willpower to say no to those temptations that would entice him back into slavery. When that happens, I always want to yell at the screen, "Stop! How many times does this have to happen before you will learn that it's not worth it?"

Yet, perhaps my frustration is not just with Pinocchio but rather with myself when I see myself falling back into those behaviors that got me into trouble in the first place. Everyone needs to recognize that temptations are always out there, and that there will always be an opportunity to fall back. But with God's power, you can learn to set those boundaries and then make a contract with yourself and Him to help you limit your compulsive behaviors. That will give you the freedom you need to do what is best, rather than what you are "bound" to.

―――――――――

Lord, give me the power to stand fast in the freedom You have provided for me.

> *Blessed be the Lord,*
> *Who daily loads us with benefits,*
> *The God of our salvation!*
> —PS. 68:19

Do you realize that even in your recovery you are carrying a load with you? If you have seen how developing a relationship with the Lord has taken away the load of guilt you were bearing for so long, this may sound rather disheartening. But it is true. In fact, God's Word says that the Lord daily puts a load on you. But before you become too discouraged, check and see what the contents of that load are because it is a load of benefits.

Each day, God provides you with the strength to deal with whatever issues that you will face that day. He provides you with the love you need to recognize that you are His child and that nothing you do will ever cause Him to stop loving you. He provides you with the Holy Spirit, who knows your needs even before you ask Him. He provides you with new, positive messages about yourself, found throughout His Word. He provides you with a direct communication link to Him at any time through the power of prayer. And this is just a small list of benefits He gives every day. So when you wake up tomorrow morning, be glad for the load that God has placed for you to carry that day—it is a load of benefits that far exceeds anything you might have ever expected in this life.

Lord, thank You for the load of benefits that You give me every day.

Choose for yourselves this day whom you will serve, . . .
as for me and my house, we will serve the LORD.
                                        —JOSH. 24:15

No matter how much Alan recognized that his addictive behaviors were destructive in his life, no matter how much he understood that God had a plan for his life, no matter how much he saw the need for accepting God's forgiveness, eventually Alan had to make a choice. He knew all the right things to do and recognized all the positive benefits of this new way of life, but those benefits would never make any difference unless Alan chose to appropriate them.

The children of Israel were aware of God's power, and they spent forty years seeing that He had a plan for them. While they intellectually acknowledged that, they were unwilling to completely get rid of the sinful practices in their lives. Joshua pointed out to them that there comes a time when they could no longer consider the options, no longer weigh the consequences, and no longer straddle the fence, trying to hang on to the best of both worlds. He laid out the choices for them, and then told them to choose their direction.

Alan decided to make that choice and then commit himself to live by it, no matter what the cost. You can continue in your addictive behaviors, or like Alan, you can choose to commit your life to God. The choice is yours. Which will it be?

Lord, help me recognize that You are the only choice for my life.

December 5 – ADMITTING WEAKNESSES

> *Likewise the Spirit also helps in our weaknesses.*
> *For we do not know what we should pray for as*
> *we ought, but the Spirit Himself makes intercession*
> *for us with groanings which cannot be uttered.*
> —ROM. 8:26

Early on in his recovery process Leo began to recognize how weak he really was. He had spent his life struggling in his attempt to make some kind of success out of his life, only to look back and see a history of failures. Even as he committed his life to the Lord, his weakness in following God's plan became evident. When he desired to do the right thing, it was a difficult task because so often he didn't even know what he should be asking for.

Yet, in His mercy God has provided His Spirit to help you know what to ask for. He recognizes that in your human frailty, oftentimes you ask for the less painful or more expedient solutions, instead of truly asking what is best for you. And since it is God Himself who is making it clear what you need in your life, then you can trust that need will be met perfectly by Him as well. Leo saw that God not only knew how to meet his needs but was able to know what needs he really had. Then He really did provide the perfect solution to his life.

Lord, help me rely on You not only to meet my needs but to help me realize what those needs are.

And He said to me, "My grace is sufficient for you,
for My strength is made perfect in weakness."
Therefore . . . I will rather boast in my infirmities,
that the power of Christ may rest upon me.
—2 COR. 12:9

In the perfectionistic life Nan had made for herself one of the most important tasks was to never allow anyone else to see her weaknesses. No cost was too great, no price too high to insure that no one sensed any vulnerability or flaw in her. Her addiction to her beauty regimen helped her build a wall around those emotional deficits and give the impression of success and control. She could boast in her successes and point to her accomplishments as proof that she was the strong, self-made individual she claimed to be.

When an individual allows God to begin controlling her life, the only boasting that takes place is in those very weaknesses that she was trying so desperately to cover. The boasting is not necessarily *about* the weaknesses but rather about what God is doing in her life in spite of those weaknesses and how God is using those very weaknesses to manifest His power in her life. It is through those places that you are weakest, those areas of your life with which you have the most difficulty, that God can truly show how powerful He is. It is easy for Him to take your strong points and work with them, but He chooses to use your weaknesses as well. What kind of God must He be if His power is made strong even in your weaknesses? The kind of God that you can trust with every part of your life.

Lord, use Your strength to help me deal with my weaknesses today.

> *And this is the testimony: that God has given us*
> *eternal life, and this life is in His Son.*
> —1 JOHN 5:11

Of all the gifts that God gives to a person who becomes His child, the one that provides the most hope for any individual is the promise of eternal life. On Kelly's difficult road to recovery, he had victories along the way. He also constantly struggled with the temptation of falling back into those old ways of thinking and responding. The life that God was giving was more productive than his old life of compulsive striving for achievement, but it was still a life full of suffering and pain, one that would always be a struggle.

Even if you do have struggles in this life, eventually there will be a time when you will be able to live happily and joyfully in God's presence forever. The knowledge of having eternal life gives you strength because that is the direction in which you are moving. When Kelly began to see this life as simply a journey through which he was passing, he gained a little more strength to deal with the day-to-day struggles. He began to ask himself, "What will this matter in one hundred years?", and that helped his focus on the peace of his future rather than the struggle of the present.

Lord, help me remember the eternal life You offer through Your Son.

*But may the God of all grace, who called us to His
eternal glory by Christ Jesus, after you have
suffered a while, perfect, establish, strengthen, and
settle you.*   **—1 PETER 5:10**

Joanie came into her counseling session crying one
day. "I blew it again," she said. "I do well for awhile,
and then something comes up that I haven't prepared
for and there I am again, right back where I was." Her
complaint is not uncommon. Often it seems that as
soon as a person feels confident about the progress he
or she is making, something happens to snatch the positive feelings away.

Mostly, that is what recovery involves—a "settling"
of the back-and-forth instability that addictive behaviors create. Making drastic changes is not an overnight
process and one of the goals of recovery is to recognize that trying new, positive behaviors in place of the
old, negative ones will take some practice before you
become proficient.

To help Joanie with her discouragement, I asked her
to tell me the last time she "blew it." She thought and
then said, "You know, it has been two weeks." When
she realized that this used to be a daily occurrence, she
saw that she was on the way to being "settled" to her
new behaviors.

_____

Lord, give me the strength to go through the settling process.

> *Praise Him with the sound of the trumpet;*
> *Praise Him with the lute and harp!*
> *Praise Him with the timbrel and dance;*
> *Praise Him with stringed instruments and flutes!*
> *Praise Him with loud cymbals;*
> *Praise Him with high sounding cymbals!*
> —PS. 150:3–5

One thing that individuals need to learn in recovery is how to express themselves in a creative way. After the need to learn ways of expressing negative emotions—anger, fear, resentment, bitterness—is learned, there is also a need to give freedom to your creative, artistic side. Your expression might be through music, perhaps singing or playing some instrument. It might be through drawing or painting or some other type of visual expression. Maybe you can write or sew or cook—whatever it is, begin looking for that way to express yourself.

Louise felt she had never had a creative thought. She had tried several different outlets but didn't feel comfortable with any of them. Then one day she came in bursting with excitement. "I've found it," she said. "And you'll never guess what it is—carpentry!" She shared how she had to put together a shelf for her daughter's room, and she found she really enjoyed it. She signed up for a class at the local vocational school and had already bought some tools. "I know I will have to be careful not to go overboard, but it is fun to know I can actually be creative." So can you—begin exploring today!

Lord, thank You for the creative abilities You have given me.

However, for this reason I obtained mercy, that in me first Jesus Christ might show all longsuffering, as a pattern to those who are going to believe on Him for everlasting life.   —1 TIM. 1:16

How willing would you be to allow your life to be used as an example of God's work? Would you be willing to allow your life to be an example of God's *patience?* When Leann finally came to the place where she decided to take the steps toward recovery, like everything else in her life, her goal was to do it as quickly and efficiently as possible. She wanted what all the greeting cards offer—a "speedy recovery."

Because of your sinful nature and the extent of the negative messages and unmet needs that you have in your life, your recovery process is often long and tedious, and there are many times that you test the patience of God by reverting back to your addictive behaviors. Leann wanted to believe that she was the exception to the rule, but in reality she also struggled with the desire to return to the old perfectionistic ways. Yet as often as she fell, she learned that God is unbelievably patient and longsuffering with her. And He encouraged her to get up and try again. And with His power, she could.

Father, thank You for being patient with my recovery.

Therefore let those who suffer according to the will of God commit their souls to Him in doing good, as to a faithful Creator. —1 PETER 4:19

In moving down the road to recovery, one of the realizations that eventually dawns on you is that it is not an easy road to be on. Travis struggled with the pain of letting go of many of the relationships from his past. He went through the grieving process and finally said good-bye to those people and circumstances that had affected him for so long. He was learning to fill the void they left behind with positive messages and productive relationships. But every once in a while that old pain would resurface, and he would question the progress he was making.

You must understand that your recovery is not dependent on the amount of pain you do or do not suffer, but rather on the faithfulness of God in meeting the needs of your lives, even when you hurt. Whatever pain or suffering he was experiencing in recovery, Travis learned to recognize that God understands that pain and that He would not allow anything to happen to him that would not be for his own good. Recognizing and believing in God's love helped Travis deal with whatever pain he felt along the recovery road.

Lord, help me deal with the pain I experience in my life today.

Rejoice always.
—1 THESS. 5:16

In Leslie's driven past there was little to rejoice about. The grief of a dysfunctional past, the loss of significant relationships, the neglect of unmet emotional needs, the wasted energy of trying to establish approval and worth, and the guilt of all the past failures did not add up to a whole lot to be happy about from a human perspective. But when Leslie committed her life to Christ, she gained a new perspective on her life that allowed her to have a whole different attitude. What made the difference in this perspective was the realization that her life was in Someone else's control, and therefore she did not have to concern herself with the outcomes of the situations she encountered.

God only requires your obedience and your trust, and everything else is out of your hands. Then He takes the negative things in your life and begins to use them to develop you in ways you never could have imagined. Leslie saw how God took her desperate need to care for other people and used it to minister in a nursing home. In that way she saw that by allowing God to take her weaknesses and turn them into something useful, she could be further down the road to recovery. If there are no circumstances that are not in His hands, then there is no time you cannot rejoice.

Help me, Lord, learn to rejoice in every circumstance of my life.

And do not be conformed to this world, but be transformed by the renewing of your mind, that you may prove what is that good and acceptable and perfect will of God.
—ROM. 12:2

You have probably seen those toys that appear to look like one thing but by bending and twisting the different parts into certain positions, you end up with something that looks completely different. A car can be transformed into a robot; a building can be transformed into an airplane. Looking at the original object, you would never guess what it might turn into, and to look at the finished product, you would never guess what it was before.

Part of learning how to practice vulnerability in Iris's life was learning how to relax her preconceived ideas of what she was and what she could do. She initially was unsure about giving up complete control of her life to God. God happens to be both Designer and the One doing the transforming so He can take a life that has no direction and a great many faults and weaknesses and by His love and power turn it into something that is productive and useful. The added bonus to this is that by allowing Him to do this in her life, Iris opened herself to possibilities she never dreamed of.

So don't let what you think about your life hinder you from allowing God to transform it.

Lord, help me allow You to transform my life into the individual You want me to become.

For all the law is fulfilled in one word, even in this:
"You shall love your neighbor as yourself."

—GAL. 5:14

Now that I am learning how to be free of addictive relationships," Marty said, "I find myself a little reluctant to get into relationships at all. What if I fall right back into the old behaviors? I sure don't want that, and yet I need friends—people with whom I can really learn to share and trust. How do I balance it?" Marty's concern is common among those recovering from addiction, and it is a valid question. How does a person balance the need for true, loving relationships with the drive for addiction?

The answer is found in this verse. The key is to have that healthy concept of who you are before getting involved with others. During the process of accepting your worth through God's love and forgiveness, you discover that you don't *need* those other relationships to make you feel better. Rather, you can *choose* to love others because you already feel loved, and you desire to share that love with others. "So," Marty said, "the more I accept God's love for me and, therefore, love myself, the more I can choose to love others, right?" You're on target, Marty!

_____

Help me, Lord, love others with the love You have given me.

> *He shall cover you with His feathers,*
> *And under His wings you shall take refuge;*
> *His truth shall be your shield and buckler.*
> —PS. 91:4

Have you ever watched the little chicks in a barnyard? At the first sign of any danger, they run as quickly as they can for the protection of their mother's wing. They instinctively know that their mother will protect them and that is the safest possible place for no one will look out for them like she will.

As you travel down the road of recovery, one of the steps you must take is to recognize those areas where you feel especially vulnerable. Betsy was still susceptible to the influences of her ex-boyfriend. On those occasions when their paths crossed, he knew just what to say to make her feel that in her insecurity, she still needed him. She knew she couldn't handle it on her own, and so she made a promise that rather than try to defend herself, she would simply run to God for security. Whatever the situation, God promises to provide the same protection that a mother hen provides for her chicks. He wants you to run to Him whenever you sense those areas of danger in your life. He recognizes that you cannot fight those battles on your own, but when you admit you are still powerless in those areas, He can give you His security.

_____

Father, help me use the protection You provide in my life.

*Not forsaking the assembling of ourselves together,
as is the manner of some, but exhorting one
another, and so much the more as you see
the Day approaching.*　　　　　　—HEB. 10:25

Whether your commitment to Christ is brand new or whether you have renewed your old commitment, fellowship with other people who are going through the same struggles is necessary. God instituted the church as a place of healing and growth as well as a place of dealing with the sin that still continues in your life. Because you need the teaching from His Word and encouragement of other fellow believers, you must make church a priority in your life.

Joan was afraid to go back to church. She felt that everyone there would know why she had been gone for so long and make a big deal about it. She also was afraid that once she became involved, she would have the tendency to overdo it again and end up right back where she was. But finally she made up her mind to give it a try and she was amazed at what she found. Not only did everyone welcome her back and say how glad they were to see her, but the pastor himself hugged her and encouraged her to take the time to just be ministered to right now. Joan realized how much she had missed what God wanted to teach her through His church.

Thank You for giving me the ministry of church, Father.

Yet the righteous will hold to his way,
And he who has clean hands will be stronger
    and stronger.
                                    —JOB 17:9

One thing that must be realized about recovery is that there are many possible detours along the road. Old habits die hard and because some of these behaviors have been providing security for so long, it makes it very easy to fall back on them when things get a little stressful. While these detours may look enticing and they may seem to be a reasonable alternative for the moment, the truth is that they lead further and further from the destination of recovery. Soon enough you discover that no matter where that detour may lead you, you always have to return back to the main road in order to get headed in the right direction again.

Lisa shared how she was dealing with the possible detours in her life. "When traveling, I saw that the best way to avoid detours was to have a reliable map and to talk to someone who had gone that way before. So whenever I face what might be a detour in my recovery, I take out my Bible (the map) and find a verse that deals with my particular situation. Then I discuss it with my accountability friend, someone who has already been down that part of the recovery road. By allowing God to use those resources in my life, I'm able to avoid many of those possible detours."

Help me, Lord, avoid the detours on my road to recovery.

But the path of the just is like the shining sun,
That shines ever brighter unto the perfect day.
—PROV. 4:18

When Troy compared the two roads of his life, he saw that the road to recovery was different from the road of addiction. In looking back over his past, Troy saw how the path of addiction had gotten darker and darker and brought him more confusion each day. Even though his compulsive drive toward success seemed to provide the answers he sought, he inevitably came up empty every time. It was a journey into darkness, where truth became less and less discernible and reality became harder and harder to see.

The path toward recovery was the opposite. The further Troy moved down that road, the brighter his future became. He was moving toward God, the source of all truth and light. His Word illuminated those dark places where Troy had not looked for years, and he realized that he no longer had to believe those untruths about himself. The brighter that path became, the more he saw how little his former life provided for him and the more he wanted to move in the direction of that light. Eventually, that path would lead to the ultimate perfection of eternity.

Help me, Lord, continue walking toward the light of Your Word today.

*And everyone who competes for the prize is
temperate in all things. Now they do it to obtain
a perishable crown, but we for an imperishable
crown.*
                                        —1 COR. 9:25

It was easy for Jeffrey to see the destructive addictions
he had to eliminate from his life. His extramarital affairs, his gambling, and his need to scream at his kids
were all destructive behaviors he could live without.
However, there were certain behaviors that he simply
could not eliminate, and therefore, these areas had to
be considered carefully to determine to what extent he
could continue these behaviors, and at what point
these behaviors became detrimental to his health.

The main area Jeffrey needed to learn balance in
was his work schedule. He realized that he still needed
to work but not to the point where it consumed him.
With prayer and meditation, he decided to be home by
six o'clock every night and make every other Saturday
off limits. That boundary allowed him the balance he
needed. Not everyone will draw the boundary in the
same place. Therefore, you cannot compare yourself
to the next person and use that as your criterion for
where to draw your line. You must be sensitive to God's
leading in your life and allow His understanding of
your situation to lead you in determining the unique
place that you draw those lines.

Lord, help me recognize where to set the boundaries in my life.

To this end I also labor, striving according to His working which works in me mightily.
—COL. 1:29

Recovery is hard work. People who have never had to deal with fighting addictive behaviors often do not recognize the great amount of effort it takes to begin to lead this new life-style. Many people think that if they simply pray about it and commit it to God, then He miraculously changes all the circumstances and removes all temptation from their lives. But that's not how it is.

While Sally learned not to minimize the power of prayer in helping her on the road to recovery, she also recognized that there was definitely hard work involved. Trying to break free from returning to that addictive exercising every time the feeling of inadequacy surfaced was a difficult task indeed. One technique that she often used was the "Make Muscles Move" strategy she had learned from her recovery group. Each time she felt the urge to stay on her exercise bike too long, she realized she could make her legs stop pumping, make them get off the machine, walk to a chair, and sit down. She still had control over her physical body. Never underestimate the power of God to work in your life, but you must continue to be aware of the work which you will have to do in order to make recovery a reality.

Lord, help me work hard in my recovery process, as I continue to trust in Your power to help me.

For I consider that the sufferings of this present time are not worthy to be compared with the glory which shall be revealed in us. —ROM. 8:18

It is almost too incredible to believe, but do you realize that God wants to use your life to illustrate how wonderful and powerful He is? Brett had struggled all his life with the feeling that he had no worth, that he had to prove his validity by climbing the corporate ladder in order to justify his existence. To accept God's forgiveness was one thing, but to believe that God could be demonstrated through his life was something else. How could God's glory be revealed in someone like him?

One way that Brett began to understand the worth and value that God gave to him was to find a way to express himself in a creative way. He found that photography was a way of identifying God's beauty and plan in nature. As his appreciation for God's hand in nature grew, Brett also began to see that he was one of God's beautiful and special creations as well. The more he accepted that fact, the more he began to express himself back to God through his photographs.

Lord, help me find the way You want to reveal Your glory in and through me.

For His anger is but for a moment,
His favor is for life;
Weeping may endure for a night,
But joy comes in the morning.
—PS. 30:5

Just like any other father who loves his child, God will have to correct you. There will be times when you will make a wrong decision or fall back to an old way of thinking, and God will need to deal with those areas. While the consequence may be painful for the moment, you must realize that it is not an indication of God's abandonment or lack of love. In fact, you can look at it as an evidence of His love because if He was not concerned about you falling back into the old destructive ways, He wouldn't be concerned about correcting the behavior as swiftly as He does.

Jason had slipped back to his old addiction of pornography and because his girlfriend found the magazine, she had broken up with him. In the past he would have been totally devastated. But now he had a different attitude. "Sure, it hurts," he said, "but it hurts in a different way than my father's anger used to be. I knew he punished me, but it was never backed up by his love. Now I see that it is *because* God loves me that He cares enough to correct me. And I can live with that."

Father, help me receive Your correction as an act of love from You.

> *You will show me the path of life;*
> *In Your presence is fullness of joy;*
> *At Your right hand are pleasures forevermore.*
> —PS. 16:11

Due to his past misconceptions, Steve had the idea that when he turned his life over to God, it would automatically become some kind of drudgery, a dutiful servanthood to a rather dour dictator. He had the idea that in order to gain God's power in his life, he would forfeit his right to enjoy whatever life God might give him.

The Scriptures show that nothing could be further from the truth. The kind of life God promises is more fulfilling than anything that you could ever produce for yourself. Not only does He promise to point you in the right direction and not only does He promise to be enjoyable company, but He also promises that you will have a good time along the way. One way Steve was encouraged to see the enjoyment was to develop some kind of recreation that served as an outlet for his energy. He decided to take up cycling, something he had always wanted to do. Although he realized he had to set limits on it as any other activity, he also found it to be a special, fun time that he shared with the Lord as he enjoyed the beautiful creation he never had time for before.

Lord, help me truly see the kind of journey and companionship You want to provide for me.

Now the Lord is the Spirit; and where the Spirit of the Lord is, there is liberty. —2 COR. 3:17

Julie was afraid that when she committed her life to God, her freedom would be gone and there would be no more choices left up to her. She assumed because God wanted control of her life, He was going to slap on handcuffs and lead her around according to His whims. By allowing God to control her life, she felt she would give up the right to make any decisions for herself.

But in looking at this issue more carefully, I suggested that Julie answer some questions honestly. How many choices did she have when her whole life was controlled by her addiction to perfection? What kind of true freedom was there when she was a slave to everyone else's desires and approval? What kind of choices did she have when she was driven to perform actions she knew were detrimental to her life? When Julie answered those questions, she concluded that by allowing God to control her life, she could be free to choose the one thing her perfectionism never allowed her to do—the ability to make right choices that lead to a healthy life. That is why true freedom for the individual is found when he allows God to control his life for that is the only place that an individual can be free to choose what is right.

Lord, thank You for the freedom I can find in You.

Draw near to God and He will draw near to you.
—JAMES 4:8

Maribeth was reluctant to begin developing relationships again. She looked back and saw how she had become so addicted to people that she was afraid she might again start needing those people more than was healthy for her. In going through the initial stages of her recovery, she had seen the need to set boundaries on relationships, and now she was being told that it was time to learn how to develop them in a new way. How could she learn to do that?

Recovery gave her a completely different perspective. Rather than trying to base those relationships on what they could do for her or she could do for them, Maribeth began to put her focus on improving her relationship with God. As she drew closer to Him, she realized that she was drawing closer to others who also were drawing closer to Him. In that way, she saw that because those relationships were based on closeness to God, she could begin to enjoy those relationships, and she saw in turn that those relationships also brought her closer to God. Each encouraged the other and both encouraged her.

Help me draw nearer to You each day, Lord.

Listen to this, O Job;
Stand still and consider the wondrous
works of God. —JOB 37:14

Sometimes in your recovery process, you may reach a certain plateau where you feel like you are not covering any ground. Because of his past addiction to achievement, Colin felt that he had to be continually moving in order to accomplish things. But he learned that sometimes God simply desires for a person to stop his activity for a while to meditate on who He is and what He has done in his life.

This was contrary to what Colin was used to, and it was especially contrary to the drivenness that Colin felt before. But that is exactly why God designed it, for so often Colin was so busy doing things that he neglected to take the time simply to let God speak to him. Sometimes he just needed to take that quiet moment and reflect on who God is. He also used those slower times as an opportunity to assess his progress over the last few months, to see what he had accomplished, and where he was going next. So at those times when your recovery seems to stall, don't be discouraged; rather, take it as an opportunity for God to speak to you in a special and personal way as you evaluate your recovery.

Lord, when You cause me to stand still, help me listen to what You have to say.

Walk in wisdom toward those who are outside,
redeeming the time.
—COL. 4:5

One of the things Carla became aware of in her recovery process was that often she was ministering to other people around her who were dealing with their own recovery. Sometimes she felt that she was going it alone, and in many ways she was, but she also saw that as she gained encouragement from others in her recovery group, so too were others encouraged by her recovery.

Whatever direction your recovery takes, you must always be responsible to God for whatever He chooses to do in your life. But you must also recognize that as God manifests that power in your life, you can be a testimony to other people by helping them through a difficult time in their own recovery process. Carla saw the importance of sticking with her recovery through its duration. Although recovery might be long and difficult, it had a purpose not only in her life but in the lives of those around her. She recognized that if God chose to use her in someone else's life, then that was only one more way that she could be assured of the worth and value that He placed on her life.

Lord, help my recovery be used in someone else's life today.

Bear one another's burdens, and so fulfill the law of Christ.
—GAL. 6:2

It is very important in the recovery process to involve yourself in some kind of recovery group. There are other people who have gone through the same situations that you have who can help you know you are not alone in this recovery process. When other members of the group share experiences that you haven't encountered yet, it will enable you to deal with those situations in a more productive way when they happen to you. It also provides you with some accountability, for there will be people there who will be interested in your progress, and they will want to know how things are going in your life from week to week. Most importantly, however, these groups provide a place where you can share feelings and feel that perhaps a little bit of the load you are carrying can be lifted among these friends who do care.

In involving yourself in one of these groups, it is important to understand that this is why God designed the church, so that each other's burdens can be shared, and the support and encouragement that anyone needs can be found. If you haven't joined a recovery group, it is important for you to do so as soon as possible. It is one more building block in the recovery process.

Lord, help me be willing to share my burdens with others.

> *Therefore I take pleasure in infirmities, in*
> *reproaches, in needs, in persecutions, in*
> *distresses, for Christ's sake. For when I am*
> *weak, then I am strong.* —2 COR. 12:10

One of the difficult realities that Craig encountered along the recovery road was that not everyone was as excited about his recovery as he was. While he saw the changes he was making as positive and healthy, his father found them very threatening. In fact, his father saw the limits he was placing on his work time and the increased amount of energy spent on his family as a weakness. He had been used to Craig's absolute commitment to work, and he let Craig know at every opportunity how he felt about the changes. In fact, his comments and criticism got downright ugly, and they became threatening to Craig's recovery.

Persecutions and reproaches are to be expected as part of the recovery process. Craig's worth is not dependent upon pleasing his father, but since he had committed his life to God, he has a responsibility to do the things that God has asked him to do. He also needed to relax the need to control his father's response and remember that while he couldn't be responsible for his father's reactions, neither did he need to live by them.

Help me endure the persecution in my life.

GUARD YOUR RECOVERY – *December 30*

O Timothy! Guard what was committed to your trust, avoiding the profane and vain babblings and contradictions of what is falsely called knowledge.
—1 TIM. 6:20

Not everyone will be supportive about your recovery. You may find there are those close to you who would try to steal away what you have worked so hard to achieve. Kara thought that her family would be as excited about her recovery as she was. What she found instead was that her parents minimized her pain, saying it was all in her mind, while her husband purposely set out to make her life miserable in order to try and get her to return to her old ways. Even her kids whined and griped that things were different. How could she hang on?

Here are four things you can do to keep on in the face of trials.

1. Focus on God's love and power because your worth *and* responsibility are from Him.

2. Keep reading God's Word for reassurance and pray for strength.

3. Continue to give and receive support from others who have also gone through recovery.

4. Remind yourself daily of how far you have come.

By practicing these principles, Kara was able to guard her recovery in the face of the toughest attacks.

Lord, help me guard what You have given me—my recovery.

And in that day you will say:
"Praise the LORD, call upon His name;
Declare His deeds among the peoples,
Make mention that His name is exalted.
—ISA. 12:4

As you continue to travel down the road of recovery, you will have many new insights and experiences along the way. As you take on the challenges of each new day, you will begin to realize more and more how life-changing God's power can be. Eventually, you will be able to look back and recognize how far you have come and how healthy you have become along the way. But in spite of everything else, there is one thing that you will definitely be able to say at that point— "Praise the Lord!"

Take time today to look over this past year and make an inventory of your recovery. As you recount the deeds that He has done and the miracles He has worked in your life, it will fill your heart with so much love and gratitude that you will want to commit your life anew and fresh to Him to take you further down that road to places that you never would have imagined. No matter how far you journey down that road, no matter where your recovery takes you, you will always be able to say, "Praise the Lord!"

Praise You, Lord, for all that You have done and are going to do in my life.

ABOUT THE AUTHOR

Director of the Minirth-Meier Clinic of Longview, Texas, Ric Engram is a licensed professional counselor. He has a Master's degree in counseling from the University of Akron, Akron, Ohio, and a Bachelor's degree in psychology from The King's College in Briarcliff Manor, New York.

Ric has practiced individual, marital, family, and group counseling, as well as administering and interpreting psychological evaluations. In addition to his counseling, he has conducted seminars for churches, schools, and community and business organizations.

Ric lives with his wife and children in Longview, Texas.